DOSTOYEVSKY IN THE FACE OF DEATH

EUROPEAN PERSPECTIVES

THE KRISTEVA LIBRARY

For the European Perspectives series list, see page 329.

DOSTOYEVSKY IN THE FACE OF DEATH

or Language Haunted by Sex

JULIA KRISTEVA

TRANSLATED BY ARMINE KOTIN MORTIMER

COLUMBIA UNIVERSITY PRESS   NEW YORK

COLUMBIA UNIVERSITY PRESS

Publishers Since 1893

New York   Chichester, West Sussex

cup.columbia.edu

Copyright © 2019 Buchet-Chastel, Libella, Paris

Copyright © 2021 Fayard

Translation © 2024 Columbia University Press

Library of Congress Cataloging-in-Publication Data

Names: Kristeva, Julia, 1941– author. | Mortimer, Armine Kotin, 1943– translator.

Title: Dostoyevsky in the face of death : or language haunted by sex /

Julia Kristeva; [translated by Armine Kotin Mortimer].

Other titles: Dostoïevski face à la mort. English | Language haunted by sex

Description: New York : Columbia University Press, 2023. | Series: European

perspectives : a series in social thought and cultural criticism |

Includes bibliographical references and index.

Identifiers: LCCN 2023022395 (print) | LCCN 2023022396 (ebook) |

ISBN 9780231210508 (hardback) | ISBN 9780231210515 (trade paperback) |

ISBN 9780231558457 (ebook)

Subjects: LCSH: Dostoyevsky, Fyodor, 1821–1881—Criticism and interpretation.

Classification: LCC PG3328.Z6 K77713 2023 (print) | LCC PG3328.Z6 (ebook)

DDC 891.73/3—dc23/eng/20230705

LC record available at https://lccn.loc.gov/2023022395

LC ebook record available at https://lccn.loc.gov/2023022396

Printed in the United States of America

Book design: Chang Jae Lee

Cover design: Julia Kushnirsky

Columbia University Press gratefully acknowledges the generous contribution to this book provided by the Florence Gould Foundation Endowment Fund for French Translation.

If people are deprived of the immeasurably great, they will not live and will die in despair. The immeasurable and infinite is as necessary for man as the small planet he inhabits. . . . My friends, all, all of you: long live the Great Thought!

—Dostoyevsky, *Demons* (1872)

CONTENTS

PREFACE

Reading is a singular adventure. Against the civilization-destroying acceleration of the electronic age, reading retains the memory of civilizations and calls for them to rebound. The "Russian ogre" takes part in this rebound. Explorer of the undergrounds of the European soul, his thoughtful carnival consumes its demons.

Dostoyevsky writes to Apollon Maykov in August 1867: "everywhere and in everything I go to the last limit; I've been going over the line my whole life."

His writing, an exuberant affirmation of life until death, snatches the internaut out of the Web in which he is endlessly engulfed and invites him to an inner experience. I receive this inner experience like a kind of intimate immunity. It does not replace vaccines, nor does it extinguish warring conflicts, but it builds the psychic and cultural ramparts indispensable to the human species' struggle for life.

Knocked out, ravished, I am carried along by this *sur-vival*. The oratorio I am offering you is inhabited by a new, total Dostoyevsky, galvanized by language. I'm introducing the man and his work into the third millennium, where at last "everything is permitted." And the web user's anxieties connect with his experience of subjectivity and freedom, which echoes hypermodern contingencies. This experience invites you to pave your own way, without fear of exceeding the last limit or going over the line.

For my part, I accompany to the scaffold this man who was condemned to death for his "revolutionary ideas." I follow his traces in the Siberian jail, where the man pardoned by Nicholas I endures four years of imprisonment in Omsk, followed by five years of exile, and where this "disciple of the convicts" undertakes his metamorphoses. "The child of disbelief and doubt," which he will remain until the end of his life, discovers and reconstructs a "national Christ" who will never leave the side of the "new narrator" now emerging from *Notes from a Dead House* (1862) and *Notes from Underground* (1864). The prophetic Siberian deportee early anticipated the prison-house matrix of the totalitarian universe that became evident in the Holocaust and the Gulag, and that still threatens today with the omnipresence of technology.

To confront nihilism and its double—fundamentalism—which plague the world without God (and *with* Him), Dostoyevsky reinvents the *polyphonic novel*, which is a wager on the power of the word and the narrative. In doing so, he was supported by his Orthodox faith in the incarnate Word. By liberating the *sentient* from objectivation and intellection, the intensity of Orthodox Christianity leads the novelist to the heart of the *destructive pathos* and the *nihilism* to which the fractured Western democracies struggle to respond.

As I continue to auscultate the "cursed Russian," as Freud called him in a letter to Zweig (October 19, 1920), I glimpse the *backstage intimacy* of this close combat. I recall the "Russian virus" in my native Bulgaria, where the second language was that of the Soviet writers; my bedazzlement as a high school student standing fixated in front of the funerary bust of the "little father of the people"; my father, faithful to Orthodoxy, advising me not to read Dostoyevsky, "enemy of the people" according to the Stalin regime; the discovery by Mikhail Bakhtin of the novelist's carnivalesque polyphony, which the young student that I was introduced into French structuralism; the Soviet dissidents who "have something of Dostoyevsky."

While Freud cuts Dostoyevsky up into four pieces (the creative artist, the neurotic, the moralist, the sinner), I go deeper into the *doubling*, the *homoeroticism* (the obsessive doubles and trios of the novels' plots), and the *limit states* into which madness and suicide, saintliness and crime flow. Through the cult of *suffering*, I identify the *jouissance* of the writing, in contact with an essential dimension of the human condition: the advent and the eclipse of meaning in and by the cleavage.

The paroxysmic investment of the narration stems from Dostoyevsky's exceptional singularity: he was able to translate his epileptic auras into a flood of language. Tirelessly supported by his Christian faith, a messiah of Russian populism, tempted by anti-Semitism, the novelist remains a fervent adept of Europe, which he doesn't stop vilifying nonetheless. A sworn opponent of Catholicism, he is just as opposed to atheism, its supposed offspring. A connoisseur of "idiotic" saintliness (Myshkin) and "stinking" saintliness (Zosima), he is opposed to the Grand Inquisitor who denounces Christianism but spares Christ from the stake (*The Brothers Karamazov*). The nihilist Shigalyov suppresses liberties in the name of egalitarianism, while it remains for Kirillov to kill himself as a way to open the path to absolute (Godless) freedom (*Demons*).

A precursor to Freud, the novelist depicts parricide (*The Brothers Karamazov*), considered as the universal desire of "all of us." And he anticipates the current escalation of *feminicide* (which strikes Nastasya Filippovna, the Cripple, the Meek One . . .) and *pedophilia* (with Svidrigaylov, and especially in Stavrogin's confession)—ultimately unpardonable crime. . . . The very traits inherent in the "ridiculous man," which the narrator admits to being himself; inherent also in the "European man" (Mitya Karamazov recites the words of what will become the European hymn); and in the universal human, definitively.

The first part of this book probes his played/played-out passions, particularly with the women in his life (Maria Dmitrievna, Apollinaria Suslova, Anna Grigoryevna Snitkina) among an archipelago

of badly treated heroines who revolt or triumph—Nastasya Filippovna (*The Idiot*), the shrieking Cripple (*Demons*), the Meek One
("The Meek One"), Grushenka (*The Brothers Karamazov*). The second
part returns to the febrile Christocentrism of Dostoyevsky the publicist and seeks its sources in the *gnosis*. His novelistic rhapsody
attests it in transforming the canonical *dualism* of the theologian into
a *swarm of emanations*: masks, words, ordeals. "Terrifying beauty," the
ultimate expression of which would be *parodia*, the counterpoint to
the sacred, vertiginous contestation.

Thus incorporated into the passions, into the history of religions
and the deflagration of ideologies, Dostoyevsky's discordances are
the truth of his storytelling, not rhetorical tactics. This undecidable
tension constitutes us; it may well survive us, perhaps.

PART I

THE FLOOD OF LANGUAGE

I admit all the same that in Dostoievsky this preoccupation with murder is something extraordinary which makes him very alien to me. I'm amazed enough when I hear Baudelaire say: "If not yet poison, arson, rape, and stabbing / It is because our soul, alas! Lacks daring."

But I can at least assume that Baudelaire is not sincere. Whereas Dostoievsky...

—Marcel Proust, *The Captive* (1923)

1

THE CONDEMNED MAN, THE SACRED MALADY,

AND THE SUN

Death ... is of all things the most dreaded, and to come to grips with it
requires the greatest effort.

—G. W. F. Hegel, *The Phenomenology of Spirit* (1807)

1.1 December 22, 1849

"Retired Lieutenant Dostoevsky, age twenty-seven, for having taken
part in criminal designs, having circulated a personal letter filled
with impertinent expressions against the Orthodox Church and the
sovereign power and for having attempted, together with others, to
circulate works against the government through means of a private
printing press, is condemned to death."

The air is compressed and vibrates with the slightest sound. The
members of the Fourierist circle Mikhail Petrashevsky, slipping on
the frost-covered steps, climb the scaffold covered with a black cloth,
on Semyonov Square near Saint Petersburg. Kiss the cross held out
to them by the priest in funerary garb. Don ample pointed cowls of
white cloth with long sleeves that reach to the ground. Drumroll.
On their knees. The executioners flourish their sharpened sabers
above their heads. Lined up three by three, the first ones are bound

to three gray stakes, hands tied with rope. Dostoyevsky waits his turn in the second rank.

"Lower the hoods over your eyes!"

"Aim!"

A few seconds . . . a minute . . . two . . . The rifles don't go off.

Fyodor has always stared at death like the sun. Numb with fear, cries and trembling, loss of his self outside self, breathless and headlong . . . And once more, that harassing, sonorous drumroll that recaptures words, conversations, narratives, calls and responses. Life persists and returns in the voices, irrefragable verbal flow, infinite, spasmic, energetic, stunning dialogue, dazzling voluptuousness. "On the contrary, the brain is fearfully alive and active, must be working, working, working, ever so hard, like a machine; . . . as soon as you start telling a story, you stop being a philosopher" (*The Idiot*, 1868). A full life is a drumroll of voices, of novels. From the moment you narrate you are neither dead nor a philosopher, you finally exist.

Much later, surrendering to the sparkling needles of the same frosty sun, so powerful that they remind him of his obsession with "prescribing a remedy of birch rods" for himself ("Petersburg Dreams," 1831), this "fantasy walker," this "idle dreamer" will abruptly feel his heart swell. Similar to that 22nd of December 1849 at the foot of the dreaded platform. A gush of blood, a suffusion of powerful sensations, "but up until then unfamiliar to me." With the absolute, bodily certainty that a "completely new world," in gestation since childhood, can and must begin. Here it is, it's "starting," in this very minute, it's striking. Henceforth, a new "I" will inhabit his new life, a life of voices sealed with images, theater of sensations-visions, scaffold of mask-wearers, moving puppets who burst out laughing. No minute is more full, sacred, and pure than such minutes, "as if inspired by opium." Of course, he'll have to close the books on sentimental, tumultuous romanticism, on the Schillers, Walter Scotts, and Paul de Kocks, they're enough to make you cry laughing. It's happening. Mortality, all the same, will not be sent off into the bloody twilight, it will be integrated into the pulsation of the serial narrative, which rebounds, languidly. The novel is a genre to be reinvented with each verbal flow, oscillating, intimate-extimate, tormented, undifferentiated, insane. Even Raskolnikov will lose himself in the foggy sun of Saint Petersburg only to blossom all the better, tied to the crimes and the punishments that constitute him, that give him being.

I remember, one January winter evening, I was hurrying home from the Vyborg side of the city... Night was descending on the city and the whole immense Neva River, flat, swollen from the frozen snow, was sprinkled with endless myriads of sparkling dots of hoar-frost in the last reflection of the sun. A twenty degree frost was setting in... I trembled and my heart was, as it were, suffused at this moment with a hot rush of blood, which suddenly boiled with the surge of a sensation which was powerful but up until then unfamiliar to me. It was as if I realised something in that minute which had up until then only stirred within me but was still not fully comprehended; as if I had had a vision of something new, of a completely new world, which was unfamiliar to me and known only through some dark rumours, some mysterious signs. I suppose it was from that minute that my existence began...

And I began to scrutinise things and suddenly I beheld some strange faces. They were always strange and peculiar figures, completely prosaic, not at all like Don Carloses and Posas, but titular councillors to the full and, at the same time, kind of fantastic titular councillors. Someone was grimacing before me, while hiding behind this whole fantastic crowd, and was tugging at some threads and springs, and these puppets moved, and he roared and roared with laughter! And I imagined at that time a different story, in some dark corners, some titular heart, honest and pure, moral and devoted to the bosses and, together with this, some little girl, insulted and sad, and my heart was deeply torn by their whole story. And if one was to assemble this entire crowd, which appeared to me then, it would have been a glorious masquerade. ("Petersburg Dreams," 1861).

The Condemned Man, the Sacred Malady, and the Sun   5

Nothing is more ardent—when the black sun of death is within reach—than the theater of childhood, a fugitive reminder of obscure youthfulness... The condemned man is an infant who suckles the Bible.

I was still a baby huddling in my mother's arms when Job's cry pierced my eardrums. A dark voice from the chest, like mine, it still strikes me: "why I can't hold my tongue in my anxiety." "Thine eyes are upon me, and I am not." Mama's all honeyed song. Maria Fyodorovna, she rocks her "little hero" who bears the "blessed given name" of her own father Fyodor Nechaev, no connection with the nihilist Sergey Nechaev, viscous proximity... I prefer to ignore that fake Jupiter, his jealous thunderbolts of anger, the greedy power of his money, that unhearing Pantocrator, my military doctor of a father, Mikhail Andreyevich... The melody of my almost twin brother effaces and absorbs them; born only a year before me, the same day as I, named Mikhail like my father, Mikhail Mikhailovich then, doubly the father, eclipsing the father, marker and foil: "we were two, I maintain," programmed doubling... Glacial cacophony of the adults, professors, and parents... Morose murmur of the poor, avid for life in the paternal hospice, sole playground in the saddest neighborhood of Moscow... The silence of the woods and the cold blue of the countryside, Darovoye and Chermashnya... An idiot woman moaning the death of her child by an unknown father... The muzhiks and their horses, the drunken brigands, and a tender laborer, the fabulous Marey who caresses my cheek until more life comes to me... The crosses and the fisticuffs... The permanent anguish about dying while asleep... I spread sheets of white paper on my bed, I ask that I not be buried until after a lapse of five days... All my senses sharpened, always inside-outside, inaccessible refuge fervor.

We have a subscription to the review *Library of Reading*: classic literature and history, popular poetry, Russian folklore... The voices from the books come back to me now: amplified, magnificent, mortiferous, resuscitated in the electric verses of the poets . . . Racine, Schiller, Goethe, Pushkin, Zhukovsky . . ."Frozen in enthusiasm and horror" . . . well, everything. And especially the ample whirlwind of novels creating a world in the world . . . The gothic turmoil of Ann Radcliffe, the sovereign feminist George Sand with her Indiana . . . The mysterious Balzac—irresistible vocation and hand-to-hand combat with his *Eugenie Grandet*, did I translate it or rewrite it? . . . His *Old Goriot* possessed by money, the most passionate of the passions, it governs the end of the world . . . The young Victor Hugo of *Hans of Iceland*, marriage of nature and romanticism . . . All in all I prefer Hoffmann, and I set out with new strength: "Yes, if I won't be able to write, I'll perish. Better fifteen years of imprisonment and a pen in hand!" (Letter to Mikhail, December 22, 1849) . . . A few strong friendships with schoolmates; Durov, housemate and prison-mate . . . And you, my brother, dear Misha, so faithful and loyal, you don't dare compromise yourself too much with me, author of a crime against the State—I can hear you from here, that's my prophet side . . . All of them revolutionaries in the soul and in the firmament of free ideas, subversive ideas that noisily agitate the West . . . I have no violent action to reproach myself for, scarcely a clandestine printing press, and all for the vocation . . . Aside from that, I'm not known for any female conquests; paralyzed by women, I swoon before the majestic Mme Panaeva, a splendid beauty à la George Sand (she again), hanging on the arm of her frivolous husband, the muse of his circle of amorous authors; first time for love at first sight and first instance of the "trio," two men for one woman, delicious torture, I will be a long-time subscriber . . . Vissarion Grigoryevich Belinsky praises me, glorious moment, I exist, I exult; he rejects me, I collapse, "knight of the sad countenance," the laughingstock of Saint Petersburg high society, pretentious neurotic hypochondriac . . .

Nekrasov and Turgenev attract me, then disappoint me . . . But nothing will erase the ineradicable passion that attaches me to Nikolay Speshnev, irresistible aristocratic libertine and already a Marxist, my terrorist creditor, atheist and communist, "I am with him and I belong to him," I see him, he inhabits me, I will make a character out of him ... Gogol obsesses me, though I thumbed my nose at his lugubrious, realistic "Overcoat" in my *Poor Folk* (1846), which was the first half-fantastic, half-social novel, that's what they said, I stick to pathetic souls, I haven't finished dealing with Gogol, I know.

Death expands, interminable minute. In the distance, the top of a church cupola sparkles, glimmerings blended with the voices, dazzling kaleidoscope of clamor. Could it be the specter of Countess du Barry alongside Sanson? "She sees him bending her neck under the blade, kicking her forward—the crowd laughing—and starts shouting: *Encore un moment, monsieur le bourreau, encore un moment!*"[1] One of my characters, Lebedev, "another sinner like her," will pray for the lady ... "What if I didn't have to die! If life was returned to me—what an eternity it would be! And it would all be mine!" (*The Idiot*, 1868)

What eternity? The Superior School of Engineering? Fine, it's done, though loathsome; indigence and deprivation ... Galvanized by the theater: Shakespeare, Racine! And always Balzac, Schiller, Hoffmann. To write, "to redeem oneself or be lost," exaltation and torments. Five years of publication already, sudden fame and total fall from grace ... The voices of his books now invade the silence of Semyonov Square, gaping black hole of the frosty cosmos. Thoughts are intonations, incessant dialogues, proliferating points of view, echoes carrying afar ...

He hears them, he sees them, a fluid rhapsody flows outward (water is his element, with the sun) in the tortured turns of a collection of letters of unrequited love inaugurated by Makar Devushkin, his first character, that pathetic rat of a minister, that ludicrous functionary (say it in Russian: *chinovnik*, guaranteed effect of morose laughter), who doesn't know he's the grandfather of the anticapitalist-man-machine in Kafka and Chaplin. His relative Varenka replies to him with kindness, "muddled friend" and abused orphan who

nevertheless marries another oppressor, with the amorous participation and faithful compassion of Makar himself, inconsolable
poor folk.

A nervous laugh dilates and twists the face of the condemned
man: the dream of the sickly and triumphant letter-writer, which
doesn't leave him when the woman he loves leaves him for another,
this the author knows well, it's his wild dream. The secret of what
has been taken for his sentimental humanism tormented by anguish
is obvious in the patronymic of the hero, Devushkin, in Russian
devushka: "young girl"! The despairing orphan is *also* he, the budding
writer! You couldn't love the *other* as *yourself* since this poor other was
your alter ego: your very own feminine self. Deep down within you
there follow undecidable oscillations and, outside of you, voluptuous
blockages. Did the enthusiasm of the redoubtable Vissarion Belinsky for *Poor Folk* pick them out when he predicted the fame and
future of a "great writer"? This famous literary critic, who considered himself a socialist, was to recant with *The Double* (1846), the
second book by his protégé, because the acclaimed author, having
ostensibly portrayed his doubling, dissected it and caressed it, madly,
tirelessly.

The revolt of the universal civil servant aiming at the system:
quashed. The lame dream of the romantic couple: temporarily
abandoned. In getting undressed (*golyí*, in Russian, means "naked,
denuded"), at the fringes of indecency, the subservient soul of the
small-time bureaucrat splits into Goliadkin the elder and Goliadkin the younger: the "dirty old rag" with "unrequited ambition"
and the arrogant snitch, the magnanimous convulsive and the
sneering scoundrel. They embrace feverishly in a secret revolutionary soirée, but it's only nothingness, *níhil*, madness, nothing.
The sentence withers irreversibly with the narration. Meaning is
lost with the character, and the risk of mental collapse descends
upon the scaffold, atrocious perception and prophetic vision of
self-destructive nihilism.

About thirty years later, in 1877, the writer will persist; he writes
that he had "never literally achieved a more serious idea" than the

one in *The Double*. With Goliadkin he sensed the demons. Already now, the condemned man hears them in Pushkin's verses:

Upon my life, the tracks have vanished,
We've lost our way, what shall we do?
It must be a demon's leading us
This way and that around the fields.
. . .
How many are there? Where have they flown to?
Why do they sing so plaintively?
Are they burying some household goblin?
Is it some witch's wedding day? (*Demons*, 1872)

The underground man (*Notes from Underground*, 1864) is the first to defy the demonic din. Lame Marya, Stavrogin, and Pyotr Verkhovensky (*Demons*) are not born yet. The irresistible thrust of the words alone, on the scaffold, embodies the urgency of giving flesh to the doubles, the shame, and the obscurity that border on crime.

Obstacles are thresholds: to disseminate, to repent, and to correct oneself, to say and say again, anguish and crisis. To listen, to listen to oneself, to undo oneself, infiltrate oneself and infiltrate you, my likeness, my brother. Cross over . . . turn in circles . . . faint, to a point barely posed . . . and rebound. Inexhaustible conversation, the non-finite is infinite. Who talks of abandoning hope? This inferno is a palliative, nothing is forbidden, everything can and wants to be for-bidden.

Two or even three who are "saved" in the beauty of their infinitely deformed reflections, discordant polyphony? The three who were tearing themselves apart in *Poor Folk*—which did not prevent the narrator from dying of laughter about it, but nothing is ever for sure in this caustic anguish—this trio continues all the better in "The Landlady" (1847), it will survive the scaffold. A solitary old man, a researcher in the history of the Church, gives his tender heart away to the torments of the tumultuous Katerina—the condemned man will retain this first name for the strong women to come in his writing, which leads him to the essential: confronting the redoubtable rival.[2] The epileptic old man, convicted criminal, tyrannizes his incest-marked daughter-wife so well that the "mistress of the house" (*hozía-ïka*) succumbs to sadistic subservience! And the triumph of feminine masochism carries off the two romantic idealists, the landlady and the tenant.

The feminine assails him, it penetrates the novelist still, while the blacksmiths encircle his feet in irons, he doesn't care. It is in the feminine that he hears the voice of his *first confession* signed in the first person singular. To be left unfinished (*Netochka Nezvanova*) because of the trial for sedition that brings him precisely here, facing death. In the name Netochka, one can hear negation, *nyet* "no" and *tochka* the "point": final point or there is no point? The patronymic Nezvanova, from the adverb *nie* "negation, lack, absence" and *zvaníie* "title, grade" from *zvat* "to call, invite, name," completes the orchestration of the negative: unnamed, ignored, without help, unnamable ... Emerging from nothingness ("I do not remember my father"), the young woman will become a singer—perhaps. A painful replica of "feminism" à la George Sand, does she seem to think that only art can still save us? Like the revolutionary aesthete on the scaffold, who lives on, survives, haunted by the voices of his characters, transcended by literature. But the adoptive father of the little memoir writer is a brilliant violinist who goes crazy, and her sickly desires are expended in suave effusions with Katia, the dominator. Sadism in the feminine becomes frenetic: "And, crying and laughing, we kissed each other till our lips were swollen."

Drumroll. It's still not the end ... The condemned man has more than one trick up his sleeve, inexhaustible romantic vein, sentimental, sadistic ... His last seconds on this earth flood him with memories of the orgasms of the young boy within him ... The trembling voice of the "little hero" he has just penned, this night, in the prison of the Peter and Paul Fortress, knowing he will have to die the next day, today ... He is eleven, splendid women caress him and a mysterious sensation invades him, something terrifying that makes the heart, the body, everywhere beat and burn ... Blushes and unexpected tears, solitude, "ashamed and even hurt" by so many "privileges" I enjoyed, I could "remember something—something which [I] now had *suddenly forgotten*, something without which I could not ... exist at all." Sexual abuse or guilty pleasures? "Lately women have been making me feel particularly afraid, and that's why I was seized with a terrible confusion" ("The Little Hero," 1849).

The condemned man feels the bullet penetrate his cranium, his neurons catch fire, his creatures, his doubles, his puppets escape, grimace, and sneer ... When all is said and done, they have always been ridiculous because they scrutinize themselves, torture themselves, interpenetrate each other. But in that fatal minute, at the threshold of the ultimate punishment, the narrator himself joins in the dance, in the end he is going to burst out laughing ... Drumrolls.

The imperial pardon arrives with an aide de camp on a galloping horse. "His Majesty took cognizance of a petition ... commutes the death sentence ... stripped of all rights ... sent to prison ... indeterminate term ..."

That very evening, from the Peter and Paul Fortress, the survivor writes to his brother Mikhail: *On voit le soleil!*[3] In French.

The convict knows by heart *The Last Day of a Condemned Man* by Victor Hugo (1829). Proud homage to the Immortal in writing. Obstinate hopes and pleasures in suffering, in loving, and in remembering. Christlike ascension and resurrection into the sun-father of the visible world.

Not only. With the imminence of death avoided, I *begin anew* to exist! In the puffy sparkle of the frozen snow, the thunderbolt of illumination only asks to return. It separates "the head of ideas" from his shoulders, and an idea makes its entrance in the chaos and blood of the pardoned one: *life*. "Life is everywhere, life is in us ourselves, and not outside. There will be people by my side, and to be a *human being* among people and to remain one forever, no matter in what circumstances, not to grow despondent and not to lose heart—that's what life is all about, that's its task ... That idea has entered my flesh and blood. But it's the truth! ... What remains is memory and images created and not yet embodied by me" (letter to Mikhail, December 22, 1849).

The voices in his stories deploy an augmented reality for the survivor: languages and images in fusion, inordinate fullness of meaning, nuclear scission-combustion of the neurons, cells, and fibers. Superior exaltation verges on the epileptic aura, time dilated, before the electroshock of the seizure chews up language, mind, respiration, skeleton. And strikes death, that limit of *jouissance*, with a new incarnate narrative of "life in us." Infinite pulsation of new beginnings, new births.

1.2 The Ultra-Deep Song of Beings

It seems young Dostoyevsky experienced only minor epileptic seizures in his childhood, plus one major seizure, called "temporal," at the announcement of his father's death in 1839—killed and castrated by his serfs, a hypothesis contested today, or dead from apoplexy. This illness, which will later take paroxysmic forms, never leaves him for his entire existence. His own notes show it. They are cold self-observations and diagnoses: "totally deprived of my senses"; "remembering nothing"; "difficulties of speech"; "I'm still confusing words."

He doesn't recover from epilepsy. Moses himself, the prophet Mohammed, Saint John of the Cross, Teresa of Avila, Flaubert also, among other giants of the civilizations, let it be known what they owe to the sacred disease. Dostoyevsky is the only one who locates, in the "abnormal phenomenon" from which he suffers, a paroxysmic, pathological augmentation of *the* specifically human capacity: the ability to *speak*, to *make meaning*, which happens only in the burning bush of all the senses. The voice that speaks, remembers, and thinks epitomizes the high point of the *jouissances*-sufferings in which it participates while tearing itself apart.

Irrefutable clarity: shipwrecked, he appears in the original fissure of our speaking species; he restitutes for us the vibrant membrane that covers it, the sonorous vestige of the ultra-deep field of being: flesh and senses fused, revivals and reversals, bombshells and eclipses. Reprieved, his verbal energy brews sentences, conversations, and stories. But please, do not rely only on these separate scraps of facts, listen to the rise and fall of meaning, its harassing vortex, guffawing, exultant, jubilant. When he regains the use of speech, the epileptic fracture holds him, caresses him, cultivates him, exalts and destroys ideas, tableaus, plots. Patient and furious stream of intelligence that hurries slowly: the sun diffracts all the shadows of judgment, the flight of meaning . . . A tsunami of exchanges, arguments and counterarguments. The sentence burns up in "it seems to me," "hmm," "almost," "how can you know," "on the contrary" . . . Obsessive reasoning loses track of its target, moves away, absurd surprises and senseless events. The narrative is not fantastic, but no way could you be realistic, thanks to fuzziness. The tidal wave of the verb exceeds the thrust of the verb. It hears itself, it runs out of breath while hearing itself run out of breath, it talks . . . Arguments or hallucinations dampen the characters— already difficult to hold onto with their three denominations in the Russian manner (first name, patronymic, family name): Pyotr Stepanovich Verkhovensky, not to be confused with Stepan Trofimovich Verkhovensky, his father, who by the way hardly knows him, not having really raised him. Each takes on, diffracts, and brings down the centrifugal, then centripetal, reasonings of his interlocutor, which overflow the tight threads of grammar. The verb unhooks from the utterance to seize on the anguish, the envy to the death, the indifference that kills, assassination and salvation, cruelty of the incarnation. No concreteness remains outside language, no demon resists it, they all find their homes in it, the flood of language lets itself be infiltrated, dilated, punctured, jubilated. The flood recedes by itself in the knot of anguish and the fracture of crime.

But not the least shadow of defeat, of resignation or renunciation. At the heart of the disaster, no nothingness: *the investment of interlocution* is keeping watch, speaking is given and received, the forbidden exults. The novel does not give up, does not abandon us; it contaminates, muddles, carries off; you are *of it*: invested. *Invested*:

from the Sanskrit *kred, in Latin credo: gift and restitution, call and response, unbearable mutuality of sense and the sensed.

Faith thus transmuted into a wager on the *Logos*, the played/played-out narration escapes from the latent, diffuse coma to come.

The voice, the most organic element of language, seizes the maternal tongue, diverts it—but not too much—refines it, makes fun of it, redoes it. Weaving of the soul and the body, suffering and *jouissance* of the hyperconnected brain in an inexhaustible serial: almost all of Dostoyevsky's novels appear by programmed tranches in the periodical media of the time (*Annals of the Fatherland*, prototype of the "big review," *The Contemporary, The Petersburg News, The Russian Word, Time, The Epoch, The Russian Messenger, The Citizen*), as was common. But in his case, the gusts of writing, with the flood of language, approach the aura of the sacred disease, which espouses him and breathes him in. Then at low tide the flood succeeds in filtering obnubilation itself, which scrambles the superheated neurons while accumulating porous sentences and stretching the partially opened lips of the speakers—absurd, stupefying capture of the loss of meaning, within the excess fullness of meaning.

This permanent "site," this catchy Facebook, smartly rhythmic, orchestrated, did not generate only realist-naturalist-romantic-fantastic novels. Yet, with their expansion-acceleration, contradiction-collapse-new beginning, they are intrinsically imposing as *thought novels* (never mind literary marketing): "that is: thought, that is: the center and the Synthesis of the universe and its outer form . . . that is: God, that is: eternal life" (*Meditation*, 1864). An odd thinker; this novelist, who gives priority to invocations and resonances, owes it to himself to excel in *composition*: "vast crescendos," "opera of the deluge," self-analysis permeable to the innumerable limit states of the men and women around him. In unison with the spasms of the social organism of that time and ours.

Consubstantial with epilepsy and its transposition-deliverance in the writing of an irrepressible dialogue, scanned solitude and magnetized alterity up to the limits where language and flesh are consumed in crime, in memory, and in paradisiacal mutuality: for more than a century and a half, readers and commentators have been fearful of or have admired this extreme experience, the double-faced (at least) man, the polyphonic work. Elucidate its magic? Mission impossible—cleavage and polyphony unseat the explanation. The therapeutic impact remains, the irreversible vocation of life at the edge of life. It has conquered its place in literary, aesthetic, and philosophical kingdoms, it dominates them, and it imposes itself in the new globalized crisis of consciousness.

Love Dostoyevsky? Dostoyevsky author of my life?[4] Two phrases too narrow to express the engulfment and the regeneration that are provoked in me, in you, by the vocal tessitura of this whirling meaning, the violence of the incarnate Word that I am, that you are, that wounds you, troubles you, and transcends you. A breathless writing that translators exhaust themselves trying to rationalize, Viscount de Vogüé, at the head of the list of the first French translators, was not unaware of its pitfalls. The hyperbolic title of the collection, "The Authors of My Life," with the overwhelming names I discovered after the fact (*Descartes* by Paul Valéry, *Schopenhauer* by Thomas Mann, *Marx* by Trotsky), were no less daunting. Many times I wanted to protect myself, give up. Until my reading of the translation by André Markowicz restored to the French language its ability to let the Telling unfold without being afraid of the sacred. And the stupendous gallery of characters, doubles and multiples, the archipelago of female solitudes, the responsibility borne for transgressions, even the pedophilia, in a world where "everything is permitted," submerged the finiteness of our confined passions.

Nine years in Siberia, of which four in the jail at Omsk, five years of exile in Semipalatinsk, first marriage in 1857 to Maria Dmitrievna, feverish affair with the brilliant early feminist student Apollinaria Suslova, first journey through Europe, death of his first wife and of his brother Mikhail in 1864 . . .

Along the way, with notebooks in hand, a sensational descent operates close by the malicious fissure, the demonic split, and their membrane in words. *The Insulted and Injured* (1861) tallies romantic souls, which it will take some time to settle up as a farce (*The Eternal Husband*, 1870, insatiable jealous man in love with his rival) or as a tragicomedy (*The Gambler*, 1866, who takes pleasure in losing, as much as if not more than winning, at roulette). *Notes from a Dead House* (1862) should be read as the *obverse* of the *inverse* that is the dazzling *Notes from Underground* (1864). Which reshuffles the cards for the irresistible takeoff.

Finally authorized to publish, and still in Siberia, the writer sticks to "recollections" to begin with, capable of satisfying the necessarily public "curiosity" and deserving the "strongly favorable" approval of the censors—above all, "very little there that is strictly personal," he emphasizes in a letter to Maykov. But the anonymous reporter he pretends to be doesn't stay for long within the limits he had imposed on himself, limits that reconcile him with the glory of his beginnings, if not more.

The *Dead House* introduces reportage into the absurdity of the penal universe: opera of male passions, Christlike grace of the Russian people. Reportage "publishes," that is, *relates to the public*, a human existence cut off from public space. The carceral system is nothing but death living a human life, a system that exhibits the immanent destructivity of the social and political "house." On the other hand, the convicts themselves, criminals, recluses, condemned for life to this death, live a life of "arch-capital interest": "A new path opens," the convict writes to his brother. It's true, the *Notes from a Dead House* (1862) opens the way for explorers of the totalitarian social contract. The carceral universe of the concentration camp is ongoing, Kafka's *The Trial*, Solzhenitsyn's *One Day in the Life of Ivan Denisovich* won't be long now . . .

But the ex-convict will quickly build support for his carceral chronicle by digging *under* the "house." Reinvigorating the reforming minds from the reign of Alexander II, the novelist outpaces the convict, the denunciator of the police state, and the secret agent of "new ideas" with a much deeper immersion. The "underground" is written *podpolie*: "underneath the floorboards," and the term commonly designates clandestinity, the *maquis*. What is unsaid in the blog explodes in enraged confessions against himself at first and all sorts of "houses," ideas, communities, or evidences, identities and sideways maneuvers included. Even more, with his second *Notes*, the author *has hold* of an absolute certainty: his salvatory furor, without a fixed literary genre but blending them all (letters, memoirs, confessions, reporting, novel), is *the internal source* of polyphony, of writing.

The survivor could have stopped there—the nervous, refractory, historical witness. Except that the clandestine thrust overflows its dismissed "notebook" at full tilt, in giving birth to a veritable human bomb. The bomb seizes the voices and their phantoms; it gives them a makeover, adds others, and recomposes them. Everything is in the recomposition. One after the other the inescapable ones arrive: *The Idiot* (1868), *Demons* (1872), *The Adolescent* (1875), *The Brothers Karamazov* (1881), with in the background the constant, indefatigable *Writer's Diary* (1873–1881).

1.3 On the Thread of Crime and the Sublime

Where do "great works" come from? From an extranormal DNA, from transgenerational memory, from education, from the social context; from a ham actor who likes to coddle the hysteria of opinion; from a hero who succeeds where the narcissistic pervert fails; from a wheeler-dealer who knows how to sell his nagging fantasies to the power of opinion, who wins by dying while alive, by living in death, after death, beyond death?

What does the globalized internaut have to do with this nihilist of a Raskolnikov or a Stavrogin, both half crazy; with a Saint Prince Myshkin flanked by his double, the enraged assassin Rogozhin; with Kirillov, Shatov, and likewise Verkhovensky who agonize or smirk, not knowing or thinking they know if God is dead or really not; with the four Karamazov brothers, who prefigure Bolshevik, fundamentalist, and jihadist terrors and take intense pleasure in attributing to themselves, or not, the murder of their father while dissecting the cadaver of national sexual identity, of universal values, of humanist harmony? While a volley of women, quite humiliated and offended, whether they are dominating and crippled, mystical or dim-witted, ridiculous but redemptive, gravitate around their men who don't have the vaguest idea what to do with them. And sometimes are able to punch through the shackles of the hallucinated passions of the males themselves. Between cruelty and grace, there seems to be no other forgiveness for crime than to write it. There remains the most radical evil of all imaginable crimes, sexual abuse of a child with murder—the dream of Svidrigaylov, the confession of Stavrogin, it haunts Dostoyevsky himself... Silence and suicides. The sun and speech collapse into a black hole. End of the novelistic. The Devil and God always face to face? Sacrifice and the sacred.

Reopen his books and listen up. When at last "everything is permitted," or almost, and you no longer suffer anguish, just liquid anxieties, no longer desires, just purchasing fevers, no longer pleasures, just needful release through all sorts of apps, no longer friends, just *followers* and *likes*, you are incapable of expressing yourself in the quasi-Proustian sentences of Dostoyevsky's demons, but you pour yourself out in your addiction to clicks and selfies? Well, you are resonating with the extenuating polyphonies of Saint Dosty, who prophesized the streaming of SMS, tweets, Instagram, pornographies and protest marches, "#outyourpig," and nihilistic wars under cover of "holy wars."

Does this mean anything to you? Could the inaudible Dostoyevsky be our contemporary? No more, no less than a fugue for string quartet and a choral symphony by Beethoven. Or the density of Shakespeare. Or Dante's comedy. Insolent challenges to the outside-of-time of time.

Translated into all the languages (sixteen versions of the translation into Chinese of *Crime and Punishment*, 1866), the "Russian giant" does not entirely convince men of letters of "good writing." "Fumes and disorders," "confusion and marvelous messes," "the first of the great incomprehensibles who only succeeded in making the incomprehensible more obscure still." But he stimulates philosophy, freedom of thought, the reinvention of the novel in Russia, in Europe, and in the world.

Nietzsche's overman admires and shares in the combustion of the "new man" found in Raskolnikov and Ivan and Mitya Karamazov. And in reverse, when the author of *Beyond Good and Evil* (1886) goes mad embracing the bloody nose of a horse being beaten, he is again literally sinking into the culpable pleasures of Dostoyevsky's *Crime and Punishment* (1866), in the form of the outraged little Rodion charging for Mikolka's whip as it finishes off the lame mare. The philosopher of the "death of God" recognizes in the Russian novelist "the only psychologist . . . from whom I had something to learn."[5]

Did the Kafka of *Metamorphosis*, with his Gregor Samsa, read *Notes from Underground*? In the eyes of Zverkov, "with his dumb sheep's brain," the underground man is reduced to an object, to an odious insect climbing among the passers-by, an "ugly fly" to be squashed as if it never existed.

Marcel Proust declined the proposal from the NRF to write about Dostoyevsky, but "the Dostoievsky side of Mme de Sévigné's Letters" fascinates him, and the interminable sentence of *In Search of Lost Time* (1913–1927) resonates like a complicit echo of the "indispensable" confessions by Ippolit (*The Idiot*, 1868) and with the reciprocal infiltrations that maintain the dialogues between Smerdyakov and Ivan (*The Brothers Karamazov*, 1881).[6]

In his courses, Vladimir Nabokov, whose great-great-uncle had become the commander of the Peter and Paul Fortress where Dostoyevsky was imprisoned before his condemnation to jail, is fiercely set against this renowned author, who is "neither a true artist nor a true moralist—neither a good Christian nor a good philosopher—neither a poet nor a sociologist." Could the genial hunter of butterflies and stalker of *Lolita* be jealous?

André Gide, on the other hand, reads him passionately. Captivated by the intimate secrets of the man and the work, which lead "to the mysterious center of the Gospel," he venerates them in memorable lectures he gives to the grateful French public.

Albert Camus lets himself be possessed by a theatrical Dostoyevsky, to the point that he succumbs to the temptation to "adapt" him for the stage. His attachment tells us a lot about the obscurity of his freedom: he imagines the pedophile Stavrogin as a "contemporary hero." Strange doubling, indeed, of the stranger Meursault.

Nathalie Sarraute borrows her "tropisms," a bit nauseating and somewhat grotesque, from the search for this specifically

Dostoyevskian *interpenetration* (*proniknovenie*), where the infinite distance between beings and things enters into total fusion, deep within cruelty.

Simone de Beauvoir takes Dostoyevsky's Elder Zosima for the epigraph of her novel *The Blood of Others*, which concludes with the philosophy of *engagement*: "Everyone is responsible for everything before everybody."

But it is Paul Claudel, in passing, and briefly, in his correspondence, who salutes "two things in the great artist" (because his "eye listens"): "the inventor and the composer," who knows how to "exhaust an idea in its ultimate consequences," who possesses "a power that has been equaled only by Beethoven."

James Joyce, modernist for the eternity, will surprise stuffy avantgardists by aligning himself with the foggy Russian: he "has created modern prose, and intensified it to its present-day pitch" by engaging two "motives," violence and desire, "the very breath of literature."

Which does not prevent Céline, on the contrary, from vituperating against "this manner of adoring prison, which nauseates [him]," "too sinister, too Russian," "police epileptism," while also applauding the anti-Semitism in "this prediction by Dostoyevsky" (after the Commune in 1871): "Once all of the riches of Europe have been dissipated, the Bank of the Jews will remain!" Could he have forgotten that, as he delivered *Journey to the End of the Night* to the publisher NRF ("five years' work"), he had said: "Crime, delirium à la Dostoyevsky, there's something of everything in my contraption, to learn from and have fun with."

Only Philippe Sollers, in "Dostoyevsky, Freud, Roulette" (1981), raises the "irritating question" about the writer's sexuality, about the artist, about his "paradoxical psychic functioning." Sollers ventures into the laboratory of the writing to note that "the epileptic seizure manifests an original convulsion in the interior of the subject, as if from within its genetic impossibility."

Whereas other novelists (such as Leonid Tsypkin, *A Summer in Baden-Baden*, 1982/2003, and J. M. Coetzee, *The Master of Petersburg*, 1995/2004) attempt to marry their imaginary to the passions of the gambler.

2

DOSTOYEVSKY, "AUTHOR OF MY LIFE"

I was thrown into this hearth: nothing remained of me but this hearth. In
its entirety, the hearth itself was thrown outside of me.

—Georges Bataille, *Inner Experience*

2.1 Outside the Limits

His eyes rivetted on the Bulgarian editions of *The Idiot* (1868),
Demons (1872), and *The Brothers Karamazov* (1881), my father advised
strongly against reading them. "Too destructive, demoniacal,
clingy; enough is enough, you won't like it at all, leave it!" In addition, he dreamed of seeing me leave this "intestine of hell," using I
don't know what verse—unlocatable in the Holy Scriptures—to
designate our native Bulgaria. To accomplish this desperate project, I saw nothing better to do than to develop my "innate taste,"
as he put it, for clarity and liberty, in French, it goes without saying, since he had had me discover the language of La Fontaine and
Voltaire. In addition to our "Russian big brother," who was "naturally" imposed on us. At the time, the dominant ideology ridiculed
the writer's "religious obscurantism," even though fervent specialists behind the Stalinist stage continued to lovingly celebrate his
mysteries—his "immersion" (*proniknovenie*) in himself and in others

(Vyacheslav Ivanov), the "plurality of his worlds" à la Einstein (according to Leonid Grossman), his "Shakespearian polyphony" (A. V. Lunacharsky) . . . Obviously, as usual, I disobeyed the paternal orders and plunged into Dosty. Bedazzled, overwhelmed, engulfed.

I will never forget how thunderstruck I was reading the two conversations between Raskolnikov and Sonya and their exchange of crosses, in *Crime and Punishment* (1866). Had she guessed what he himself wasn't even sure he had done? Crimes or deliriums, the murder of Alyona Ivanovna, an obscure pawnbroker "rich as a Yid," had wrested the "detective novel" from literature to reveal the miseries and abjections of our century. And the cross the nervous student refuses, then accepts in the end, was it Sonya's cross or rather the one she had received from Liza, the second victim?

This gift of a gift, this forgiveness, did it unite him, both fascinated and disgusted, with his own feminine tendencies? To achieve the renewal of his destiny as a hero? With "Napoleon in perspective," Rodion hallucinated the ultimate freedom of a "louse" turned "overman" by putting to death a superfluous human being.

I could understand, envy, argue, but in *living in the text* this disruption of norms and laws to the point of wiping out the "ultimate limit," I lost my footing.

Later on, returning to Dostoyevsky in French, I came upon a passage in his *A Writer's Diary* of 1877 about the successes of a neologism of his invention. The neologism was abundantly used by Turgenev, unbearable though admired rival: *stushevatsya* ("to disappear, to be annihilated," from the Russian *toush*, in German Tusch, designating India ink). The engineering student, who worked to sketch various drafts, plans, and military constructions, drawn and shaded in India ink, excelled in the art of "shad[ing] a given surface well, from dark to light to white—to naught": "sinking imperceptibly into nothingness," such is the evasive, fleeting subject that the young Dostoyevsky was. His neologism revealed, to anyone who wanted to hear it, the exquisite excitation retained in the act of writing, the extenuated sound of his voice engraved in the map of the maternal tongue, the intense pleasure of being "the wound and the knife," the steely stylus that scarifies me, mastery conjugated with collapse. Or how to "annihilate oneself with fluidity."

But the *stushevatsya* produces neither an "elegant washdrawing" nor a painting on Chinese silk from Dostoyevsky's pen. This word impregnates the pitiful embraces of Mr. Goliadkin the elder with his double, Mr. Goliadkin the younger (*The Double*, 1846). It *sweats* in the "sin" that gnaws at them, *tickles* the fleeting "glance," *brushes against* the crowd that "surrounds" them, then *sinks* with delectation, like a "pâté in the mouth" of its shadow, substitute trash . . . In the discreet polyphony of this neologism, I then perceived what the *Writer's Diary* did not say, but which the novelistic flood of the entire oeuvre carried forward, insidiously: triumphant expansion of the sentences breathlessly released (*tush* also means "fanfare" in Russian); convulsive saraband of consumed bodies (*tusha* refers to flesh and meat); *tushit* means "extinguish" or "smother"; seductions, lures, and pleasures of the take; or caressing pictorial techniques. In French, *toucher* ("to touch") turns into a charmer when one is touched/touching, but it becomes libertine in *faire une touche* ("to seduce"). Irrefragable *jouissance* of the writing.

The young student in French philology and comparative literature did not know she was the prisoner of this *stushienie/stushevatsya*. I was upset, disconcerted. And I hastened back to my La Fontaines, my Voltaires, my Hugos, who were to lead me to Sartre, Beauvoir, Camus, Blanchot, the New Novel, Sollers. An exile rather more exhausting than the prison with the underground in Dostoyevsky's white nights. Cutting intoxication of eroticism, lucid sublimation in the French manner, in French, and freedom risked like a unique transcendence.

2.2 Polyphony According to Bakhtin

The second edition of Mikhail Bakhtin's book *Problems of Dostoevsky's Poetics* (1929/1960) was an event—for specialists, amateurs, and well beyond.[1] This was during the "thaw." The promised freedom of thought was taking its time to arrive, but it did have a way of slipping into criticism and theory of literature, the secret lung of shackled philosophy.

The initiated had known the first edition for a long time, but with the new one, Bakhtin's *Dostoevsky* turned into a social phenomenon, a political symptom. At the center of this agitation was my friend and mentor, Tzvetan Stoyanov, a famous literary critic, Anglophone, Francophone, and obviously Russophone. He had already introduced me to Shakespeare and Joyce, Cervantes and Kafka, the Russian Formalists and the post-Formalist breakthrough of a certain Bakhtin. Now, day and night, aloud and in Russian, with Bakhtin's book in hand, we could again immerse ourselves in the novels of Dostoyevsky. I felt the vocal power of the tragic laugh, of farce within the force of evil, and that contagious, intoxicating flow of dialogues composed into narratives which Bakhtin calls *slovo*, translated by "word." To be heard, through the lexicon and the syntax, like an incarnate Logos, the Word handling the Biblical deliverance in a new plurivocal, multiversal narration:

"For I am full of matter, the spirit within me constraineth me. Behold, my belly is as wine which hath no vent; it is ready to burst like new bottles. I will speak, that I may be refreshed: I will open my lips and answer. Let me not, I pray you, accept any man's person, neither let me give flattering titles unto man. For I know not to give flattering titles; in so doing my maker would soon take me away" (Job 32:18–22). Hadn't Dostoyevsky known Job as a baby?[2]

The Russian Formalists had unraveled the labyrinths of *story*: they had reduced it to a binary morphology or a sort of grammar in which the *subject* addresses an *object* in the trial of the *verb*. They would be an inspiration for French structuralism. Illuminating analyses, to which the Bakhtinians were opposed, attentive as they were to Hegel while rejecting Freud in their attempt to elucidate the enchantment and toxicity of narrative poetics.

In the novelistic *slovo* (word), Bakhtin's interpretations identify a deep logic: the logic of *dialogue*. The human voice is born in dialogue—initial, unending, undecidable *conversation*. I speak only ever in twos, foundational alterity-proximity. We *con-verse*. A stabilizing-destabilizing structure, because "*the dialogue allows him to*

substitute his own voice for the voice of another person" (213). There follow
identification and confusion. But also projection, introjection, and
sometimes mutualities—invasive or fruitful, closed or open, crimes
or ecstasies. Only the narrator finds his way in it, at best, because he
is not really the author but another species of dialoguer, a sort of
third party who takes the risk of getting involved in the narrative
that proceeds from the interaction and is composed of thresholds,
impasses, and coups de théâtre, repeatedly, infinitely.

The plurality of voices thus discerned and recomposed orchestrates the interior and exterior debate in each of Dostoyevsky's
metaphysical detective stories. For instance, about *The Double* (1848):
"The whole work is constructed, therefore, entirely as an interior
dialogue of three voices within the limits of a single dismantled consciousness. Every essential aspect of it lies at a point of intersection
of these three voices, at a point where they abruptly, agonizingly
interrupt one another . . . One and the same word, idea, phenomenon is passed through three voices and in each voice sounds differently. The same set of words, tones, inner orientations is passed
through the outer speech of Goliadkin, through the speech of the
narrator and through the speech of the double, and these three
voices are turned to face one another, they speak not about each
other but with each other. Three voices sing the same line, but not in
unison; rather, each carries its own part" (220).

Dialogue having become the deep structure of *being in the world*
according to Dostoyevsky, "Everything in his world lives on the very
border of its opposite" (176), and meaning erodes but is reborn,
masked/unmasked, carnivalesque misalliances and somber, thoughtful laughter. For "Love lives on the very border of hate, knows and
understands it, and hate lives on the border of love" (176): Versilov's
love-hate; Aglaya and Nastasya Filippovna's love-jealousy; Katerina
Ivanovna's sacrificial love for Dmitri Karamazov; Ivan's guilty love
for Katerina and Liza; Alyosha's fearful love for Liza; Dmitri's parricidal love for Grushenka. "Faith lives on the very border of atheism, sees itself there and understands it, and atheism lives on the
border of faith and understands it," Bakhtin insists (176). "Loftiness
and nobility live on the border of degradation and vulgarity (Dmitri

Karamazov). Love for life neighbors upon a thirst for self-destruction (Kirillov). Purity and chastity understand vice and sensuality (Alyosha Karamazov)" (176).

Regenerating a current that runs through European literature, Dostoyevsky invents "the uniquely original and innovative form of the polyphonic novel" (178). For one thing, he manages to "carnivalize" ethical solipsism: since humans cannot do without the consciousness of the other, contraries that disunite (life-death, love-hate, birth-death, affirmation-negation) also tend to contract and converse in "the upper pole of a two-in-one image" (176). Example of a masterly figure of carnival: Prince Myshkin, saint and idiot. His mad love for his rival Rogozhin, who tried to assassinate him, reaches its summit after the murder of Nastasya Filippovna by the same Rogozhin, when the final instants of the princely consciousness sink into insanity.

But, on the other hand, the polyphonic novel also opens up the intimate scene and its defined epoch to the space of a *universal infinite*, which the *mysteries* of the Middle Ages also aimed for. The capital discussion between Shatov and Stavrogin in *Demons* (1872) evokes it: "We are two beings, and we have come together in infinity . . . for the last time in the world. Abandon your tone and take a human one! At least for once in your life speak in a human voice."

2.3 Seriousness of the Carnival

With his nervous laugh, disarming and disruptive, Tzvetan Stoyanov punctuated, accentuated, and liberated the farce of nothingness and being, dispelling the confused melancholy of my first readings. Bakhtin had convinced us that Dostoyevsky had charted an unheard-of course: neither *tragedy* nor *comedy*, more corrosive than Socratic dialogue and not even *cynical*, although he had borrowed his recasting of genres from a third-century BCE cynic, Menippus of Gadara, and from the medieval and Renaissance Menippean satire, which the literary theoretician also showed informing the work of Rabelais.

No cynicism, then, for one who knows how to die laughing, with civilization starting to feel its mortality. Dostoyevsky was revealing to us the seriousness of the carnival, a vitality we needed, twenty-five years before the fall of the Berlin Wall, to break up the senselessness underlying ambient pretentions about "making sense." Even more seriously, and beyond the political context, Tzvetan's laugh helped me accept the carnivalesque dimension of *inner experience* itself, which Dostoyevsky places in counterbalance to beliefs and ideologies.

In the meantime, Tzvetan Stoyanov devoted himself to the ultimate dialogue that Dostoyevsky had put into play in his relations with Konstantin Pobedonostsev. This ayatollah of Orthodoxy, jurist and professor of law, with a long face and a waxy complexion, whose portrait by Repin gave us a chill, had ended up at the rank of General Prosecutor of the Holy Synod. Unmovable pillar of the reigns of Nicholas II and Alexander III. The writer needed him to protect him from the "censor pigs" (as he called them), who were threatening the seventh book of *The Brothers Karamazov* (1881), in which the former convict, henceforth sublimated as a faithful of Christ, had taken the liberty of transforming a Russian monk into a literary character: the famous Elder Zosima of the stinking cadaver, who harbors "Karamazovian profundities." Among other carnivalesque visions, sudden catastrophes, and truthful lies. In their correspondence, which becomes more and more intimate, the writer assures the General Prosecutor that "[my] ideas are very close to [yours]," going so far are to promise that in his speech on Pushkin, he will develop "*our* convictions," not without specifying that he cares less about the "ideas" than about the "artistic pictures" of his novels. The "director of conscience," son of a literature professor, very much likes to read, knows about the impact of literature, and is quite willing to bask in the light in the vicinity of the genius, while manipulating him.

Because the problem of God makes "the child of the age of disbelief and doubt" "suffer consciously or unconsciously all his life."[3] Kirillov also proclaims, in *Demons* (1872): "I cannot think something else, I think one thing all my life. God has tormented me all my life."

Dostoyevsky, a former Fourierist, henceforth spokesperson for the theophorous Russian people, is convinced that only the Orthodox faith of the tsar-father and of the muzhiks can embody Christ's message, on the condition of overlooking his dangerous mystery. His novels bear its precious and truthful evidence. Might he have displaced God into all humanity? The novelist, dying, bequeaths to his son the Gospel that the women of the Decembrists had given him on the road to the prison.

Dostoyevsky and Pobedonostsev: complicities and manipulations, again and always! On this subject, which is central to any totalitarian regime, the first volume of Tzvetan Stoyanov's research, *Le génie et son maître* (2000), as impassioned as it was meticulous, contained veiled allusions to the connections intellectuals in Bulgaria risked with the forces in power at that time. It was to be followed by a second volume devoted to the novelistic ruses of the genius who ceaselessly fine-tuned his art of parricide, under the auspices of the Holy Synod. Tzvetan Stoyanov died in 1971, in dubious circumstances, and the second volume never saw the light of day, as if in echo and in ultimate dialogue with Dostoyevsky, who never wrote his *Life of a Great Sinner*. But his entire oeuvre is that *Life*.

Europe, embarrassed by Russia, struggling with its multilingualism, suffers in its Orthodox part. It has not yet taken the measure of those penetrating voices that have made it happen, that will make it endure. Tzvetan Stoyanov's voice is one of those.

Expecting the fellowship for doctoral studies on the French New Novel, I took the plane to Paris with five dollars in my pocket (the only ones my father had found) and, in my suitcase, Bakhtin's book on Dostoyevsky.

Paris was talking about language, discussing phonemes, myths, and kinships . . . elementary structures and generative syntax, semantics, semiotics, the avant-garde, and formalism . . . Exile is a trial and a chance, I dared to ask: "Gentlemen structuralists, do you like poststructuralism?" I heard Émile Benveniste insist on the *enunciation*, which carries the *utterance*, and Jacques Lacan play with the *signifier* in the unconscious. Bakhtin's postformalism inspired another view of language—intrinsically *dialogic*—and of writing—necessarily *intertextual*. Roland Barthes's seminar, the journal *Critique*, but especially the journal and the series of *Tel Quel* books by Philippe Sollers, then the École des Hautes Études, the Université Paris VII, New York, and many others gave me the chance to develop them.

I turned away from Dostoyevsky's themes only to commit myself to the writings of Mallarmé, Céline, Proust, Artaud, or Colette, using Dostoyevsky's *polyphonic logic* and my own intimate understanding. Attentive to the surprises and the exploits of styles and forms, this approach focuses from the start on *revolutions in language*, which reveal and manage pivotal tremors in civilization, in depth and often in opposition to social movements.

Once again I brushed up against the mouths of darkness that had disconcerted me in my father's library; my semanalytical seismograph,[4] dialogism and intertextuality included, palpitated with the crucible of these toxic experiences both in the texts and in me, but they did not let me cross their thresholds. The interpretation, even when exquisite, of an orchestration as convulsive as Dostoyevsky's procures an approach to the tenuous, cautious (Georges Bataille would say "indecent") pleasure of uncovering once and for all the strangeness that augments oneself. To tame it, to make it one's own. Would all that remained for me be a return to metaphysics—which had in any case programmed all the linguistic, hermeneutic, and philosophical tools on the sly? Or rather, in the "post-truth" era, was I going to go in search of "something that, not being God," disappears in the jubilatory night of the suffering sinner, in the impossible wager of the moralist? Neither the one nor the other; psychoanalysis would open new horizons for me that were considerably more stimulating.

2.4 Freud: Reader of Dostoyevsky

In inventing the unconscious, Sigmund Freud discovered a distinctive, unheard-of human trait: *sex haunted by language* (the expression comes from Philippe Sollers). It is this very trait whose polyphonies

Dostoyevsky composed, without realizing it, thus revealing himself—after the fact—as a precursor to Freudian concepts, anticipating the post-Freudians themselves. The author of *Beyond the Pleasure Principle* (1920) and *Civilization and Its Discontents* (1930) probes the forms of this voluptuous furor of speaking beings, laundered through dialogic thrusts, in his "Dostoevsky and Parricide" (1928).

The founder of psychoanalysis, who recognizes that he "[does] not really like him" (in a letter to Reik)—because "my patience with pathological natures is exhausted in analysis"—nevertheless places the novelist "not far behind Shakespeare." While regretting that "he was condemned to this failure by his neurosis" and that "the greatness of his intelligence and the strength of his love for humanity might have opened to him another, an apostolic, way of life," the Viennese doctor concludes: "The future of human civilization will have little to thank him for."

Through (and in spite of) the lens of oedipal desire (possess the mother, eliminate the father) with which he diagnoses this convulsive man and his inevitable sadomasochistic ambivalences, reinforced by a constitutional bisexuality that is the source of a repressed homosexuality, Freud doesn't forget Dostoyevsky's "mechanism for abnormal instinctual discharge . . . laid down organically." The writing, he believes, reveals his psychosexual traits, all dominated and maintained by the pathetic consciousness of guilt and an unpayable debt to the father, lord and God, which oblige the neurotic artist to "claim to be playing a Christlike role" and to "become a reactionary."

Freud's set-to with the "moralist sinner" is considerably more than a toxic aggressivity that awakens the reader knocked out or blinded by the text. The Viennese doctor seizes hold of little Fyodor, confused with his excited and disappointed young mother. The child masturbates to the death, and that's not merely an expression. Pleasure to the death for real, for the paternal punishment is omnipresent, emasculation is precisely the equivalent of putting to death. The little boy is afraid of dying while asleep, of being buried alive. According to biographers, "frightful, unforgettable, and torturous things" take place in this family; and the little child will have illnesses that are not really epileptic. *Morbus Sacer* will declare itself only at age eighteen when his father dies, in 1839. As if the punishments inflicted on the convict were not sufficient to satisfy the culpability of the neurotic Oedipus-son, he mortifies himself even more: the seizures start again in Siberia and henceforth mark his existence. Annunciatory exaltation and mortiferous explosion. Body and soul consumed in the finally total orgasm. Do we not call coitus "little epilepsy," even "little death"? Freud specifies that the convulsions, like the sexual processes, have a toxic origin. A jubilatory and terrifying annihilation, unless it's a self-engenderment *at the same time*: the putting to death of the old body—impotent, sickly, *feminine*, castrated, and ashamed—to attain the "perfect man," the new man, beyond Myshkin and Mitya Karamazov. The re-birth. And re-begin, like the Man of Sorrows, in infinite Time.

Freud's brief soundings into his Dostoyevsky divide him into four parts: the creative artist, the neurotic, the moralist, the sinner. We should read these soundings in consideration of *all* the writings of the founder of psychoanalysis.

When he approaches "this accursed Russian" (Freud's letter to Zweig, October 19, 1920), Freud is in the process of modifying his conception of the psychical apparatus. Repression, Oedipus complex, and neurosis no longer suffice. In *Beyond the Pleasure Principle* (1920), Thanatos emerges as the active double of Eros. It's the "work of the negative," call it *negation, denial,* or *forclusion,* specifying the speaking being. *The Double* (1846), *The Gambler* (1866), *The Eternal Husband* (1870) had been there already . . .

The drives for immediate satisfaction and pleasure are deferred, held back, engrammed in *mnemonic traces*; these mnemonic traces accord with those of internal and external perceptions, to be composed, recomposed, redone, and undone. That is the degree zero of thought. Matter gives up immediate pleasure and constructs "beyond" it a "substitute." It is the capacity to engram, represent, memorize, think, speak, play, write. A *neo-reality* arrives, at the cost of a tearing away, a jump, a generating cut: Freud calls it "a revolution in the mind" in his "Formulations on the Two Principles of Mental Functioning" (1911).

This psychical preformulation initiates the original repression, which makes possible the human capacity to speak and to think. The assumption of libidinal components dispenses a specific new pleasure, which accompanies the creation of the symbol of negation and of all the symbols that will ensue, and the being appears in the form of nonbeing: thoughts. The repressed person is taken up in a sort of independence with respect to the repression, suspension-inscription of the flesh in the flesh of words, *sublimation*. Sublimation opens new fields of investment, procuring that "gain in pleasure" that is *jouissance*. Lacan avoids this psychosexual economy by pivoting around "the purely topological origin of language": "Is the speaking being speaking because of something that happened to sexuality, or did something happen to sexuality because he is the speaking being?" (*Seminar 19*, 1972–1973).

Because of "secondary repressions" imposed by the context of family, society, and history, the mosaic of the "heart of hearts" is added and tends to cohabit with the volcano of the drive and its crust of perceptible meaning. They don't leave the neurotic in peace. The neurotic is expected to "succeed in his synthesis," "his unity," but they torture him with more or less bearable symptoms between desire for Mom and putting to death of Dad. Until the unconscious itself and its formations shatter into pieces and the speaking being yields to the "original gap," "limit states," and revolution of the "void."

We will call this place where the neurosis erodes and the Dostoyevskian demons flood in: "cleavage" or "split," "cut," or a "re-splitting of the subject." Freud's disciples pushed their treatments into these regions to support the "ejection out of oneself" (Bataille), "limit states" and "collapses." Toward possible transformations (W. R. Bion), understood as psychical growth, renewal, even rebirth (D. Winnicott, A. Green). Death to oneself and resurrection? "*Surrection!*" It's James Joyce's word: "Array! Surrection" (*Finnegans Wake*, 1939). But Dostoyevsky beats him to it, in attributing the fury of this reversal to the narrator who would engage in polemics with Chernyshevsky's "clandestine" Lopukhov. For having confronted and integrated the "bottom of the underground," "the spiteful man," "the sick man," "the most unpleasant man," "the paradoxical man," "emerges the most alive" (*Notes from Underground*, 1864).

The underground is not outside us, it is inside us. We are *doubled* daily by the absolute separation between diurnal life, which tends toward peace, and the wild destructivity of the dream life. *Doubled*, we also participate in the ideology and the mystique of the groups and communities that conserve their internal connections by ejecting their reprobate onto others. Some are "split": limit states that "deform" themselves to avoid the rupture of the ego: "In this way the inconsistencies, eccentricities and follies of men would appear in a similar light to their sexual perversions, through the acceptance of which they spare themselves repressions," writes Freud, in "Neurosis and Psychosis" (1924).

So much for the "purified pleasure ego," which still haunted the supercilious Viennese doctor, reader of Dostoyevsky! Welcome to the "split ones" with their "private madness." Hoping they will not scatter about as avatars on the Web, but will attain eventual kaleidoscopes of malleability, crossings, and sublimations.

2.5 The Flesh of the Infinite Void and of Words

Long before, and very early, Dostoyevsky had realized that the epileptic explosion, its auras, its pains, and its fears, put him in contact with an essential dimension of the human condition: the advent of meaning and its eclipse. He was able to register, in story and voice, the hypersynchronous firing of the neurons, the noisy, strangled respiration of the seizure, the discharges still full of energy. A sort of verbal *stereotactic* that neither *defends* itself from these discharges nor *forgets* them, but rather encloses them in the funnel of emptiness where symbol, language, and thought are constituted. The schizophrenic persists in doing the re-splitting, but he sinks into the gap, and the *real* is confused along with the *symbolic*. The paranoiac makes the effort to reorganize them as a delirium into which his unsymbolized traumas are integrated. The writer, neither schizophrenic nor paranoid, is the one who acquires the conviction that the fault is destined to consume the very gap that generates it; that he owes it to himself to *suffer* and to *quit* the gravitational waves in which each word, behavior, and story reveals their split being—dialogic, polymorphous, inexhaustible, and pitiable, dying, surviving. To capture in words the flesh of the infinite void and of words. Genesis (1:2–3) arises out of the Abyss (*tehom*) that haunts the poets' paradise, "won from the void and formless infinite" (Milton, *Paradise Lost*, 3:10–12).

The paroxysmic investment of the narration, taking the place of other capacities for love and suffering maintained but subordinated to writing, necessarily stems from Dostoyevsky's exceptional singularity. But it also belongs particularly to the Christian faith that sustains him before and, above all, during and after prison. Which permits him, through its immanent dialectic, to use it to the point of contorting it for the benefit of his Word, of his extravagant survival as a man and a writer. His *optimism* and his glorification of the *energy* of thought (so admired by André Gide) are incomprehensible without his Christlike faith (*vera* in Russian) in the incarnate Word. His novels are Christlike, his Christianism is novelistic.

Russophone readers can hear the Sanskrit sources of this word (*vera*), which brings them neither to "belief" or "credit" nor to the "link that ties and unties" in the Latin words *credo* and *religere*. *Vera* points rather toward the *true*, the *just*, the *faithful*, to dominate the *fire* and *ferment* managed by the guardian of the seas: Varuna "of a thousand eyes," that god of the Indo-European pantheon turned into the very popular Svarga of the Slavs.

A psychoanalyst before the notion existed, the "moralist sinner" accomplished an unprecedented exploit when he succeeded in piercing the fog of neurotic phantasms in which his pre-Siberian writings kept him. He discovered their *underground*: the ultimate threshold of primary rejection, the empty center of the schism, the re-splitting of the subject. He needed the stroke of a double-edged blade, those two *Notes: from a Dead House* (1862) and *from Underground* (1864)—delicate incision, raging dissection—for the voice of his great novels of the last years to be liberated, on the other side of neurosis.

3

IN THE STEPS OF THE LIBERATED CONVICT

The law of self-destruction and the law of self-preservation are equally powerful in humankind... You're laughing? You don't believe in the devil? Disbelief in the devil is a French notion, a frivolous idea.

—F. M. Dostoyevsky, *The Idiot* (1868)

3.1 Passions Played/Played-Out

The metamorphosis begins in the *Dead House*.[1] Tortured flesh, instinctive anguish about oneself: "Ideas and even convictions change, a whole person changes too," the convict writes to Totleben (March 24, 1856). Howling of the dirty cattle, "they would have eaten us," desire to resemble them. Was he really flogged by Kryvtsov? Scars from the blows of the birch rods, "I was the disciple of the convicts" (he supposedly confided to Nekrasov, according to what his daughter said). "Prison killed many things in me and made other things blossom." Tenderness of the bodies deformed in the mists of the baths. An enormous, giant spider as big as a man, called Gazin—he enjoyed cutting the throats of little children. The criminal Orlov, a titan of a man who had a perfect command of himself, necessarily treated me with scorn as a little boy—feeble, submissive creature that I am, inferior to him in all respects. Evil is a somber grandeur, demonic spirituality. As absolute as pleasure, the proof of which lies in those convicts who disguised themselves as women to perform on the boards a Don Juan on the Volga. And the love of the young Muslim Alei, as pretty as a young girl, "Ah, how well he speaks!" when he learns to read in Russian.

The neurotic fragmentation is not going away, but a new narrator is emerging: the common law criminal Alexander Goryanchikov, condemned to forced labor for having killed his wife. He is a convict along with the others, a man like the others, who recounts his life in the prison. It is not enough to double oneself, it is possible to reunite with the death drive, absolute emptiness hemmed with certainty, which becomes a joy, the joy of being able to play the men/play them out: to write them.

With the Gospel in hand, his only book, the convict is doomed to masculine promiscuity and the love of the Russian people. Upon leaving Omsk, the writer discovers women, marriage, and torturing passions. After five years of reclusion, he continues to serve his time in Semipalatinsk, a Siberian town with Asiatic camels. Enrolled as a simple soldier in a regiment, said to be "indifferent toward women, almost [having] antipathy for them," he falls in love with the frail Maria Dmitrievna Issaieva, née de Konstant. Dostoyevsky obtains a promotion for her husband, a poor alcoholic instructor, who dies soon afterward. Vergunov, handsome hunk, gross character, whom Dostoyevsky also helps in his career, wins the widow's favors. But Maria agrees to marry Fyodor. On February 6, 1857, in the Orthodox church at Kuznetsk, and Vergunov is the best man. In spite of the violent epileptic seizure that day, and the bride's disgust, the trio continues, Dostoyevsky finds the rival "more likable than a brother." It's Maria who is plagued by jealousy. The couple breaks up, Fyodor will look after Paul, his wife's son from her first marriage. Broken love continues to tear him apart: "My life is distressing and bitter," he writes in 1858.

This doesn't prevent some fanciful passions. Like the feverish friendship with the actress Alexandra Schubert, wife of his doctor, Dr. Stepan Dmitrievich Yanovsky, a friendship he'll have to renounce, as he does with all his chaste fevers that burn for the impossible in the shadow of the third person. Next comes the enigmatic vagabond, Marfa Braun, partner of the essayist Pyotr Gorsky. She has traveled the world over, in sketchy company, on foot and by boat. This young writer, a migrant before the word existed, undocumented and homeless, seizes the heart of the master. But the master proposes a happiness so weighty that this phantom of a woman prefers to fall back on Gorsky.

Sophie Krukovskaia-Kovalevsky, daughter of the famous general and soon to become famous as the first woman mathematician, was so attracted to the suffering genius that she learned to play Beethoven's *Pathétique* sonata for him; then realized, in consternation and embarrassment, that she had never been in love with him. The "terrorist" mutated into a journalist next declared his passion to her older sister, Anna Vassilievna Krukovskaia, fervent adept of the "new ideas," of natural sciences that claim man descended from the apes, and furthermore keen on literature—she had sent two stories to the master of the review *Epoch*. For three long months, the underground man had so assiduously courted and oppressed his muse that she refused to marry him.

But it's the wild Apollinaria Suslova who literally pushes the underground man into his entrenchments. A daughter of serfs (recently freed by Alexander II), she is a "Russian beauty in European garb." This nihilist and feminist student sends the writer a letter of frantic admiration. She was his first passion; it will last six or seven years—stormy, humiliating, interrupted by breakups and separations, while passing through Paris, Berlin, Rome, and Naples where the couple stays.

The young woman's diary evokes the "offense" she says she was subjected to—evanescent desires and unhealthy pity.[2] Apollinaria is pretty and sensual, Fyodor is ugly and wants to marry her. And here's the trio once again: in Paris, she gives in to Salvador, the handsome Spanish student, to compensate for "the lowly aspects of character that no talent can make up for." "Will my pride ever desert me? No, this couldn't be. I'd rather die." She's aggravated: "I hear about F[yodor] M[ikhailovich]. I simply hate him. He made me suffer so much, when it was possible not to suffer." She fumes: "As I remember what happened two years ago, I begin to hate D. He was the first to kill my faith." She takes revenge: "I feel very sorry for him."

Hysterical reprimands on the part of a woman, as he interprets it: "You can't forgive me that you gave yourself to me, and so you are avenging yourself." Or Karamazovian truths from the novelist who, "uncouth and bitter, delights in the suffering and the tears of other people" (according to Nadejda Suslova, the sister of his mistress). And who is already playing his heart out at roulette and makes his proud lover pay for it.

Apollinaria remains Dostoyevsky's most tumultuous affair. The rebellious woman will marry the philosopher Vasily Rozanov, twenty years younger than she, and will end up devoting herself "to the people" as an instructor in the country.

For his part, Dostoyevsky the journalist will continue to support "the need for higher education for women in Russia, a need that is most urgent at this moment in particular, in view of the serious pressure among today's women to be active, to be educated, and to participate in the common cause . . . In fact, it is only higher learning that is serious, attractive, and powerful enough to settle what is almost an agitation that has begun among our women. Only science can provide answers to their questions, strengthen their intellects, and take their heterogeneous thoughts under its wing, as it were" (*A Writer's Diary*, 1876).

But the humiliated lover never tires of probing his erotic fixation, tainted with fetishism, in *The Gambler* (1866) for example, where Apollinaria Suslova is called Polina: "And I don't understand. I don't understand what's so good about her! Good-looking she is, though; yes, it seems she's good-looking. Others lose their minds over her, too. She's tall and trim. Only very thin. It seems to me you could tie her in a knot or bend her double. The print of her foot is narrow and long—tormenting. Precisely tormenting. Her hair has a reddish tint. Her eyes—a real cat's, but how proud and arrogant she can look with them."

Nicolas Strakhov was a close friend of the writer's ("you are the only one who has understood me," the author of *Crime and Punishment* had said to him) and a faithful collaborator with *Time*, but he gradually breaks with Dostoyevsky. In a late letter (1883), Strakhov denounces him to Tolstoy as "bad, envious, perverted, and he passed his whole life in upheavals which made him pitiful and would have made him ridiculous if he had not been so malicious and intelligent."

With an underground laugh, *The Eternal Husband* (1870) exposes the pathetic pleasures linking two rivals who claim to love the same woman. The novel becomes completely carnivalesque and invites us to uncover the derision intrinsic to the earlier writings and those to come. Whereas *The Gambler* (1866) indulges in a cruel vivisection of inaccessible *jouissance*, the hallucinated double of the sexual orgasm, for one who, "having lost the faith, does not dare not to believe." Even if only in the chancy luck of the roulette, absurd suicidal melancholy.

3.2 Crystal Palaces

1862. The two and a half months in Europe—Berlin, Dresden, Wiesbaden, Baden-Baden, Köln, Paris, London, Lucerne, Düsseldorf, Geneva, Genoa, Livorno, Florence, Milan, Venice, and Vienna—confirm the solitude of the writer who doesn't know how to travel. And they prepare him to break with the "humanitarian" spirit, which hadn't disappeared in his attachment to the convicts he fraternized with in the *Dead House*. "I am alone and they are all": the formula has not yet been struck, but it can be read in the disappointment that what he perceives as a new European catechism provokes in him: "To amass a fortune and possess as many things as possible." In Paris, the only thing he likes is the architecture. "The Louvre is a superb thing, and all that embankment, right up to Notre Dame, is an amazing thing." Without its "admirable monuments," the City of Light would be "an awfully sad city," for "The Frenchman is quiet, honest, polite, but insincere, and money for him is everything." "You will never dissuade the Frenchman, that is, the Parisian (because, you see, in essence all Frenchmen are Parisians), from his belief that he is the foremost man on the face of the earth. Except for Paris, however, he knows very little about the face of the earth. Indeed, he really does not want to know." It amuses him that French eloquence has become bombastic in the right-thinking of the Second Empire: "It suddenly struck me as funny. The high-flown word debases everything."

London, on the other hand, fares much better. This contemporary "Baal" has granted itself a new palace, sparkling pavilions of glass, brand new towers and cupolas that absorb the *termite nest*, the *chicken coop*, the *herd*, in a triumph that thinks it's titanic. But "you feel that here something has already been achieved." The Crystal Palace is ready for the *Notes from Underground* (1864) and the Grand Inquisitor. Neither nature nor works of art attract the attention of this very special tourist, who will look at them more, intermittently, during his other trips to Europe (1869–1871) with his second wife, Anna Snitkina. The writer is interested only in *people!* London swarming with crowds, half-naked, savage, famished, the Sabbath of "white Negroes" in the working-class neighborhoods of Whitechapel, the thousands of "women for sale" in Haymarket where the mothers "were bringing their young daughters into the business." The meetings with Herzen and Bakunin only mature his faith in the theophorous Russian people whom he heard moaning and exulting, even in the wailing of the "cruel man" in the katorga in Siberia. Before defining himself later, and definitively, as an "old Russian European."

The second trip unleashes his passion for gambling and his thunder against the West. Against Catholicism first and above all, because it betrays the mystery of the Christ by establishing the political power of the papacy: "in the West Christ has been lost (through the fault of Catholicism), and because of that the West is declining." "Jewish Germany" is "a people who have used up all their energies, because after such a spirit, after such learning—to trust in the sword, blood, violence." A catastrophic vision inspired by the Franco-Prussian war, or vague prophecy of National Socialism to come? When it's only "professors, doctors, students [who] are most excited and *proud* of all." His greatest anger, though, strikes hard at French socialism:

"For the whole 19th century that movement has either been dreaming of paradise on earth (beginning with the phalanstery) or when it comes the least bit to action . . . demonstrates a humiliating inability to say anything positive . . . They chop off heads. Why? Exclusively because that's easiest of all. To say something is incomparably more difficult." And he delivers the coup de grâce of the Paris Commune in sarcasm: "The burning of Paris is a monstrosity: 'It didn't succeed, so let the world perish, because the Commune is higher than the happiness of the world and of France'" (letter to Nicolas Strakhov, May 18, 1871).

For ten years, this man disappointed with Europe will make his little review, *Time*, the center of Russian thought. Against the revolutionary materialists of *The Contemporary*, he needed to create "a new form, truly our own, taken from our soil, popular sources and spirit." He's a Slavophile because he's in love with the Russian soul, but in the manner of a *pochvenik* (from *pochva*, "earth, terroir," which his adversaries would now translate as "of his origins"), although a reformer. It's a *history aesthetic*, neither ivory tower nor utilitarian ideology, that Dostoyevsky is creating and imposing: "the beautiful is useful, because in humanity there is a constant need for beauty and the supreme ideal."

The polemist adopts Dobrolyubov's sentence: "Art is always contemporary and real, it has never existed otherwise, and above all it cannot exist otherwise." "The Word is a great thing" becomes his motto, in contradiction to various political commitments. It could have been the underground man's motto, if that insect had been able to understand himself and have a motto.

Censorship cracks down, *Time* is forbidden by order of the tsar end of May 1863. *The Epoch*, which replaces it, won't last, but the fever of journalism doesn't let go of the ex-Fourierist and ex-convict. It is therefore in the conservative review of Prince Vladimir Meshchersky, *The Citizen*, where Dostoyevsky becomes the director for a year (1873–74), that his first *Writer's Diary* comes to life. Not without having been sentenced by the court of Saint Petersburg to a fine and two days of imprisonment, for having published "information" about "highnesses"!

3.3 The "Hampered Ego"

Maria Dmitrievna, the writer's first wife, dies on April 16, 1864. Dostoyevsky's brother, Mikhail Mikhailovich, dies on July 10 of the same year.

Facing the remains of his wife displayed on a table, as was the tradition, the widower drafts a funerary meditation. More like a justification of the *Underground Man*, the project of which dates back to 1862 but whose *Notes* won't be published until January 1864.

"To love thy neighbor as thyself, according to the commandment of Christ, is impossible," proclaims this Desdichado.[3] From the outset, it is the Ego that causes obstacles. But does it really exist? Man is unfinished, in a perpetual struggle and in permanent development. The violence of desire pierces through and annihilates any *duality*, the husband *and* the wife, Masha *and* me. The Holy family itself is abnormal and egoistic, the only valid *doctrine* is that of the sword: "I came not to send peace, but a sword" (Matthew 10:34).

As for the Christly ideal, "our future ideal," does it not teach the *annihilation* of this Ego in the fusion with the all? "Love each thing as thyself." However, only Christ is capable of this "full synthesis" of being. Does the impossibility come from the Ego or from Christ? Such is the question that will return with the Grand Inquisitor. Start by planting the sword in the obscure and pretentious Ego, rummage into the rubble of its loves and its hatreds, confront its crystal palaces, sacrifices, murders, and crimes. Suffer, suffer a lot, "call this state a sin" to write all this, because "we know men don't die completely." With the vicious truth of its undergrounds, it can contemplate a "full synthesis" of being in the "infinite diversity," "in Analysis."

This meditation beside the cadaverized love, with its intense Christly tonality, sketches an imperious and fearless transvaluation of Christianism. The writer envisions the wounds and the potentialities of humanity and constructs living neo-realities with them. An exuberant vitality emanates from this widower who is less unconsoled than questing plenitude. But it does not predict the triumph of the Nietzschean overman towering over the fissure in being, which was to carry off the mad philosopher. Without being an anarchistic rejection of marriage either, Dostoyevsky's reticence toward family reveals rather the panic of a fragile body before women, femininity, and the feminine within oneself. Later, the attraction of the supernatural must have made him dream, along with his friend Vladimir Solovyov, of a "real resurrection of former generations," "putting an end to reproduction." Angelic fundamentalist transhumanism.

But the novelist devours the thinker, and the sword of the underground man begins to attack the obsessions of the neurotic stuck in three-sided love affairs, as well as the spasms of the gambler ruining himself—like a true Russian!—in the casinos of Europe. *The Gambler* (1866) and *The Eternal Husband* (1870) show its scars.

3.4 The Whims of Chance: Money and the Synagogue

The narrator is the gambler himself, Alexis Ivanovich (*The Gambler*, 1866). Young preceptor to the children of General Zagoryansky, he becomes infatuated with Polina Alexandrovna, the stepdaughter of the general, and becomes a gambler only to please her during the family's stay at Roulettenburg.

The prototype of this fatal miss, who toys with the narrator and causes his fall, would be Apollinaria Suslova, the wild feminist student whose memoirs let it be understood there was a troubled and violent affair with the novelist.[4] In *The Gambler*, the young woman represents the implacable *maternal dominion* from which Alexis desperately attempts to free himself by winning at the casino. Very quickly, however, wanting to impress Polina, he becomes addicted to gambling. The desire to penetrate the young woman's secret and the magic of the roulette become so entangled that humiliation and hopelessness sweep the narrator-gambler (doubling and redoubling the author) into a "pleasure unlike any other, except that of the whip when it slashes your back and tears your flesh apart."

This burning image betrays the convict: it is not the naïve preceptor, it is Fyodor Mikhailovich who experiences like this the whims of chance that the prisoners of Omsk indulge in. It is he who shudders at the voice of the chief croupier proclaiming "*Les trois derniers coups, messieurs,*" "*Passe,*" "*Manque,*" "*Rouge.*" To win to the point of losing, be stunned, no longer remember anything. No thoughts, hallucinatory lure of the win, and nothing but the monstrous jubilation of the loot, unmerited power—"I no longer know how to say it." Even more orgiastic, more stunning still, is losing, the *zero* that scans the infinite expectation of luck with a negative ecstasy. The author Dostoyevsky's requests, as he cries over his debts and implores his best friends, wife included, to provide him urgently with the sums required to place his bets again, will continue for years in his letters.

The convicts, thirsty for alcohol and beaten with lashes of the whip, manage to obtain money to gamble with in their *Dead House*, and they spend it, laughing. For "in this debauchery, there is a laugh of freedom," which Dostoyevsky hears. With no "going out" except after a long term, or never, this secluded humanity got drunk on a sort of grimacing freedom: to win only to lose to no avail. The convicts' pleasure in playing the winner loses, the loser wins is a relief because it parodies the knout roulette on the lacerated backs of the convicts. Hadn't the writer emphasized in his correspondence that "his representation of the convicts" is a "CONCRETE and extremely detailed representation of the roulette"? To give free rein to intoxicating sadomasochism would be a freedom for the convicts, then? "Our Sade," Turgenev calls Dostoyevsky in a letter to Tolstoy; and Apollinaria Suslova, annoyed and bitter, lets that be understood, while sparing herself any sexual allusion.

Money—debauchery and liberty—is one of the obsessional themes in Dostoyevsky's writing, like the "trio" and the "rape of the little girl." "Money is everything" and "Everything is permitted," he proclaims, bearing witness to the galloping capitalism sweeping the old Russia of the nineteenth century. Everything is permitted ... with money! Even freedom, this game, a game with money, playing with money. The convicts had understood that and made fun of it with all their hearts. "What does a convict place higher than money? Freedom, if only a dream of freedom." "Spending his money, he acts as if already free."

Does the psychopathological drama of gambling cover a metaphysical experience? Dostoyevsky-Sade becomes Dostoyevsky-Pascal. Isn't *placing a bet* making a *wager* to win, to pull through, to be free? Betting is a way of praying, of *believing*; and in the financialized globalization, *life*, this *lottery*—compulsive auction winning/losing, winning/winning, losing/winning—was going to become the new religion. After having lost everything but one *gulden*, Alexis did not dare not to believe. He bet on the zero: emptiness, nothing...And he won! How can one not bet on the lack when that's all one has to dare with? Readers, dare to bet, dare to believe!—says the gambler, in essence.

Modern humanity is being born around Dostoyevsky, and through the writing of this gambler, it is already a humanity of concentration camps as well as gambling. Everyone a *convict: prisoners* of the economic and administrative constraints, *confined*, we would say today, by liberty-killing procedures. But *convicts* doubled by *gamblers*, their mediocre version, who have a need to believe, even if only in emptiness!

The story of *The Gambler* (1866) becomes pathetic or ridiculous, depending on those involved: the superrich invalid grandmother who also becomes addicted to gambling, ready to swallow up everything, trembling with pleasure; Mlle Blanche the adventurer, who turns out to be a typical French prostitute who will marry the general; de Grieux, the Frenchman, imbued with his "elegant national figure," which allows the narrator to rail against the soulless *Gallic cock* one more time; or the knowledgeable Mr. Astley, finally an Englishman, whose perhaps dull reserve the narrator appreciates and who is needed to save Polina when she falls ill and almost dies in this storm, but whom he will certainly marry.

Echoing the immemorial maternal dominion, mistress of the "having" for lack of the "being," the beautiful hysteric embodies the power of the dominator which "surpasses the limits of slavery and obliterationism," more redoubtable than a "man, naturally despotic." Alexis would be ready to kill if Polina gave him the order to; and to kill her also, for having asked him to. The specter of feminine/

maternal domination, confused with the passion for money, culminates later in the character of the hideous moneylender whom Raskolnikov will have to assassinate to be free.

In his fog, which he calls "Schillerian," the novelist continues to confront the multiple stations of this rather carnivalesque cross, taking deathly pleasure. Sentimental and romantic neurosis that the narrative begins to dissipate, however, reassuring the gambler that he is not incapable of "an instant of firmness"—the proof of which is that he did not dare not to believe. An incorrigible winner who never tires of betting on nothingness. To die laughing for!

"Everything is money" and "everything is permitted," his nihilists affirm, then. Subjugated by this "all," a modern totality, the writer himself yields to the fantasy of the Jew, who in possessing money would also possess all the powers at the same time as an impregnable mastery on their variations, vices, and manipulations. A *hatelove* of Jews runs through Dostoyevsky's works. On the one hand, a populist political anti-Semitism without complexes ("The Jewish Question," *A Writer's Diary*, 1877). On the other, a continuous veneration of the biblical message. The Jew: threatening rival and brother likeness, but none the less supreme authority. As the "cold shower" of the synagogue shows.

The Gambler (1866) had ventured a burlesque writing of pleasure compressed into pain. Writing is only another way of playing on the green baize, which does not ennoble this vice but shines a bright light on it and confronts it with the sacred: zero, circle and spiral, all or nothing. God is in the implacable wager. Jouissance also, and yet...

A new secretary, and future wife, Anna Snitkina takes down the dictation of this novel, which must be urgently published, debts are mounting. Compassionate and faithful, she will pawn her entire dowry, then her last earrings. And the addiction continues.

Until that special day in Wiesbaden in 1871 when, wanting to confess for the *n*th time in an Orthodox church, ashamed and anguished for having lost everything, Dostoyevsky finds himself in a synagogue. "It was as though I'd had cold water poured on me... A great thing has been accomplished over me, a vile fantasy that *tormented* me almost 10 years has vanished . . . Now that's all finished with! . . . I had been bound by gambling. I'll think about serious things now . . . And therefore *the serious business* will move better and more quickly, and God will bless it."

Did he perhaps hear Job, whom he has known by heart since childhood? This late Job that the young Elihu reconciles with Yahweh: neither guilty nor innocent, repudiating transgressions and mortifications, the ordeal over with, the patriarch is reprieved, and he can stand face to face with duty. Which is to say that the presence of God is inscribed, *signed*, in the songs of the night. And that the *Sheol* (hell) is also a passage (a canal) that is an integral part of life, not just any life, of "living life" itself!

Dostoyevsky will never be reconciled. But for the time of a cold shower, Yahweh sent him a sign. The Unnamable recognized him, *elected* him, almost, perhaps. The writer will no longer go to the casino, suffice it to say. When one has touched the abyss, the split, the underground within oneself, and the ecstasies of the green baize, only the oeuvre relays the lottery. Writers know that writing is a life and death game of chance. Sollers says so, calmly, in titling one of his novels *Portrait of the Gambler* (1984). Homoerotic hateloves continue to hold sway in *The Idiot* (1868), *The Eternal Husband* (1870), and *Demons* (1872) in the passions of Myshkin the absolute for the vulgar Rogozhin, in the eternal trios that keep the husbands alive or in the demons agglutinated around Stavrogin.

The man blessed by God in the synagogue will keep his promise not to gamble anymore, this time. Anna Grigoryevna confirms it. Unseen in her role as stenographer, pragmatic and effective, faithful fan and spouse, submissive before the Eternal to her eternal genius, she endures and scrupulously notes the attacks of epilepsy, registers comments, facts, and gestures, then restores them in a biography that will be a reference for the following generations. Innocent and modest, Anna Grigoryevna is only twenty when the suffering master marries her, he's forty-five, an advanced age at the time. They will have four children; Sonya and Alexis die in early childhood, Fyodor and Liubov will live to their fifties. Conjugal duty? Not only. Fyodor astonished his wife by encouraging her to buy fashionable frilly things, trivialities without interest for her. The "narrow, long trace" of Dunya's foot tortured Svidrigaylov in *Crime and Punishment* (1866). And the specter of Stavrogin raping little Matryosha could not keep from roaming the Dostoyevskian underground of the roulette.

3.5 The Carnival of the Couple: An Underground Laugh

That "ugly novella" *The Eternal Husband* (1870), which cost him "the work of a convict," does not place a cuckold and a Don Juan face to face. The worldly Velchaninov, cruel seducer and liberal aesthete, is pursued by "a gentleman with crape on his hat," who is only the provincial functionary Trussotsky, the husband. The husband of "that woman," Natalia Vassilievna, whom he had thought to be madly in love with and for whom he felt only hatred when he remembered her, turns out to be "in that degree of vexation in which the most restrained people sometimes start saying unnecessary things." " 'And what?' he thought, 'what if it's not in fact he who is bothering me, but, on the contrary, I him, and that's the whole thing?' "

The feminine figures may change—Natalia, Lisa, or Lipochka— "that woman" is always already "dead" after having been the one who dominates. If not, she will soon die, and necessarily, as a deliverance, or be content with dull melancholy formulas: "we two stand on the sides of that grave," "only it's terribly funny all the same." During this time, the lover and the husband embrace and lavish their attentions on each other, joking about their "precious connection, in which the deceased woman constituted so precious a link." Their jealousy is a sneering hatred. The lover "is taken with a real excitement"; the husband, "an appendage of his wife," "spat as if he had been befouled by something." "Yes, he loved me *from spite*; that's the strongest love." The roles are reversed, the husband lives a life of debauchery, he plays the clown and his master's fool. The carnival reaches its highpoint when the offended-offending husband "put two fingers like horns over his bald forehead . . . looking into

Velchaninov's eyes as if reveling in his most sarcastic impudence." And mocks his new office boss, who is "some sort of Jupiter." The two rivals' "orgasm" finally reveals its macabre face in their ultimate confrontation: "one could hear only their heavy breathing and the muddled sounds of the struggle." Blood of the lover, obtuse smile of the husband. It was not coitus, just a throat-cutting with the lover's razor but committed by the husband, who only had the *intention* of it, not even the *idea*, which had not escaped the lover.

One year before *The Brothers Karamazov* (1881), Dostoyevsky had noted: "Memento: For my whole life, write a Russian Candide." The laugh in *The Eternal Husband* has nothing to do with Voltaire, whose supposedly candid sarcasm had sustained his struggle against the "universal reason" of History. *The Eternal Husband* just shows the influence of prison and the debauchery of males in detention. Criticism hears in it remorse, mystical fusions, the doubling of a finally denuded Goliadkin. Chaste or piquant allusions that have trouble filling in the constitutive gap, cruel threatening truth of the underground man.

In fact, Dostoyevsky casts a bright light on the *sin* attached to *faith*, that "mysterious center of the Gospels," which attracted André Gide to the author of *Demons*. The irrefragable lovehate of the males propagates like a cosmic ray of the inexorable, irreparable, universal split. Without remorse and without compassion; no more teary sentimentality like Goliadkin's (*The Double*, 1846) or like Vanya's and Natasha's (*The Insulted and Injured*, 1861). A laugh, also underground, replaces them. Pitiable, insane, the comic drives off the pathos when it runs into one of the faces of borderline Janus and the other sends back gusts of tears, a furtive convulsion. Thus, when the eternal husband takes the train with a finally trustworthy wife, because he "took her from our local vicar," the former lover notices that the newlyweds are also leaving in a trio with the uhlan Mikenka. "Something wavered as it were and suddenly snapped in Velchaninov, who had been laughing so much only a moment before." Nothing remains of this electrical laugh but "something" of a rupture, powerful and feverish distress.

4

BEYOND NEUROSIS

To breed out of *humanitas* a self-contradiction.
I call Christianity . . . the one immortal blemish of mankind.

—Nietzsche, *The Antichrist* (1865)

4.1 "At the Bottom of the Stinking, Abject Underground"

"I am a sick man . . . I am a spiteful man." The "underground man" lives in a "corner" (*ugol*) under the "floor" (*polye*). The word *podpolie* suggests "what is under the floorboards"; it doesn't suggest any sort of burial in the ground, but designates the clandestine, the *maquis*. This denizen of the hideout, resistant and outside the law, makes his fury known. In a rage he fires off the confession of a sick man, his diseased liver, the well-known seat of melancholy, having become in his case the organ of hatred, anger, abjection, and other inextinguishable nastinesses. These he frankly doesn't so much seek to be rid of as to give vent to them.

A miserable mouse with a broadened consciousness who slaps himself, whips himself, makes fun of himself, and delights in himself, this ridiculous man does nothing but hit his forehead and his fists against a stone wall, the impregnable barrier of universal reason as summarized by the expression "Two and two make four." No compromise ("infinitely recurring zero") could possibly please him, for the simple reason that it's the law of "all of us," the impregnable fortress of the "us-all-ity." This "bad actor" of the nineteenth century has already invented a word: "the global men," *obshchechelovyeky,* he writes, foreshadowing the fantasy of a compacted and globalized humanity in the third millennium. And that revolts him.

The ground, the floor, the foundation of all the laws of nature and of mathematics that secure humanity needs to construct its chicken coops—Versailles in the past, "crystal palaces" now—to protect itself in rainy times . . . All that . . . But *What's to Be Done?* The materialist Chernyshevsky, who inspired Lenin, has just published his road plan under that title. Without taking into consideration the bilious entrenched Dostoyevskian who is not among those whose goal in life is to stay dry. "As long as I'm still alive and feel desire," the cruel one proposes to root around to find out what desires are made of, if it is indeed true that desires still exist. But there is a new obstacle considerably more dangerous than the "stone wall," it is the shame "swarming inside," feelings of guilt and forgiveness, volatile things that agitate the unhappy consciousness (the "mouse") and settle into melancholy, a fraud and a dodge in addition. Of course *The Gambler* (1866) and *The Eternal Husband* (1870) attempt to settle accounts with him, with this neurotic "mess"— laughing scornfully. But it is in *Notes from Underground* (1864), "glacial despairing hope" of the enraged man, that the "whip" of the cleavage that provokes him is affirmed, his existential and novelistic truth.

The devious moans, this "salt" of neurosis that blends contradictories, the same and the other, pleasure and suffering, into "one doesn't know what, one doesn't know who and what for you," no longer amuse the rebel. The anger turns against the "heart or whatever was going bad," like a spirited horse getting rid of the "bit in his teeth." A different writing develops, bringing to light its sovereign energy, and takes on the morons of romanticism whose refuge is in "all that was beautiful and sublime!" And even takes on the future philosophers of "nausea," "the gentleman who, in his faint-hearted anxiety, had sewn a German beaver onto the collar of his old overcoat," who will make of him an untimely hero.

In the structure of the narrative itself, a sort of new science is announced—neither gay nor sorry but poignant and ardent—the science of the split, to be exact. The clandestine writer discovered it as a result of curing himself by writing, a trial that seeks a chance to "be good." Plowing into the "wet snow," the experiment takes the form of a confession that pulverizes right in their faces the obsessive phantasms of earlier Dostoyevskian prose, starting with the model obstacle: any kind of master who treats you with scorn, a cliché of the paternal figure. Then the pals and their officer with a name like an animal's, Zverev, which recalls the name of the prison chief (did he beat him with birch rods, or is that only a dream, a desire?). Finally, "mad love" with Liza, the disgusting prostitute, hated and fatally loved-disloved, impossible love . . .

Except that the narrative explodes. The aggressivity unleashed from the underground transforms it into pathways, into open, undecidable itineraries. And the memory of passions experienced—recently, in the prison, in childhood—an indelible "imprint" of the former Dostoyevskian world, rises toward the unknown of "living life."

"Whip it! Whip it!" shouts the narrator to his coachman driving them to a woman one shouldn't love, to take savage revenge on himself, on the impossible, on the real itself, to be reinvented. The ice of repression starts to melt, and its wet snow yields to the brasier of elucidated drives.

These *Notes* are not literature. They take stock—temporarily—of a violent self-reexamination that achieves the *re-splitting* of the antihero, beyond neurotic links: edge to edge with the drives and the senses, where the speaking being, the *parlêtre*,[1] surges up—or collapses. The *Notes* palpate the vital plasma, the constitutive protobiota which is none other than the singular capacity of the unhappy consciousness—of the "insect," of the "mouse," of the "ant"—to mutate. To be and to disappear. In touch with henceforth unbound passions: redoubtable *unlinking* that sweeps away the boundary between good and evil, the self and the other, the feminine and the masculine—paradoxical coexistence of contraries risking crime and delirium. Raskolnikov and his punishment, still latent, in gestation, are anticipated here. As is the furious as well as scrupulous negation of this destructivity in the polyphony of a writing that recomposes it as truth.

Readers have preferred to hail "the philosophy of cruelty" that attacked the sentimentality of romanticism and prophesized the totalitarian latencies of the humanist, socialist, and nihilist utopias, before bowing down to the "incomprehensible genius of the novelist." My purpose is to accompany this writing that assumes the psychosexual experience of the *split*, while integrating it into the minute analysis of emotions and nuances of thought among his contemporaries and his epoch.

These *limit states* of unlinking, re-splitting, and cutting have become accessible to researchers only in the century following the disappearance of the author. Dostoyevsky appropriates the experience of these limit states in a gesture of survival, which reinvents the *novel of thought* inhabited by the *split*. It is not enough to say that his comitial state left his intellect intact. The writer introduced the "psychical revolution of matter,"[2] which he experienced, in the art of thinking through novels. It is here that his incommensurable originality resides. The voice of the thinker, ideological and orthodox, forms an integral part of it, among the other voices of his polyphonic narration.

What inhabits him is not the lyrical invocation of Lautréamont, even though *Maldoror* (1869) and the *Poésies* (1870) borrow the same *fin-de-siècle* vocabulary.[3] The French poet will even arm himself with a "steel-thonged whip" "to spin him like a top" (64) and lambaste the "Great-Soft-Heads" (232), the "poetic moans of this century [that] are only sophisms" (223). In Dostoyevsky, the energy of the *unlinking* of the drive has been transfigured into a feverish though obstinately meticulous *dialogue* with the carnivalesque *stories* of "blubbering humanity" (Lautréamont, 226), unsolvable narrative meditation, prey to his desires for death, for his possessions. No triumph, either, in this breathless vitality of the narrative, nor categorical Nietzschean overview.

The imperious push of the work grants the embodied word authority over the various ways of being in the world: "I've only taken to an extreme that which you haven't even dared to take halfway; what's more, you've mistaken your cowardice for good sense." From "monstrosity," it is a matter of extracting "the most alive," "men with real bodies and blood of *our very own*." No "living death"; enough with the fathers who engender us, "dead themselves." Soon "we'll conceive of a way to be born from ideas." *The Brothers Karamazov* (1881) will take care of it, having incited directionless humanity to "take from life all that it can give."

The writer's family life will accept and adapt; passions and ideologies of the time, opposing it, will let themselves be infiltrated. The work connects with our own "stone walls" and the internal swarming of our globalized *maquis* and masks.

4.2 Matricide, Crime, and Forgiveness

Does Rodion Romanovich Raskolnikov (*raskol*, etymologically from the verb *raskolot*, "split in two," designates the schism, derived from schismatic movements with a mystical tendency in the Russian Orthodox Church; also *villiki raskol*, designating the great schism of 1054 between Orthodoxy and Catholicism), does RRR, then, the principal character of *Crime and Punishment* (1866), a student separated from the university, living in extreme poverty, haunted by "certain strange and unfinished ideas," commit the "double murder" of the moneylender Alyona Ivanovna and her sister, the innocent Lizaveta? In his hovel, more exactly a closet, where he ruminates morbid dreams, he undertakes an *essay*, all the while distrusting himself: how to arrive from *ideas to actions* as such.

Did he do it, did he only dream of *that*, and if *that* does indeed exist, how can *that* be spoken of? Impossible admission, or "mute admission" in the infinite cohabitation with the death drive, always this in-between. The narrator of *Crime and Punishment* relies on the figure of Christ to identify in RRR something like a "humility out of conviction," "without reasoning." He endeavors to make the voices proliferate, to multiply realities. The polyphonic writing is his conviction, his faith. This writing is truly the spirited horse who escaped from the underground and the "wet snow," to invent for the first time a detective novel, one that is psychological and metaphysical at the same time, but *without an ending*.

More trenchant than a confession, the third-person narrative surpasses and superposes places and times, compiles the points of view of the killer himself with those of his various doubles, reasonable accomplices (Razumikhin) or cynical scoundrels (Svidrigaylov). He complicates his task, illuminating it without resolving it: *how to narrate* a thing about which one has neither a clear idea nor a personal opinion? Is it a question of reconstructing the murder, its motivations and aims? Or rather of harking back to the gestation, before the birth of the idea of killing? How to cohabit with this initial cruelty of all new thoughts, whatever they may be, when they pierce the indifferent solitude of the affective fog to make meaning with another thought, with others? And to grasp the new shock, the ideal that, by definition, suppresses the mortiferous ratiocinations of the "dead man" and *innovates* ideas, science, the life of humans for their greater happiness? "It's too ideal, therefore cruel," said Vanya in *The Insulted and Injured* (1861). In this sense, innovators are cruel criminals, since they destroy our consensus, our norms, and our laws. How to narrate *that*?

In osmosis with the "confessions" of the young man, the narrator insidiously destroys his hesitations, his remorse, his shame, and his smirks before, during, and after the decisive act, the role of which was precisely to unbind him from the tergiversations of his confused thinking clouded over by the "imperfect ideas" floating in the air. He assimilates these ideas, and like a meticulous cannibal, the writer integrates them into what he calls his "artistic point of view."[4] But only to wring their necks, slice into the dubious introspection, and lead the investigation. As the psychologist-judge Porfiry Petrovich runs the police inquiry, complicit and competitive (with Raskolnikov and the narrator), the "artistic point of view" becomes detective: the narrator reveals the putting into "sometimes monstrous form of the very processes of representation," of the *engendering as such* of thought.

His RRR doesn't have any ideas, properly speaking. Nothing "in his head" but "a baby chick pecking its way out of the egg," electrical discharges, lightning flashes of clinging obsessions. And then the brain wave, it appears as if from outside. The sordid mumblings of a drunken student, excited by his "bitch" of a moneylender: "Murder her and take her money and then use it to dedicate yourself to the service of all humanity and to the common good." "One death and a hundred lives in exchange—it's a matter of arithmetic!" Something that RRR had himself fortuitously slipped into his article on the "right to crime," signed with *just one letter*, for a periodical. The filthy allusion by a lubricious little man had suddenly seized hold of his extraordinary nightmare of the night before, the mare being beaten by blows from Mikolka in a fury, in front of his father and him, Rodion as a child, with the crowd shouting in laughter: "Take an axe to 'er, that's what! Finish 'er off now!" Ideas arrive when other voices—fearsome, exciting—pierce the underground of sleeping passions. Some find resources there and move ahead with innovating finds. Others lose their way, are caught, get confused, and the split turns to the outside, *that* topples into acting out. A "decisive act," RRR hallucinates as he executes the crime.

Crime (in Greek *krinon*, from *krei*, the root of "crisis" and "criticism") is a judicial decision that screens, separates, and sorts, based on the ability to define, to discern, to critique the tested one, the testing, the crisis. Languages derived from Latin insist on the razor's edge of reason as judge.

But in Russian, crime (*prestuplenie*) *makes the step* (*stupen*: "threshold, step"): he leaped over the threshold, the step, the edge. Language lets one hear from the start the *transgression*: shame and guilt.

In the interstices between the two edges of the split, Raskolnikov escapes from the limits, and his crime plunges him into psychotic alienation. The narrator slips in, he likes to maintain the transgression through reiterated crescendos. Polyphony does not judge, it is content to transform, and the dreamy reading becomes hallucinatory.

Rodion grew confused from the moment he wanted to resolve the question. Fatal absurdity! His confused article distinguished two human categories: the *ordinaries*, who submit to the existent (what is said), and the *extraordinaries*, who invent new languages, new ideas. Newton and Kepler founded a science; Lycurgus, Solon, Mohammed, and Napoleon changed society's laws. Whatever these new conceptions and realizations may be for their specific fields, they "violate"—by their own legislating tendences—the old laws faithfully and commonly observed before. The new language can generate realities just as violent, if not more violent; some are even perpetuated in ignominious massacres exalted as consecrated myths only because of their success. But after the fact, and temporarily, because posterity also has its judgment, that's how *that* works. Napoleon, RRR's icon, idol of his madness, is the best example. In one of his despairing sneers, the antihero himself asks if he isn't crazy. But how to know?

Having included psychology in the law, the inquiring judge Porfiry Petrovich manages to channel the storm of suffering that ravages the suspect student. Porfiry, a psychologist hence dubitative, seems to have the young man under his skin ("my sweet") and has understood everything: "He's a murderer." In the absence of proof and for all evidence, this man of the Law begins to wallow in his science of the soul, which he communicates to his client, all the while aware that "these psychological means for defense . . . cut both ways."

Although done in a conversational tone, this psychological expertise destabilizes RRR. He no longer recognizes himself in his article and admits there are pathologies, "neuroses" like his, opinions, in short, that act out processes immanent to the "alembic" of humanity, a secret anthropological alchemy that today stems from the unconscious. For his part, he requests "the right to permit his conscience to overstep . . . various obstacles, and only in the case that the execution of his idea (sometimes, perhaps, one that would benefit all mankind) requires it."

Does Porfiry, in a deformed echo of the underground man, believe in the "chemical decomposition" of suffering into guilt, the instigator of a conscience? His emphatic empathy with the suspect's emotional states ends up also exciting in RRR the consciousness of his mistakes: "If someone has a conscience, and if he acknowledges his mistake, then let him suffer. That's his punishment, in addition to hard labor," as the presumed guilty party puts it himself. This impersonal "he," designating a third party not in the conversation, a nonperson, nevertheless suggests that the improbable couple of the psychologist-judge and the murderer, on which Porfiry's mission rests, is only a legal fiction. "I" am not in it, "I" give the slip to the binomial "crime and punishment," "I" am sticking with my right to the "extraordinary" affirmation, which is intimately connected with the death drive. RRR will stay with it, delirious and disengaged, until he meets Sonya.

His vertigo worsens, also his insolent laugh and his cold hatred; his "sorts of thoughts," mere "snatches," only hint at the disappearance of objects, starting with those that testify to the crime. The killer recognizes only a "threatening danger" (*ot davivshei opasnosti*), ultimate indicator of his compressed melancholy, and he frees himself from it by calling it *spasenie davivshei opasnosti*, "almost good to feel." Triumphant "instinct for conservation" riding the crest of what's felt and sorted out, far from the spoken and the adjudged. A "perversion" or a special "case" a little "too natural"?

The improbable court psychologist runs out of breath, the *narrator* no longer needs his competencies. What can a Porfiry Petrovich understand about a double murder (and of women, to boot!), about suffering, about that particular suffering? Who can even guess it, a torture so underground that the narrator doesn't dare formulate it himself? He nevertheless ventures into the conjunction of the word and the flesh and reopens the wounds of passions that resonate with the mythical imaginary and call to the reader to deploy her own perceptions embedded in the kaleidoscope called Raskolnikov.

Over and above the political obstacle of men, with their disciplines and their parties, below the social brake with its prohibitions of incest and other rules about the exchange of women, this double crime is a sort of matricide, leading to the *unnamable*. The Greeks had celebrated it in the *Oresteia*.

The murder of Clytemnestra makes no sense; it is neither political nor social. In killing Aegisthus, the usurper of his father's throne, Orestes restores the patrilinear filiation on which the social and political cohesion of the country is built. The murder of Clytemnestra could potentially have a *societal* meaning: it takes on the arch-memory of a *prior* domestic society, a matrilinear one. More profoundly, though, through the latter, this murder attacks the internal fecundity of the hominoid link, the mother-child *reliance* that assures the life of speaking beings. Pursued by the vengeful Erinyes, condemned by the Athenian judges, the matricidal male will be freed by Athena.

This tragedy does not appear in *Crime and Punishment* (1866). Only "rays of light" thread through it (this metaphor flows frequently from Dostoyevsky's pen); he contemplates them in the portrait of Saint Cecelia in Munich. A sinner, Sonya Marmeladova, is the one who will introduce them into the multiverse of the narrator, with his RRR. Why she? And how does she lead him to an *experience*—here the term must be taken with all its Dostoyevskian connotations—that denies neither the *putting to death* of women (the one with possessions and the innocent one) nor the meaning of the *crime* in the sociopolitical field?

The narrative does not lock them into the category of a *blasphemy*, even less into the category of a libertine *transgression* (Dostoyevsky had published fragments of Casanova's escape from the "Leads" in Venice) that would authorize the morbid inversion of incest (with the mother) or the incestual (with her representations: the sisters, the close relatives, even the women from preceding generations). While the unconscious according to Freud is constructed around castration anxiety and oedipal revolt, the murder by Orestes *frees up* the violence of the separation from the maternal content. *Imaginary* matricide, the unformulatable wave carrying the risks vital to the newborn, is a psychic projection at the foundation of self-autonomy. But it threatens to take permanent form as a bloody *acting out* in the service of the death drive, when it isn't guiltily dispersed into bitter tears about death in oneself. Orthodox faith kneels on "wet mother" earth, and the icons show themselves only to call the faithful to kiss them, to let themselves be diluted by all the senses in an oceanic fusion with the absent object.[5] Dostoyevsky constantly visits these deep regions of Orthodoxy, leading him, in company with his young friend Vladimir Solovyov, to the mystical pilgrimage to the Optina monastery in the last years of his life.

4.3 The Unnamable and the Atoms of Silence

The antihero needs Sonya-Sofiya to remain on the threshold of the passions that the following novels are going to confront. *Crime and Punishment* (1866) progresses through purges in the azure patience (Dunya) of the atoms of silence (Sonya), which increase the chances for freedom. The citizen Rodion Raskolnikov accepts the condemnation to the penal colony. What awaits the criminal is an abandonment without end, without vengeful or weepy Erinyes, thanks to the suggestion that Rodion and Sonya form a couple. Sonya offers the punished man a maternal reliance made of silence but attentive to the word of the Gospel they read together. Dostoyevsky's characters are made for talking: explanations, disputes, confusions, scandals, killings in dreams and quite often for real, all while talking, and for something to talk about later. Power and powerlessness of the Word.

The sinister stories of Raskolnikov and the Marmeladovs crisscross. The mother, dejected by the fate of the young man's sister, the sweet Dunya, writes him letters she posts immediately; they are a torture for him. The "counselor with a bottle," with the burlesque name of Marmeladov, incarnates the impossibility of being a father. His second wife, Katerina Ivanovna, poor unbridled bacchant, indebted and tuberculous, dies while rushing off "to look for justice." As for the drunkard, he expires after having in all innocence drunk the thirty kopeks his daughter had earned by prostituting herself. "Her sins, which are many, are forgiven; for she loved much" (Luke 7:47), he mumbles in an approximate Slavonic. Sonya is engendered by this bankruptcy of the father, which the spectral maternal hysteria fails to manage. The scene that follows is of cosmic exactness.

Face to face, body to body: Sonya-Sofiya's "bitter anxiety," her "insatiable suffering" against Rodion's studied insolence, his "laugh . . .

somehow forced." She hears his "unsteady voice, which seemed to come from far away." "Tell me," she cried. "You're leading up to something." Suddenly he is transformed, covers his face with his hands (shame advances, invisible), goes to sit on her bed. An appeal for sexual intimacy and unbearable collapse. At that instant, the surgeon-narrator plunges the scalpel into the wound: "some scathing hatred" for this "twin sister" passes into the young man's heart.

The love he perceives in Sonya's gaze becomes confused with the ax he unhooked behind the old woman's back, when he felt "he had not a moment to lose." Then Lizaveta's face becomes mixed in with Sonya's, powerless little girls, abused, raped; Stavrogin's Matryosha will be added to them. Thunderstruck, she and he, two children, or three, or more, "almost even with the same *childlike* smile." He: "I said . . . I would tell you . . . who killed Lizaveta." She: "How do you know?" He: "I know." She: "Did they find *him*?" He: "No, they didn't." She: "So how do you know about it?" He: "Guess."

She has guessed: "Everything was that!" Because it was he, because it was she, *that* has been guessed now.

"A sword shall pierce through thy own soul" (Luke 2:35): the word of the Gospel speaks in this "unsteady voice." She kneels before him: "what have you done to yourself?" Sonya *guesses* that Rodion has cut out, with a saber, with an ax, the feminine thing in himself. The threatening feminine: the dominating mother, expert in the *domin-ion* that for her takes the place of eroticism; the depressed, resistant mother, petrified as a *dead mother*; impregnable, irresistible, inaccessible visions of the *Thing*, of the "umbilicus of the dream." The horror of separation, the dawn of the other. Fused with the omnipotent child in him, with the impotent *infans* in him. As omnipotent and impotent as it, the *Thing*.

What is "guessing?"

A third ear that hears the "fluids of life" boil. Unsteady hearing for the unsteady voice, Sofiya hears it without understanding and without explaining; she purges it with her questions; *now* she holds with him, *together*, she embraces the time of judgment: "I'll go with you to prison."

He, Rodion, is reliving the infantile experience of the primary separation: tearing himself away from the felt/sensitive content, fusion-defusion; neither subject nor object, abject.[6] The little human is born unfinished, a *neotene*, dependent and panicked, who tears himself from his maternal container, disgust, vomiting, and spasms of laughter. His Ego is born in abjection, which will pursue him the moment he manages to be reborn, which is to say to love.

She, Sonya, like Martha and Mary (who are one and the same in Orthodoxy, since Mary Magdalene will prevail only with the Catholics, for the greater delight of Marcel Proust, fond of "little madeleines"), Sonya sticks to her guns, especially in prison—to each his own—which threatens when one least expects it . . .

From bodily maternal reliance, which in the optimal development of the child leads to speaking and thinking, Sonya-Sofiya retains only the *hearing that guesses*. It's primordial, enormous, salvatory. She joins in the trauma of the old child, RRR the prideful, who was boasting: "to kill for myself, for myself alone! I didn't want to lie about it, even to myself!" The mute avowal of the murder reaches her, *that* speaks to her, to her as well. In repeating within her, *that* makes sense. She makes him understand it and returns it to him.

Gift and *forgiveness*, the dawn of interpretation is first of all a question: "what have you done to yourself?" She for-gives the one who, through a decisive act—like Napoleon!—wanted to be done with the "old vermin," the usurer matron; with, at the same time, that "impotent bitch" that he himself was and no longer wanted to be. A different *that* begins in the new mutuality between *him* and *her*, a transference that shares the unsayable *that* of the mute confession.

This space of for-giveness is found neither in religion nor in morality. Neither complaint nor compassion. The new *that* emerges in the narrative carried by the "loud and ecstatic voice, trembling," of Sonya-Sofiya, who is reciting the resurrection of Lazarus, "as if she had seen it with her own eyes." The text reincarnated by the reading becomes the medium for the for-giveness, it recognizes and authorizes the trusted, recovered copresence of the two pariahs. Rodion is not (yet) disposed to succumb to the psychologist-judge Porfiry Petrovich, who addresses him like this: "do you believe in the raising of Lazarus? . . . Do you believe in it literally?" Simply speaking, the voice of the sinner, reawakening and reviving the canonical text, installs a new reality between the two outcasts: the *imaginary*. In the palpable energy of legal fictions, the potentiality of the phantasms reopens the possibility of a life. Their theatrical liturgy prefigures the calculated hallucination that movie screens, tablets, and financialized videogames impose upon modern internauts.

I wasn't far from finding the ending of *Crime and Punishment* (1866) overdone: a *deus ex machina*, this mass where the murderer and the prostitute need to read the Eternal Book to bless their communion!

"There is no rhetorical link between [Sonya and Raskolnikov]," scoffed Vladimir Nabokov, severely. Indeed, no rhetoric justifies or explains the magnetic attraction of these two outlaws. Their parallel, unheard-of ways of desiring are notable for gaps, laconic flashes, black holes of the Word. There do not exist consecrated eloquences for *that*, just indices deposited in myths and more or less sacred codes, to be animated by agreement. For the moment, and on the other side of the "religion of suffering," the "artistic point of view" proceeds with this *for-giveness* that the narrator composes and reveals.

Only then can RRR *denounce* himself, by giving the enunciation of his crime a significance that explicitly convokes the *aesthetic*. Confessing the crime does not mean making *that* public, submitting it to public opinion. Even less does it mean taking advantage of it, as Porfiry proposes so as to lessen the punishment.

In a feverish confession to Dunya, RRR specifies that, by committing his crime, he only wanted to "place [himself] in an independent position, to take the first step," and that this "idea" of independence "was not at all . . . stupid" even though it disgusts him: "it wasn't the correct aesthetic form." *That* displeased him, *that* was not beautiful!

Based on taste and disgust, aesthetic judgment is pre-reflexive and primary, it initiates shame and guilt. RRR takes responsibility for the *ugliness* of the murders he committed: "It's the form that's incorrect." But he doesn't admit the *criminality* of his actions, which he sees as necessary for his affirmation, for the "independence" whose duty is to repair the "powerlessness," the independence that the mortiferous revenge of his freedom imposes upon him. Or is he also suggesting that exaltation seizing upon the "form," which burns the heart and aspires to the power of an ideal beauty, may lead to failure, to revenge, to crime, in the end?

"The fear of aesthetics is the first sign of weakness!" So it would not be the aesthetic experience itself but the "fear" of an aesthetic that terrifies and provokes the "powerlessness" of his criminal abreaction.

Against the "independence" claimed in sociopolitical terms, which is inevitably exposed to a necessary moral judgment and entails the judicial condemnation, RRR finds himself leaning toward the aesthetic, at least in various forms—like a sign of complicity with the narrator-author! Whatever the underlying "fear of powerlessness" may be.

For his part, the narrator, rid of the fear, promises devastation, eclipses, and recoveries of thought, for endless writing.

"The book as attack," Stéphane Mallarmé (1842–1888), a contemporary, will soon write. *Crime and Punishment* (1866) is another. It reveals that thought, with its back against the death drive—that inner lining of the life drive—separates itself from the affects of power and of destruction by the putting to death of the depressive position. Which is equivalent to a hallucinatory matricide, common to the two sexes, but differently.

Sonya Marmeladova had the genius to recognize it in herself and to for-give it in Raskolnikov, thus helping him to be reconciled "out of conviction" with his own suffering femininity.

Sonya-Sofiya repairs and satisfies maternal reliance which she had lacked. Remaining untouched is the sexuality of the female lover. Always as a function of the eroticism of the brothers, it gravitates and weakens in various declinations of feminine hysteria, which will continue to strike the narrator of the novels to come.

5

THE GOD-MAN, THE MAN-GOD

Thus playful madness may mock mockery itself,
Seizing singers suddenly in the holy night.

—Hölderlin, *Bread and Wine*, III (1880)

5.1 His Characters, His Doubles

HOMOEROTICISM

Prince Lev Nikolayevich Myshkin is an "absolute child," even were
he to live to a hundred. His childish confidence and his "extraordinary truthfulness" "pierce through people." Gifted with inner contemplation and telepathy, this "bright spirit," "an angel [who] cannot
hate," feels "love without selfishness"; a "strikingly handsome" man.
"But . . . without this ceaseless devouring of one by another, it would
have been totally impossible to organize the world." Trapped in the
innocence of the Child Jesus? An odd bird all the same—awkward, a
candid blunderer, breaker of vases. Grotesque, demented, epileptic,
fearful of his reason which escapes him in "contrary gestures." Does
he really have a "principal idea"? "The sense of proportion just isn't
there either, that's the main thing." A useful idiot to amuse those
ridiculous cannibals who devour each other, the way people used to

eat monks and children during the great famines of the Middle Ages. They openly make fun of him, not without recognizing his "principal intelligence, spontaneous, different from secondary intelligence," says Aglaya, General Yepanchin's younger daughter, who wants to run away from her family to join pure love. In describing another patient in the Swiss establishment where he was cared for— "In my view he wasn't insane, he was simply terribly distressed"— the prince was defining himself. A mouse (*mysh*, for Myshkin) from the underground, caught up in the turmoil of leonine passions (*lev*, "lion," his first name). The most pathetic of the Dostoyevskian masks, tender complicity with the ludicrous, the holy impotence of man.

Parfion Semyonych Rogozhin, the taciturn bad boy, "is fearsomely quiet" (Nastasya Filippovna says with a shudder), "only his eyes speak, he doesn't know how to move his tongue." A young uncultured and sanguinary merchant, inclined toward violence, sex, and dirty money. He lives with his delirious old mother who is ready to bless her son's vices in a dark house that smells of blood. The dwelling is haunted by his father, who died on a pile of rubles, surrounded by paintings and castrated men. Rogozhin is headed toward crime. Boss of corruption, he prefigures the mafioso oligarch, globalized by acts of fraudulent speculation in the billions and assassinations with poison; or traffickers in arms, drugs, and human beings. But he meets the Idiot, and this proximity will reveal to the gangster that the Man of Sorrows also inhabits him.

From the start, in the train, the surprising promptness of their conversation literally amalgamates the blond prince and the swarthy merchant. Their trajectories come together, they crisscross and reject each other around a beautiful woman "who has fallen": the bewitching, tried and tested, sublime, crazy Nastasya Filippovna. She had lived with Rogozhin, Myshkin consoles her, the two men realize they are "brothers by choice." The prince reads Pushkin with the trafficker, they exchange their crosses. The more they flee each other, the more they find each other, in the same corridor, the same stairway, the same park, inseparable. The killer spies on the gestures of the Idiot, who guesses the killer's drives and his threatening gestures, which will plunge him into the cerebral orgasm of the epileptic seizure at the instant Rogozhin prepares to stab him:

> Rogozhin's eyes glittered . . . His right hand rose and something flashed in it; the prince did not think of stopping him. All he remembered was apparently shouting:
> "Parfion, I don't believe it!"
> Then all at once everything seemed to open up before him; an extraordinary inner light flooded his soul . . . Then consciousness was extinguished instantly and total darkness came upon him. . . .
> Spasms and convulsions rack the entire body and all the facial features. A frightful, unimaginable scream, quite unlike anything else, bursts from the chest; it seems as if everything human is annihilated in that scream, and it is quite impossible, or at least very difficult, for the observer to imagine or concede that it is the man himself who is screaming . . . It must be presumed that it was this impression of sudden horror, accompanied as it was by all the other terrible emotions of that moment, which paralysed Rogozhin, so saving the prince from the inescapable blow of the knife which was descending upon him.

Vibrant flesh deprived of a body, icon of crucified beauty, Nastasya flees the marriage ceremony planned with the Idiot, refusing to let pity make her a princess. She joins Rogozhin, who is persuaded he can possess her only if he prevents her from being—by immolating her. Horror of the primal scene, night of the death drive. She: cold, impenetrable; or flooded with an inaccessible pleasure. He: unleashed animal, or a petrified one, plunging his blade under the left breast of the young woman, just a flow of blood. There remains only for the "old brothers" to stay by the dead woman, in two beds set up very close to the cadaver. The boor hears a spirit walking, he smells an odor, the "spirit" is an "odor" (in Russian, the same word, *doukh*, designates them both). The Idiot sees cards: "I wanted . . . those cards! Cards . . . They say you played cards with her?" Rogozhin takes them from his pocket and hands them to him: "these cards he held in his hands and had been so pleased about, could avail nothing, nothing at all now."

So much for Nastasya Filippovna. The male twins are appeased only in their Christly collapse, the assassin is restored to his madness and lets himself be caressed at last by the idiotic tenderness of the absolute child, the prince. Without intermediary: no object, no other, no third party. Mortiferous triumph of the erotic implosion: unavowable, acted upon, fatal.

Myshkin believed that beauty would save the world and joked by saying, in front of the *Dead Christ* by Holbein, that "a man could lose his faith looking at that picture!" Rogozhin is not joking. Smiling "sardonically," he reminds him that "in Russia there's more unbelievers than in other countries" because "we've gone further than they have." Very far, indeed, in this homoeroticism without an Other, which the "two brothers" in nihilism embody each in his own fashion. And which gives neither the right nor the opportunity for a woman to live and to construct her self not as the other of the other, but in her difference, heterogeneous autonomy to be conquered without end.

SAME, SAMENESS, "SELF-LOVE"

On the long road to identity—interminable incarnation—primary homoeroticism is an incontrovertible experience: primary creative capacity for the reunion with oneself through a projection-identification with someone of the same sex, which proceeds by imitation-rejection, identification-destruction. By taking up the relay from maternal reliance, and before the identification with the loving father of the individual prehistory, homoeroticism avoids incest and orients the destructive drive toward the affective quest for the *same in the other*. An *other-same*, degree zero of alterity in the same sex as oneself. This homoerotic psychic energy—fusion, destruction—precedes the choice of a sexual object (according to Tausk and Ferenczi). Narcissistic chaos, reflected back by the other-same, as omnipotent as it is threatening, overflowing with sensorial marks, images, sounds, and gestures, anterior to languages, loaded with *meaning* (ludic/semiotic), succeeds in constructing itself like a *projective territory*. Before stabilizing in *meanings* (cutting/symbolic) through the identification with the initial third party, the father. The perception of the same in oneself occurs only in the *projection* of the same in oneself onto the other: calming jubilation of the *sames* (of the *self-loves*). The life drive needs the *same* (*self-love*) to be sure of itself, to develop, to become singular in its path toward the other, its objects, and its laws. Our qualities of strangeness do not cut out or disappear but are completed and compensated in their resonance, in their echoes—oratory rhapsodies, carried by the *voices* rather than captured by the *image*, drowning the "mirror stage." What was foreign to me becomes mine, coallegiance of incompatibles, homeostasis of differences, tiresome competition, calming reabsorption of hatred into the *exaltation of the sames* (*self-love*). Corrosive destructivity, always ready to rail in anger, revolt, or crime.

Contrary to the *narcissistic double*, which is a snare, a pretense, and a specular mirroring, *homoerotic sameness* installs a transitional and transitive tension tending toward thirdness. The other-same sketches an ideal Ego, personified, interiorized, and singular, and prepares the encounter with the Ideal of the Ego, the Father who is *loving*, before he becomes *law-giving*.

Delicious and mortiferous traps of homoeroticism, which can become complacently addicted to the psychic presence of the other-same, a pernicious collage that perpetuates anguish. Whereas the denial of homoeroticism inverts into the persecution of paranoid delirium, which needs the fantasy of self-engenderment (Judge Schreber diagnosed by Freud). Or claims to seek revenge in indifference by blocking the goal of its orgasm, whatever the sex, to stop the anguish of being born from a man and a woman, for a time.

This experience of *sameness* catches up with the word when it becomes dialogic, at the very instant when it claims its maximum singularity, penetrating-penetrated, interiorization-projection of the voices and polyphonies of the messages heard or addressed. Bakhtin scrutinizes these messages in Dostoyevsky's "artistic" specificity, as he says, to distinguish him from "the philosopher," even and especially if the text abounds in philosophical utterances.

Homoeroticism works between two men (Myshkin and Rogozhin) as well as between two women (Aglaya and Nastasya); but also, outside of sex and with the help of psychic bisexuality, between a man and a woman: two *sames/selfloves* (Myshkin and Nastasya).

Aglaya and Nastasya Filippovna share the same tropisms: magnetically attracted to the Idiot, they love each other, detest each other, are jealous of each other, and grow exalted in "a single thought as great as love." "You are mine now" (Dostoyevsky made the same declaration to Speshnev, his fascinating friend from the revolutionary circle): "I am with him and I belong to him."

Myshkin and Nastasya, amalgamated from the first glance, know that the word "love" does not suit them; "pity," instead, for a mad rebel (according to him), "pride" instead for idiotic purity (according to her). Same other, other-same, temporary complementary vitalities, doomed from the start to the impossible, condemned to the piercings of Rogozhin's knife.

We are all homoerotic when we understand we are unfinished, needing to be re-created. And it is to artists that speaking humanity entrusts the task of invoking and keeping open its jubilatory and risky foundations. Whereas homosexuals put them into action and take charge of legalizing them. Adolescence revives their ambiguities embedded since childhood, it detours their fantasies and desires into ideologies and totalizing ideals, as paradisical as they are destructive. The *psychosexual homoerotic sameness* is played and played-out in love to the death in the firmament of ideas. Sick with ideality, the adolescent firmly believes that absolute satisfactions exist and, belied by reality, destroys and self-destroys to reach them. This believer in paradise is madly doubled by a nihilist.

HOLBEIN'S *DEAD CHRIST*

The Dostoyevskian man is haunted by his living cadaver. More abysmal than the underground of the suffering consciousness

("After all, suffering is the sole cause of consciousness... Consciousness is man's greatest misfortune"), it's his natural mortality, lacking any beyond and deprived of resurrection, that torments the male voices of the carnival.

Orthodox faith, more than the other branches of Christianism, grants particular importance to Jesus's descent into hell, which the Greek language designates by the substantive *kenosis*, meaning "nothingness, inanity, nullity," but also "senseless, deceptive." (The adjective *kenos* means "empty, useless, vain," the verb *kenour* "to purge, to cut, to annihilate.") Is annihilation due only to Christ's humanity, or does it affect the divinity itself, THE divinity? "He that hath seen me hath seen the Father; and how sayest thou then, Show us the Father?" says Jesus to Philip, before the Passion (John 14:9). Christ's *kenosis* prefigures modern times' confrontation with the "death of God." "God is dead, God himself is dead," this is a prodigious, terrible representation that "represents to the representation the deepest abyss of the scission," writes Hegel in *Lectures on the Philosophy of Religion* III (1821). But what therapeutic power also! It is because the Son, the Father, and the Holy Ghost are themselves mortal, annulled through the intermediary of the Man of Sorrows who thinks even in his suffering to the death that they can be reborn. Thought can begin again—but under what conditions, with what trials, risks, and limits? Nietzsche, who explores the sickly psychology of Christianism and the "childish idiotism" in the Gospel as well as in the "Russian novel," did not fail to note that complacency about *kenosis* gives to human and divine death on the cross "the freedom, the superiority over any feeling of *ressentiment*" (*The Antichrist*, 1896).

The seriousness of Hans Holbein's *Dead Christ*, a unique minimalist representation of the *kenosis*, nearly sparked an epileptic seizure in Dostoyevsky at the Basel Künstmuseum. Like the eye of a cyclone, zone of low pressure around which the storm rotates, carrying off everything, the painting makes the *sames/self-loves* revolve in *The Idiot* (1868), *Demons* (1872), and "The Dream of a Ridiculous Man" (1877). "No hint of beauty" in this tortured cadaver, no sign of the Risen one, "who had vanquished even nature" by pronouncing "*Talitha cumi*" and "Lazarus come forth!" Death, in Holbein, is the ultimate truth.

Confronted with his mortality, what remains for a man given over to the "new ideas" and structured beyond repression by the cleavage?

He becomes tempted to take the vacant place of the Creator and, through the ultimate revolt against the laws of nature that have programmed his death, take his own life *himself*. Apotheosis of the omnipotent *sameness*, of negative narcissism, this nihilism culminates in the reasoned suicide of Kirillov (*Demons*, 1872). But his elliptical language seems to be compacted now by death's ineluctable control.

The freedom to think about freedom, promised by Christianism, as Ivan Karamazov's poem about the Grand Inquisitor proclaims, seems to be another solution that better matches the time of speaking beings who are living but confronted with their mortality. All the same, this solution runs the totalitarian risk of attaching "a man to an idea," thus prefiguring the single thought into which Ivan Karamazov encloses himself. Or of frankly unfurling to the left, like the universal communism of a Shigalyov. Yet it is through *thought*, but *incarnate* thought, on the condition of its being attached to dreams, that the Dostoyevskian man seeks to save himself, even if it too runs the risk of failing. Either by "double thoughts" (Myshkin, *The Idiot*, 1868), or by mortiferous nightmares (Ippolit, *The Idiot*), if not more piteously by comic aestheticism (Stepan Trofimovich, then the worldly writer Karmazinov, *Demons*, 1872).

Crueler yet than the organic tortures probed by the Marquis de Sade (1740–1814), who also rebelled against the Supreme Being, the anguish of mortality is a ravaging jouissance. A secondary character bears witness to its omnipresence, the rich manufacturer Jeremy Smith (*The Insulted and Injured*, 1861). Father of a "romantic and unreasonable" daughter, whose affair with Prince P. A. Valkovsky (an adventurer who ruins Smith, his daughter, and his granddaughter Nellie, the epileptic illegitimate child of the prince) he will never forgive, the old man has the dignity and rigidity of Christ as seen by Holbein, like an intimate phantom, an old acquaintance of the narrator himself: "I was startled too by his extraordinary thinness; he had almost no flesh on him, and it was as if the skin were glued onto his bones. His large but lusterless eyes, set in some sort of blue rims, always stared straight in front of him, never looking to the side, and never seeing anything—of that I'm certain . . .'What's he thinking about?' I went on reflecting. 'What's in his head? And is he, in fact, thinking about anything at all? His face is so deathly that it expresses absolutely nothing.'"

This ambulatory cadaver, this dead body living a human life, is programed by the laws of human finitude, to be sure, but he is above all devoured from the inside by his obsession with the prince who dishonored his daughter. Incapable of getting over it with a pardon, Smith lets us guess that it's his hypnotic desire for the offender that vampirizes his nothingness as a living-dead, and he drags his daughter and his granddaughter Nellie into it. The insulted and the injured gravitating around this dark story nevertheless seem to savor their setbacks without realizing their own abysmal inanity.

The narrator, a writer like Dostoyevsky, takes a different course, like the family of the Ikhmenyevs who, in circumstances analogous to Smith's, end up forgiving not the cynic but the young victim. A subliminal message runs through the text: forgiveness is possible to the human being—that being for death—if and only if, in Dostoyevsky's Christly logic, man believes in resurrection. Infinite hope in the perfectibility of humans, necessary wager on eternal life. But the intransigent Smith refuses forgiveness. The *Dead Christ* that the narrator contemplates with Myshkin and Rogozhin (*The Idiot*, 1868), which he paints with Holbein's brush under the morbid features of Smith, appears "truly dead" only if he is like him, neither forgiven nor forgiving, incapable of signifying and pronouncing eternal life. Not to be confused with the *writer's* Christ, the "most courageous" and the "most beautiful" (letter to Natalya Fonvizina, February 15, 1854).[1]

Having survived the comas of his epileptic seizures, having seen himself condemned to death, dying and no doubt already dead before being saved by the "miraculous" tragicomedy of pardon granted at the foot of the scaffold, for Dostoyevsky the anguish about death surpasses the male anguish about castration. In the evangelical message of the *kenosis* and the resurrection, the death anguish resonates with his own experiences of mortality.

Death remains for the novelist the *absolute evil*. Dostoyevsky implacably condemns the putting to death a human being is capable of, whatever the pleasures of suffering or the reasons may be that lead the hero to suicide or murder. He doesn't seem to distinguish between the two, he would seem to lean toward the pain that, because it may be erotic,[2] seems to cultivate and hence humanize violence, in the artist's eyes.

In contrast, Dostoyevsky does not forgive the cold, quite "proper," and irrevocable death inflicted by the guillotine—there is "no greater torture." "Who can say that human nature can bear a thing like that without going mad?" The face of "a condemned man in the minute before the guillotine falls, while he's still standing on the scaffold before lying down on the plank they have," makes Myshkin think of the Basel painting: "Christ himself spoke of such agony and terror."[3]

The Mortal Male, Thinking and Ridiculous

Myshkin had to be an epileptic like Dostoyevsky to probe the capacity for making meaning—thunderstruck power-powerlessness that grabs the body in the three stages of the epileptic fit. After an aura of paranoid omnipotence, absolute passion, and infinite grasp of the *same* with his *self-loves*, there follows a collapse of meaning and of breath, approaching death, phantoms of suicide and of murder. Then it's the foggy reemergence of the crushed body and language, finally here, present, intermittent.

It took an Idiot for the diffraction of the idea, mortal in itself and a double of the loss of self and a double of crime; and it took an Idiot for the idea to recover its source in dreams, in all innocence, so as to finally become a *real idea*. Always heavy with risk, perhaps with promise—for later or never. This phenomenon may abandon appearances—and even the hyperconnected screens of the generalized spectacle—to assimilate the murderous gaze of Rogozhin, the righteous suffering of Nastasya Filippovna, the hysterical contortions of Lebedev, the vengeful impotence of Ippolit. It doesn't seek to inform or communicate, just to make suffering shine and thereby exult. Nor to see or to seize, but to embody, in approximate bursts, the flood and the ebb of speaking. The always unfinished gestation of *signifiance* advances and retreats by thresholds and rebounds, intermediate spaces half dream, half reason, instilled "between us," between two phantoms. Language is for it a medium in which "something" lets itself be glimpsed, it is delirious, it darkens, it can be guessed, *mereshchitsya*, to say it in one word.

Prison promiscuity having disinhibited the constitutive homoeroticism, the vicissitudes of the narrator's love life underlie the two movements that traverse the maturity of the oeuvre. Explorer of the pleasures-and-sufferings of *sameness*, the narrator accompanies and analyzes his unbearable immersion in nihilistic psychosexuality. Orthodox thinker, the journalist-correspondent wagers on the purity of the faith and tries to develop its mysteries. Ultimate doubling in the writing, these two movements contradict and complete each other. In counterpoint to the spiritualist surges of the believer, the cruel novelistic polyphony of the limit states in the novels reveals their plural truths, pitiless underground of "superior" reveries.

Thus Dostoyevsky shares many of the ideas of his young friend, the Orthodox theologian Vladimir Sergeyevich Solovyov (with whom he will retreat to the Optina monastery in June 1878). The paradisical "transhumanism" developed by the mystical spirituality of Nikolai Fyodorov attracts him also. This cosmist philosopher contrasted class struggle in the West with the intrinsically Russian feeling of mutual love and union. Against *subjectivity* leading in his view to indifference, he advocated *projectivity*, susceptible of dominating nature but also of achieving the universal fraternity of the living and the dead. Dostoyevsky for his part envisages a utopian synthesis where the limits of the Ego are erased at the heart of an amorous fusion with others, culminating in the suspension of sexuality, the generator of tensions and conflicts. The characters in his novels tirelessly pursue this illumination, in theater, in crime, in serious or grotesque "real ideas."

The writer's meditation upon the death of his first wife, Maria Dmitrievna, bears precisely on the possibility or the impossibility of love-forgiveness, consubstantial to the "construction of his individuality, to the superior and supreme development of the individual." Dostoyevsky's reflection takes off:

> after the appearance of Christ, as the *idea of man incarnate*, it became as clear as day that the highest, final development of the individual should attain precisely the point . . . where man might find, recognize and with all the strength of his nature be convinced that the highest use which he can make of his individuality, of the full development of his *I*, is to seemingly annihilate that *I*, to give it wholly to each and every one wholeheartedly and selflessly. And this is the greatest happiness. In this way the law of the *I* merges with the law of humanism . . . both the *I* and the *all* . . . mutually annihilated for each other, at that same time each apart attains the highest goal of his individual development. This is indeed the paradise of Christ. . . .
>
> But in my judgment it is completely senseless to attain such a great goal . . . if man will no longer have life when he attains the goal. Consequently, there is a future, heavenly life.
>
> We know only one trait of the future character of the future being which hardly will center, that is, in the bosom of a universal synthesis, i.e., God—we do not know . . . But there, being is a full synthesis, eternally taking pleasure and being fulfilled, and therefore, time will no longer exist.

The impossibility of sacrificing the Ego out of love for a different being (I and Masha) produces the feeling of suffering and the state of sin:

> And so, man must unceasingly experience a suffering which is compensated for by the heavenly joy of fulfilling the Law, that is, by sacrifice. (*Meditation Before the Body of Maria Dmitrievna*, April 16, 1864)[4]

But the "artistic point of view" goes against this defensive philosophy. The character of Myshkin is a flagrant example. At the end of *The Idiot* (1868) the prince falls back into his congenital idiocy. In spite of his compassion, the carnivalesque accents added to his failures in society and in love do not make of him a Christlike figure. A phenomenon of disincarnate purity, quite unconscious and complicit with his unconscious, destructive *sameness*, as enacted by Rogozhin. We have to wait for the *starets* Zosima in *The Brothers Karamazov* (1881) for this failure of embodiment to be surmounted by the spiritual and eventually carnal seriousness of the "Russian monk."

The polyphony of *Demons* (1872) will reveal the potentiality of the death drive, as essential as it is poignant, grotesque, and finally unfathomable. As is also the troubling complicity between Tikhon and Stavrogin during the latter's confession.

What opens next is a new self-analytical pathway, to which "Marey" and "Vlas" bear witness. It will lead the narrator to place the *murder of the father* in the center of a possible new beginning for man—woman included—which the "ridiculous man" considers somewhat improbable, burlesque, intensely desirable.

One among the *self-loves*, a mouthpiece among others for the band of young nihilists hateloved by Myshkin and Rogozhin: Ippolit, victim of terminal tuberculosis. He identifies with the *Dead Christ*, and he philosophizes, whereas the Idiot gets mixed up in his "double thoughts," and his assassin's grimace freezes in "terrible silence." "Is it possible to perceive in an image what doesn't have an image?" this orphan of iconophiles, this postmodern asks. Lying in bed, his only horizon the dirtied wall of the Meyer house seen through his window, the dying man has a nightmare: a gigantic tarantula, supernatural scorpion, is going to mortally bite him. His mother attempts to intervene, as well as the dog Norma with the powerful jaw: she munches and crunches the voluminous insect, but it stings her tongue as it ejaculates. Ippolit protects himself from this orgasmic devouring by "yelping" a philosophical profession of faith, a nihilistic protest without effect, with the pretentious title (in French) of *Explication nécessaire*.

But the dying man's critical mind represses his mordant anguish about fellation-castration, he rises up against the obscure laws of tarantula/nature that sows death before his eyes and professes a negative theomorphism. Simultaneously struck down by the *kenosis* of Christ and exalted by the work of death in him, a mystical jubilatory horror, Ippolit bids farewell to a Man. He nonetheless remains haunted by the omnipotence of the Man-god ("I admit the existence of eternal life, perhaps I always have"), the holder of absolute Meaning in the Paradise of nature's total domination. This ascendency makes him doubly powerless: to think of future life and its laws ("how could I be held responsible for failing to make sense of the incomprehensible?"); and to take pleasure in his own senses ("What is there for me in all this beauty... that even this tiny fly buzzing in the sunbeam near me, even that is a participant in all this festival and chorus, knows its place, loves it, and is happy, while I am the sole outcast"). The assessment continues, and a melancholy bitterness takes hold of him: "What do I want with your nature... when all this feast that has no end has begun by excluding me alone?" along with a last alternative: "to kill anyone I liked, ten people at once even." There follows the pitiful scene of the failed suicide, the pistol lacking a percussion cap.

The murderer will be someone else: Rogozhin. As for the Prince, total stranger to "people... driven by a single idea," and usually incapable of expressing his question in words, he nevertheless observes that Ippolit had taken this business about the "fly" and the aborted fetus "from his words and tears of that time." The idea of a killing means nothing to Myshkin, other than the face of a woman who is also a monstrous criminal, but "now [people are] more edgy, more mature, more sensitive, able to cope with two or three ideas at a time... the man of today has a wider apprehension."

Dependent on expiatory Orthodox faith, neither the theomorphism of Ippolit nor the disembodied purity of the Idiot have any inkling of the "third kind of knowledge" according to Spinoza, the "enjoyment of existing" (*Ethics* III), "having so to speak no fear of death" (*mortem vix timeant*, *Ethics* V), in which divine nature does not present itself as "a power" but as a "fullness of enjoyment." However, the panting, the abandon, the burrowing, the spasms of laughter and tears, the triumph and the eclipse of their sentences let it be understood that a continuous, *unconscious* jouissance (*naslajdienie*) powerfully maintains these speaking beings.

Their disenchanted consciousness can be radicalized, demonic and derisory, into terrorist actions and burlesque catastrophes. Kirillov will take the spirit of theomorphism to the highest level of absurdity by advocating and committing suicide as the supreme freedom: "it makes no difference whether one lives or does not live, then everyone will kill himself, and perhaps that will be the change . . . the physical changing of the earth and man. Man will be God" (*Demons*, 1872). Without the Creator, man alone is uniquely responsible for the meaning and duration of his life. Up against the God-man (the Christ), the Man-gods in their various nihilistic versions are not the "possessed" (as some of the translations of this title suggest, wrongly). More clinical, *Demons* reveals the chimeras that consume humans prey to their mortiferous drives and to social disturbances. And Pyotr Verkhovensky, son of the failed writer Stepan Trofimovich (who concedes: "I've been lying all my life"), pretends to be a leader of suffering souls and succeeds in convincing them to put to death one of the *sames*, Shatov, in order to prepare the "great evening," while also having accelerated Kirillov's suicide.

In a nightmare, Ivan Karamazov himself receives the devil in the form of "some gentleman" who "instills disbelief," naturally, but ends up "sow[ing] just a tiny seed of faith" in Ivan. He will have achieved his purpose when the man, between belief and disbelief, ends up believing the Devil (Evil) actually exists. The "new man" will have the right to become a "Man-god," scaling the obstacles that formerly stood before the "man-slave." "There is no law for God . . . everything is permitted," Kirillov proclaims. Another theomorphist nihilist, the seminarist Rakitin in *The Brothers Karamazov* (1881), taking a "divine" point of view, repeats an idea of Miusov's (the brothers' uncle) to deliver his credo that "everything is permitted"—an apocalyptic transhumanism that prophesizes the end of man. Ivan seizes hold of the idea. Mitya gets involved. But *The Brothers Karamazov* won't stop there. The novel deepens a retrospective return to the memory of "accidental families" (*sluchainoie semeistvo*, "families of chance") and the relations between the sexes, initiated by *The Adolescent* (1875), in the search for new carnival resources at the heart of language.[5]

MEMORIES OF CHILDHOOD: MAREY AND VLAS

Professions of faith in live contact with the people and the memories that constantly return and are corrected during prison—"I repeat: it was a hard school" (*A Writer's Diary*, 1873)—bring up scenes of a hallucinatory *sameness*. Writing also reinvents this sameness, after the fact. Screen memories or intense work of the memory: "These memories arose in my mind of themselves; rarely did I summon them up consciously . . . I would . . . [add] new touches to things experienced long ago," at the heart of a metamorphosis that the writer affirms having lived among the convicts. *Notes from a Dead House* (1862) having been written "using an invented narrator, a criminal who supposedly had murdered his wife," whereas "I have scarcely ever spoken in print of my prison life," the *sameness* recovered in the past would thus be re-created—starting with the *sameness* lived in the prison and then afterward.

In "The Peasant Marey" (1876), little Fyodor, barely nine (we are in 1830), who "liked nothing better than the forest," has an "adventure" deep in the bushes. The narrator-rascal, "absorbed in [his] own business," relives this childhood as he writes it decades later. He picks up little creatures, snakes and lizards, hits the frogs with his walnut tree switches, drinks in the damp *odor* (*zapakh*) of rotting leaves. And hears in the distance the cry of Marey who *labors* (*pakhat*) the earth, struggling and jubilant: "Gee-up!" Little beasties and humans blended, decomposed, whipped, smelling, penetrating, penetrated, the *sameness* swells and breaks, a mad cry of terror is torn from the child: "Wolf!" (*volk*). Where could this panic, this call, come from? While Marey calls his dog Volchok ("little wolf"), the panicked child screams in fright and runs to take refuge in the arms of this master of the woods. Who immediately strokes the cheek of the little adventurer. Forgotten are the "big bad wolf," the terrifying snakes and lizards are transformed into the "thick earth-soiled finger" with which, in a tender and timid gesture, the man "gently touched my trembling lips"—in accompaniment to "a broad, almost maternal smile." "Something quite different had happened, and had I been his very own son he could not have looked at me with a glance that radiated more pure love, and who had prompted him to do that? . . . Was he, maybe, especially fond of small children?" *To love* with urges that are not (yet?) abuses, but with these *samenesses* between the serf and the "little master" that make Myshkin say, in recalling his life with the children in Switzerland, "The soul is healed through contact with children." Ivan and Alyosha Karamazov are also much taken with children.[6]

Does the malady of adolescent ideality begin in the "mystical horror" that Dostoyevsky's intuition identifies at the living center of Orthodox faith? He must have thought so, as he made the wager—a "comical" one—that the salvation of the "new man" claiming to live without faith will come "from below" and not from the "liberals."

The lightning-fast descent into mystical horror connects with another hallucinatory scene, a scene of erotic blasphemy. Two audacious village lads, feverish with the faith that fascinates them and that they abominate, thus sick with the ideality they need, play at challenging each other ("Vlas," in *A Writer's Diary*, 1873). Vlas's friend tells him to take the Eucharist out of his mouth, to place it on a stick driven into the earth, to load his gun, raise it, aim at the sacred object, and shoot. An unconscious communion of the *sames/self-loves*, erection and penetration by bullet. The thoughtless insolence of these excited rascals desecrates the Man of Sorrows who inhabits and exalts them. "They both felt that they had need of one another so that together they might put an end to the affair." Horrified by these "vices" and finding them "agonizingly delightful," one of the two, Vlas, senses them, but "external" to his spirit. In an incredible vision-accusation, and complicit with his companion who was the initiator of the blasphemy—"what heights I reached!"—the one who could have been "truly . . . a village nihilist," "paralyzed by fear" in the face of his "infamy"—but not for his companion's—admits it to his *starets*; then "Our Vlas became a beggar and demanded suffering."

Dazzled by the unsustainable complicity between the "victim" and the "tempter," the writer traverses Orthodox faith with this complicity and returns once more to Mme du Barry, who begged her executioner at the guillotine, *"Encore un moment, Monsieur le bourreau!"* Mystical horror lies at the heart of this malady of ideality that burns the *sames/self-loves*: "the most colossal power over the human soul."

LANGUAGE, AN EROTICISM WITHOUT AN ORGAN

A grand staircase and a train station become one, the present and the past overlap: Myshkin and Rogozhin; Aglaya and Nastasya Filippovna; Nastasya, Myshkin, and Rogozhin share emotions and behaviors. The characters lose their contours, their porous, contaminated identities in flight. Loves, hatreds, jealousies interpenetrate, fuse, or reject each other. Exchanged glances, voices and gestures form "spaces," receptacles for *semiotic* indices. They are anterior to and transversal to the emergence of the *symbolic*, ideational constructions hooked to *vision*, the most intellectual of the senses, which poses and designates an "object" for a "subject." *The Idiot* (1868) is a novel about the *irresistible* power-powerlessness of ideas.

Or else "ideas" expand and run out of breath, with dubitative adjustments, and suspend judgment by touches, by sketches, and precautions, the better to attract the *between: perhaps, maybe, something, I don't know what, I'm not sure what, he wasn't sure what, for one reason or another, for such and such a reason*—which Dostoyevsky is fond of. Arriving finally at this apotheosis of uncertainty: "it seemed as if perfectly certain, perhaps."

The ridiculous man, who carries on from the "spiteful man" (*Notes from Underground*, 1864) and the *Idiot* (1868), knows quite well that being *is* nothingness, or actually, more innocently, that "to be myself is a joke." All the same he doesn't kill himself. Because he has a dream—a hallucination—that it is possible to transmit "desire," the "living image" of the impossible and the unrealizable. And he persists in sharing the unnamable. But this jokester has no other way of constructing his "sermon" or accomplishing his "walk" than to upset syntax and logic: "truth whispered to me that I was *lying*, and guarded and directed me . . . After my dream, I lost words. At least all the main words, the most necessary ones. But so be it: I'll go and I'll keep talking, tirelessly, because after all I saw it with my own eyes, though I can't recount what I saw" ("The Dream of a Ridiculous Man," 1877).

Or else the absurdities and incongruities sizzling in "your dream" enmesh in "your reason," provided it is "extremely concentrated" and "wily," so that they enter "completely" into reality and make you smile at an idea that "is actual." What is the "actual idea" (*mysldeistvitelnaia*), or rather the experience of an ideation in action (*mysldeistvie*) (*The Idiot*, 1868)?

The real idea is the substance, the root of eroticism according to Dostoyevsky. Don't look for it in the body, sexual organs, erogenous zones, areas of the brain, neurotransmitters and other such organic settings, susceptible to marketing in the financialized and globalized "crystal palaces" where "two plus two make four." Of the thrust of sexuality, scarcely evoked, vaguely implied and yet omnipresent, there remains only "the extraordinary strength of the impression" (*vpechiatlenie*, from *pechat*, "seal, imprint, trace"), the psychic point that pervades this kind of thought turned "real" by means of crazy grafts. As a result of which the *real idea* has the quality of belonging to your life, to "something existing in your heart now, as it has always done"; "the impression is vivid," "joyful or agonizing," "new, prophetic."

Only the smile, permanent watcher, detaches the *real idea* and preserves it from alienation, nightmare, or delirium, without for all that keeping instances of acting out from ensuing. Such is the incongruous sending of the love letter that Nastasya Filippovna addresses to Aglaya. Myshkin, the true receiver of this osmosis of jealousy between the two women, comments on it as if he were its author and uncovers *passion* in it, the quintessence of the *real thought*. Which leads ineluctably to the ultimate challenges posed by the *real* (*distvítelnost*) that are rape, suicide, murder. Impossible to think of, except in the *real thought* that is the carnival of the writing.

Dostoyevsky's eroticism, deployed in the folds of language, does not ignore the body but disseminates it—seizes it and turns it into *pre-forms* to be recomposed in the polyphony of the speaking beings (*parl-êtres*). The body is not really "forgotten" in Dostoyevsky, as people often say. But the image of the body, portraits, and physical details are often lacking for essential characters, who are barely sketched or on the contrary strongly outlined, letting themselves be submerged by the voice of ideas. Western art has accustomed us to corporal realism, to the "figure" and to "figurism." *Figure* takes its roots from *fingere* (to model), *fingulus* (potter), *fictor* (modeler), *effigies* (portrait). Erich Auerbach, in "Figura" (1938), recounts the history of repre-sentation as it was forged in our civilization since the Hellenization of Roman culture. Varro, Lucretius, and Cicero take *figura* to mean the external appearance, the contour, but also the grammatical form, the plastic form, the geometric outline, and they arrive at this most radical of Latin inventions: the "rhetorical figure," a Greek idea perfected by Quintilian. The Fathers of the Church, from Tertul-lian to St. Augustine, will give the term "figure" the meaning "prophecy in action." Less allegory or metaphor, the figure then becomes a "*bodily action* of the being in action." Sarah and Solomon, real and historical, are "figures of the future" in the context of the Church. The opposition figure/truth is in the process of being abol-ished; something else is hidden in the figure: a truth always already there and yet to come.

We are nowhere near the *icon* and its *economy* which justify repre-senting the divine, in Byzantium. In *Of the Trinity*, St. Augustine had already reversed Psalm 39, verse 6—"Surely every man walketh in a vain shew: surely they are disquieted in vain: he heapeth up riches, and knoweth not who shall gather them"—by rewriting it as: "Though man is disquieted in vain, surely every man walketh in the image." He gives it an ontological character: man is destined (*hapax*) to *vision* (representation, contemplation, theory), even though the image is preserved only by the movement toward the one by whom it is imprinted. The iconophiles, like St. John of Damascus, develop the principles into a new credo: "He who refuses the image refuses the incarnation."

But what image?

The discussion on the fate of images in theology, as in politics, is known as the Quarrel of the Iconoclasts and the Iconophiles. It marks the Orthodox faith and Byzantine society from the sixth to the twelfth centuries. The work of the patriarch Nicephorus (758–828) develops the complex notion of the *icon* (which cannot be found in Plato or Aristotle) to avoid the idolatry, the fetishistic, superstitious, and talismanic abuses of images, establishing the image in the universe of spirituality. It's the concept of the *economy* (*oeikonomia*) of the image (*eikon*)—note the homophony of the two terms—that allows Nicephorus to overcome the resistance of noniconic and iconophobic proto-Christianism. The term "economy" evokes management, cunning, benevolent design, disposition, the divine plan. Consequently, to represent would no longer be to "imitate" or to "copy," which would amount to circumscribing, but more radically to *inscribe* a mark, a notch, an infiltration. Like the *mandylion* that *imprints* the Holy Face and returns us to the gesture that marks, to the notch that cuts, to the passionate bleeding of the Man of Sorrows—and of the woman.[7]

The *figure* and the *icon* thus determine the fate of two representations in the West. The icon inscribes the unrepresentable and the void in an image with relative resemblance. The figure seeks resemblances in the duration of human history, even forcing them, so as to leave their promise open.[8]

Dostoyevsky's imaginary, his eroticism without organs, belongs to the *figurism* of the European novel, of course; but he inflects it toward Orthodox *iconism*, more resonant with the split in the subjectivity that speaks. He invites us to communicate with the invisible—uterine or mortal—while also trying to understand it, to interpret it, to deliver it to us. He thus achieves elliptical and disfigurative presentations like great modern artists after him who, through their specific processes, also lead us to the *dis-being* of a suffering or an ecstasy.

Thus the "corporal" particularities that the novelist attributes to his characters are inscribed like *iconic* traces in the textual polyphony.

Like Dostoyevsky, Stepan Trofimovich Verkhovensky venerates the Sistine Madonna and believes in the Supreme Being, but he is addicted to alcohol and to cards, and he is noted for his vulgar laugh, his lachrymal incontinence, and his cholerine outbreaks (acute diarrhea). The narrator likes to reveal how comical his expressions are, in which the repressed body gets into language only in the figurative sense that the retired professor gives it. After having affirmed that "he threw himself into the embrace of this friendship" with Varvara Petrovna, he rectifies: "God forbid that anyone should think anything idle and unwarranted; this embrace should be understood only in the highest moral sense." In contrast, the very respected father of Pyotr Verkhovensky sometimes may reduce allegories to their basic referent: his letters to his friend are "literally wet with . . . tears."

Myshkin, on the other hand, is totally deprived of a body, but the ungraspable landscape in which he evolves—the wintry cold of Saint Petersburg where the prince is buffeted, shoved, insulted, hit—reveals the disintegration of the epileptic Idiot even before the reader learns of his illness.

Ivan Karamazov, one of Dostoyevsky's most famous characters, author of the "poem" on the Grand Inquisitor, the "man of ideas" par excellence, is completely invisible. But not for his brother Alyosha, who notices that he "swayed as he walked, and that his right shoulder, seen from behind, appeared lower than his left." A minor disharmony, infinitesimal suggestion of his malaise, quickly forgotten, until, in an ecstasy, Ivan unveils his double, none other than the Devil. But disguised as a visitor, who is only a Russian nobleman—the height of irony—as ordinary as possible and "*frisant la cinquantaine*," another way of "swaying."[9]

In contrast, the debauchery of Fyodor Karamazov, the root and symptom of the disasters of his progeniture (Dmitri, Ivan, Alyosha, and Smerdyakov), is revealed from the start in the vicious details of his physiognomy, such as "the long, fleshy bags under his eternally insolent, suspicious, and leering little eyes"; and his "Adam's apple, fleshy and oblong like a purse, [which] hung below his sharp chin, giving him a sort of repulsively sensual appearance."

Whether it's forgotten, diminished, or outrageously caricatured, the body like any figurability (of an object, a landscape, a behavior . . .) can be *seen* before it is *felt, heard,* and *sounded* in the tourney of dialogic interpenetration. Almost all the interlocutors of the Dostoyevskian polyphony become "all red," "wring their hands," "cry out," "collapse onto couches," suddenly go pale, go "white as a sheet," "shudder," and "convulse" as their *medium princeps*, the signifiance of language, deploys to construct itself and link them *between* bodies and senses, flesh and ideas. Inexhaustible, unsolvable organizations-disorganizations of differences and strangeness.

With *The Idiot* (1868), Dostoyevsky's novels open broadly to the discussion of ideas that renew and examine the archeology of the religious man and his nihilistic invert. But they also do more, considerably more. In inscribing *eroticism* in the engenderment of the capacity to *speak* and to *think*, in placing into narration the copresence of *eroticism* with the sway of the *idea* and the *cruelty of the ideal*, this Russian fin-de-siècle text rejoins today's postmodern need for *ideality*, our *fundamentalisms* as well as our *disenchantments*. And reveals the sadomasochistic pleasure that underlies them, torn between the obscure abyss of desire to the death and the impotent virtue of purity.

Eroticism without organs does not weave webs or even rhizomes: no networks and even less of social networks. It comes to terms with the *void* through surprise encounters, amalgamations and detachments, which are wiped out by indifference, consumed in crime, in aleatory progression and chaotic homeostasis. While the disobjectifying of the body, rooted in incest and the confusion of the sexes, leads to the implosion-explosion of the feminine in self-outside-of-self.

Eroticism without organs is thus the eroticism of *writing* itself when it attains the extreme limit where art and text really begin, literature being surpassed: man's *symbolic expense* recovering-recreating his cursed part, his perversion. And Dostoyevsky becomes one with Stavrogin to *shake up* the "values" of the Saint Petersburg *salons*, as well as his own repression on which is built the fiction of the author he also is.

However, this bodily disobjectifying should not be confused with the "deconstruction of the couch" and the "de-divination" of man and his "little beast that itches him mortally," which Antonin Artaud is fond of, for instance in *The Theater and Its Double* and *The Toxic Little Bone*. Closer to Cy Twombly's pictural *gesture* (discussed by Roland Barthes), Dostoyevsky's writing reveals its eroticism by "lying around." Almost an inelegance that "seems to be levitating" at some distance from the *figurable*, if not the *visible*—body, object, idea, untying them. The *active idea* flowing from the novelist's pen becomes erotic because it is written . . . as if "half-heartedly." Not out of *disgust*, which is often present (and Raskolnikov speaks of it), but thanks to the recomposition of the traces left by a defunct culture—by the myths and words of an incarnationist and resurrectionist Christianism. His polyphonic dialogism breaks neither the precision nor the logical sequencing of such myths and words. It *recharges* them, filling them with a trembling atmosphere, indeterminate and inexhaustible accumulation of reasons and drives, not at all enigmatic, since everything is said at length and patiently, to remain vague. In the Dostoyevskian *vague* that approaches death and yet remains a living vague. Unexpected for an Orthodox, common in the Japanese Zen. Sudden breaks punctuate it, provoked by wacky, aberrant, and ludicrous changes. They unscrew the narrative, suspend narration, intercept the weave of the reader's reception; the reader is awakened to radical nothingness, which is not a dialectical negation. The eroticism of the writing "no longer lives anywhere"; eroticism and writing are both "absolutely superfluous."

5.2 Disfigured Destinies of the Second Sex

Nastasya Filippovna: "Heaven Alone Knows What Is Living Within Me Instead"

Her mother "had deigned to burn" for the entire domain of the Barashkovs. Nastasya Filippovna deigns to burn with her "monstrous passion" all through *The Idiot* (1868)—proud, haughty, pensive, explosive, consumed. She fascinates, from the start she haunts the connection between the two protagonists, Myshkin and Rogozhin; her photo precedes her, her legend as a little girl saved then kept as a mistress by the vicious Totsky accompanies her, her wild character revives and interrupts the story. But she is not of this world: "I have renounced the world . . . I have almost ceased to exist." Worse, or better, nothingness has seized her: neither identity nor ego, altered: "heaven alone knows what is living within me instead."

With a superior education, in French, of course, but also in diverse disciplines, even judicial ones, this woman "both knew and comprehended a great deal," including the value of money (like Dostoyevsky's women in general). A reader, a student in a sense (yet another painful memory of Apollinaria Suslova), in an ambiance marked by good taste and elegance, not without her benefactor having "inflicted" on her what he calls the "original act." Enclosed in the consciousness of her "disfigured destiny," at first Nastasya Filippovna stands like a budding feminist unbeknownst to herself, against "this man for whom she harboured so inhuman an aversion." Especially when he announces his intention to arrange her marriage to that respectable civil servant whom she also knows, and to give her at the same time a comfortable capital as a dowry, so the benefactor can get married himself without Nastasya being in a "position to do any harm."

The "woman-object" refuses to let him do it and "outs her pig," a pathetic anticipation of "Me Too," necessarily within the limits of the time. Hysterical and proud of it, she begins by shouting right into his face that she "[cares] for nothing, least of all herself," and that "[her] whole life was hanging on a thread." That makes her abuser understand that his prey is ready to kill, with prison and Siberia in perspective, or to kill herself before the altar while she's at it. For the moment, worldly comedy authorizes the outraged woman only worldly laughter and venomous sarcasms. Her devastated pride forbids her this marriage, merely to be mean and to amuse herself and not out of revolutionary convictions. Shut in, this melancholy woman plans revenge, far beyond what her corrupt keeper imagines. The proud extravagances of the kept mistress reveal the "new woman," "solemn and dominating"; she fascinates men who "fear her terribly," some try to "exploit" her, to use her as a "trump card." Nastasya will become a "gambler" out of spite, apparently out of disgust, but actually for no reason. She raises the stakes, the competitors up their antes: Rogozhin the lover vs. Gania, the possible husband paid by the abuser; it starts at 8,000 rubles; it reaches 100,000; she throws them into the fireplace; the package burns, it's pulled out of the flames, only 7,000 rubles remain; that's fine by Gania, she gives them to him, crushing snub. The rebel persists in refusing marriage. With Gania, it goes without saying, all the more since the Prince also says "no" to this priceless business. She also resists marrying the Prince for a long time, leaving the narrator to think that her monstrous pride is much superior to the rank of princess.

In fact, Nastasya Filippovna is the theoretician of this sort of love outside sex that amalgamates her with Myshkin, not just through the intermediary of Aglaya (two women who love the same "innocence of an angel"). She herself explains the unfathomable "enigma" of her gaze ("a kind of darkness, profound and mysterious. Her gaze rested on him, seeming to propound a puzzle"), when she describes her vision of unobtainable love. In counterpoint to the *Dead Christ*, which exposes males to the anguish of death, the proud beauty's favorite painting is a *Lone Christ*. He is listening to a child, His hand posed on its head, "his gaze afar." "A thought as great as the whole world dwells in his look; his face is sad. The child has fallen silent and leans his elbow against his knees and, cheek on hand, raises his head and stares intently at him, wondering as children sometimes do." "That's my picture!"

This image of the infantile divine, of the divine infantile—impotent omnipotence—could be Lev Nikolayevich Myshkin's favorite painting. Fusing with the Idiot, Aglaya, and Christ, Nastasya Filippovna yearns to oppose "the abstract love of humanity" which "comes down to loving oneself alone." She demands a "love without selfishness" in which you are "capable of loving not for yourself but for the one you love," and she comes out with this formula, which could be the motto of the *self-loves*: "love is a great leveler." However, as if conscious of the destructivity that is brewing in this *sameness* lacking an "other," she begins by declaiming to Aglaya, "You are now all mine, I will be close to you all my life" (the "you" is plural and includes Myshkin)—and suddenly adds, "I shall soon be dead."

The timeless purity of the self-less and sex-less twinning emerges in brusque and brutal breaths. From the moment of their first encounter, Nastasya treats the prince like an idiot: "In any case, how can you get married, you'd need a nurse to look after you!" It happens that he defends himself by whipping in the face an important person who insults him. When the *without-self* cohabits with the Ideal of loving only the *other-same*, what remains for him is the shame of the impossible, on the margins of this living world. The most lucid *self-loves* accept and master the work of death in themselves. The Idiot accepts himself as the revealer of the vulnerability inherent in the elementary social connection, in the always unfinished thought-idea-word. Nastasya Filippovna forces herself to play the marriage game, knowing that it's only a "one more minute, Mr. Executioner!" addressed to humans dominated by their desires exposed to destruction. She will rely on the passion of Rogozhin, who awaits her with his knife.

As a feminine alter ego of the Idiot, and beyond her refusal of the market corruption that perpetuates the affront done to women, even when they are felt to be "superior," Nastasya Filippovna shows that "there is no sexual relation," whether it's understood as an organic commerce (with Totsky, with Rogozhin) or as a communion outside sex with Myshkin. *That* does not exist without confronting the incommensurable difference, without losing in the war of the sexes.

It is not "feminine castration" that makes this femme fatale seem to suffer. Nor does she complain about the condition assigned to her by social history, that of being the second sex inferior to the masculine, even if her *pride* can be understood as a *denial* of castration no less than as a revolt against social sexism. A successful *denial* according to her limits and those of her time, which lead her to play games with men in unison with their sadistic destructivity, of which she reveals to them the masochistic lining, all the more fulfilling. "She's mad!" the Prince diagnoses. "'Who knows about that, perhaps she isn't,' said Rogozhin softly, as if to himself"—not as boorish as it seems. Like a Proserpina whom Zeus condemned to spend six months of the year with Hades in hell, Nastasya Filippovna, always conscious of the death drive, utilizes the two self-selected brothers (Myshkin and Rogozhin) as her executors and, definitively, her victims. With her, in her wake, the murderer will sink, completely delirious, the Prince will return to the brute state of Idiot. A "seeker," Lebedev will say of her, but "without goodness," and for once he is right.

Dostoyevsky could have made Vigny's verdict his own: "The two sexes will die each on their own side." Nastasya Filippovna does not feel capable of confronting the sexual "shame" that is toxic to her pride and her entire epoch. And since Myshkin, when all is said and done, reveals himself as sublime, their delicious and dramatic sublimation condemns these two "celibates of art" to the disaster of insanity (for him) and death (for her).

Although the *narrator* ceaselessly instills laughter into this grandiose pathology, the *author* for his part accumulates frequent epileptic seizures and losses at roulette; he keeps scrupulous records of them in the *Notebooks for the Idiot*, in company with his stenographer-wife, Anna Snitkina. An odd narrator, who introduces himself only as a "calligrapher," another celibate of art, whereas the devoted spouse shelters and preserves the creation of the definitive text of the novel, between attacks of morbidity in the person and the work of her husband.

Proud "Little Demons" and "Firm Like Saints"

The parade of *proud* and *rebellious* women includes three Katerinas: Katerina Ivanovna in *Crime and Punishment* (1866), Katerina Nikolaevna in *The Adolescent* (1875), and Katerina Ivanovna in *The Brothers Karamazov* (1881). Of noble birth, free and tormented, these eternal "phallic women" (more eternal even than the "eternal husband") impose respect for their autonomy. Though they tend to be ridiculous and lose their power at the end of the day, since they don't have Nastasya Filippovna's gnawing fortitude. Dostoyevsky likes them, lets them fascinate him, and doesn't spare them.

Dantesque furies and indispensable signposts, the *mothers* traverse the entire Dostoyevskian carnival, they are its messengers. Always *between* unnamable tears, with which they inundate the kissed hands of servants of the church, and their society faces; *between* logorrheas of love and despair, *between* imploring God or justice, and the rush for money . . . Interminable but fulfilling ordeals for their children, little, grown, and old, who always hang on their breasts and their souls, right to the end . . . The *melancholy distress* of Pulkeria Alexandrovna Raskolnikova, the mother of Rodion, the son who wanted to be a Napoleon. The *ridiculous emphasis* of Mme Yepanchina, wife of the general and cousin of the Idiot (Myshkin), who nonetheless expresses the author's conviction that the ongoing chaos is a religious crisis. The *maternal madness* of Katerina Ivanovna, the mother of the little Marmeladovs, stepmother of Sonya-Sofiya: broken by poverty, she devours all her children by giving them over to mendicity and prostitution. The *pathetic domination* exercised by the regal Varvara Petrovna Stavrogina, who, taken in by her son, the unpredictable Nicolai Vsevolodovich Stavrogin, thinks she can anticipate, manage, and control everything, except for the suicide of this child who has dispossessed her of her own pain.

They relay and dominate the anonymous mothers who invade the monasteries and kiss the holy ground of Mother Russia. "Our society does not have any foundations," Dostoyevsky warned. But it does. He set out to seek the "foundations," "internally and morally," in Russian mothers whom he praised thus: "the mother, a Russian type (immense character): they are crushed and submissive, and as firm as saints" (notebooks for *The Adolescent*, 1875).

Only one adolescent, "the little demon" Liza Khokhlakova (*The Brothers Karamazov*, 1881) continues certain aspects of the "febrile and lunatic" heroine of *The Idiot* (1868), Nastasya the seeker. Liza does not stop at breaking her own finger between two doors (later, Ilyusha bites Alyosha Karamazov's)—a sign, through carnivalesque displacement, of the phallic competition that feeds adolescent concupiscence. More tomboy than the brothers, she senses the universal eroticism of parricide: "They love that he killed his father," the cheeky woman cries to Alyosha. Her hysterical curiosity takes her to the most obscure zones of nihilistic ideologies, of extremist deliriums, of religious persecutions. It's Liza who, suddenly, in an implausible turn (frequent in Dostoyevskian narratives), formulates one of the morbid, murderous fantasies that fan the flames of anti-Semitism and anticipate the Holocaust: "Is it true that Jews steal children on Passover and kill them?" Alyosha merely replies, "I don't know."

These perfidious lines break into the narrative with a gust of obscure, implicit fantasies. To the cruel legend of the seducer Jew, rapist and criminal (fascinating like Stavrogin?), medieval anti-Jewish literature added the fantasy of the Jewish man with menstrual flows—to make him pay for the blood lost by (a feminized) Christ? These legends cohabit with the ones about Jews as manipulators of money, inexhaustible power dominating universal marketing—obsessive theme of Dostoyevsky's writing—through and above which the stunning wish to win to the point of losing attempts to go one better (*The Gambler*, 1866). The reader is taken hostage by the lascivious poses of this orgiastic imaginary: Liza's, Alyosha's, the narrator's?

A lubricious excitability corrupts the adolescent girl, at the very heart of her morbid aspiration for purity, a "malady of ideality" in the feminine, which Dostoyevsky explores and leaves in suspension. Alyosha's "I don't know" cannot be received only as a literary procedure of the author's, who might be said to use this evasion by the youngest of the Karamazovs to give free rein to his cherished polyphony. Liza's excessive enthusiasm makes the "ideas" of this little person infantile and caricatural, as she is "possessed" by the demon of destructivity with which Nastasya Filippovna also played, but seriously and the better to sacrifice herself. Although in other circumstances Alyosha does not deprive himself of preaching peace and other associated moral values, his fawning attitude reveals the effectively demonic hold hysteria, turned into *mortiferous unlinking*, exerts on humans. Dostoyevsky's ideological position can be heard here beneath the words, the position he assumes in the political debate and develops in his *Writer's Diary* (March 1877): *his* Jewish question, which he considers a "necessary explanation" of his hate-love of Judaism. The novelist's polyphony disappears, and the writing of the journalist becomes the herald of his own "malady of ideality."

In proposing the Russian people as a "theophorous" people, the author inevitably comes up against the temple of the Bible. And he makes himself complicit in the rejection that led to the extermination of that absolute rival, the Jews, now turned into a superfluous foreigner and scapegoat. It is up to the novelistic writing to continue to deconstruct the psychosexual sources of this phantasm, of this abjection.[10]

THE CRIPPLE: DELIRIUM OR PAIN?

By her handicap, "her bad, shorter leg," Marya Timofeevna Lebyadkina, in *Demons* (1872), embodies castration. About thirty, thin to the point of sickliness, little dress of worn cotton, tender and quiet gray eyes, and a secret joy that sometimes laughs with a sly laugh, without dissipating the unease her skinny face inspires. With her scant hair in a mini-chignon, with "a small knot no bigger than a two-year-old child's fist," she lives withdrawn in a dark corner of the kitchen. It's not really the "repulsion one usually feels in the presence of such God-afflicted creatures" that she arouses, but compassion. Which she should have for herself, since this woman continually tries to erase her birth defect, to repair herself armed with a mirror that never leaves her side—wrinkles coated with white makeup, lipstick, blackened eyebrows. She attempts to beautify even the poor Shatov—a revolutionary who lives like a monk, who has slapped Stavrogin—by doing his hair, because he doesn't have a comb. Strange stranger, coming from a Carmel order, she withers away as she draws cards that infallibly predict a wicked man, betrayal, and death.

This miserable "bric-a-brac," with its fragile seriousness, could have become the prototype of Picasso's Weeping Woman, if Mlle Lebyadkina were not devoted to the Virgin, "the hope of the human race," in her view, which leads her to think like a melancholy Spinoza: "in my opinion, ... God and nature are all the same." And embracing the Mother of God, kissing the ground and crying her heart out, until the sun sets: "so big, so splendid, so fair," "do you like looking at the sun?"

She is, at bottom, ecstatic. Her sadness submerges her babble evoking the infant she (may have?) had, all pink, with little fingernails, sometimes a boy, sometimes a girl, not baptized, no husband, she carries him into the forest to the pond . . .

Delirium or pain? Guilty of infanticide, of invalidity, of being a woman, of not being a mother . . . Marya Timofeevna is one of those "shriekers" in the memory of the Russian people and in Dostoyevsky, who lament, crazy about God. Like Fyodor Karamazov's second wife, the mother of Alyosha; like the peasant woman who sees the Elder Zosima to confirm the loss of her little boy of three, Alexis, "a name of God"—the name of the last son Dostoyevsky has just lost . . . Marya Timofeevna's tears contain "no harm," they flow toward the sun in joy, it's good, except that it's sad.

Shatov did not slap Stavrogin because this atheistic nobleman whom he loves, and who has "meant so much in [his] life," has slept with his wife; nor because he seduced his sister, Daria. But because he married Marya Timofeevna, the Cripple, "so disgracefully and basely," "out of a passion for torture, out of a passion for remorse, out of moral sensuality." "It was from nervous strain ... The challenge to common sense was too enticing!" This man of the people, the most zealous about the Dostoyevskian idea of the "theophorous people," is indignant about the sadistic tendencies and the "debauching of children" that his "genius" is addicted to, who feels "the same pleasure of good and evil, of the ugly and the beautiful."

The burlesque is waxing crescendo: the arrival at the church of the Limping Woman, powdered, adorned with an artificial rose used to decorate the cherubim at Palm Sunday; the exclamation, "What, you're lame!" by Varvara Petrovna, the mother of Stavrogin, after having wrapped her in her black shawl, "in some magnetic sleep"; Liza, whose betrothal with Stavrogin is being planned, side by side with the Cripple in the Stavrogin parlor ..."Is it true that she is ... your lawful wife?" mama dares to say. Nikolai Vsevolodovich's denial rings false: "Consider that you are a girl, and I, though your most faithful friend, am nevertheless a stranger to you, not a husband, not a father, not a fiancé ... [I] will take you to your house myself," says this mystifier to the invalid. The poor thing comes forward and of course trips, almost falls, catches herself on an armchair, and finally, helped by Stavrogin, leaves the scene limping. Hanging on the arm of the man with the wan mask. While Liza, the "libertine" and "partisan of the new rules," is seized with a convulsive movement, "as if she had touched some viper."

The vengeful truth of delirium, like the ultimate arm of the collapse that stands up to the torturer, like the bursting of the wound that bubbles against the knife, explodes in the last encounter Stavrogin has with his scorned spouse. He comes to tell her that he is making their marriage public, they will go live in Switzerland in an austere place. The Cripple is still taken with her fateful presentiment: she will be killed, a knife is being proposed, she dreams of a Prince, of *Him*, in the third person, "I'm afraid I myself may well stop loving someone ... I don't know what I'm guilty of, that is my whole grief forever." Suddenly, she addresses the visitor: "Hm ... you've grown fatter," asks him to get up and come in again the way *He* would, the Prince; but she sees only an old owl, not a falcon like *her* Prince: "Away, impostor! Grishka Otrepev, anathema!" (a heretic damned by the Church). "Ohh, idiot!" he mutters.

Thus ends this nihilistic blasphemy, the improbable marriage of "moral sensuality" with the ungraspable Limping Woman. Going out into the night, Stavrogin runs into the convict Fedka, who just misses stabbing him; he stops Fedka's knife (the one Marya hallucinated?), and throws him some banknotes, into the mud. Fedka understands the message. Soon he will be murdering Mlle Marya Lebyadkina along with her brother and burning down their house.

Since there cannot be love in a world without God, the ideal of the Madonna, insulted, is extinguished in unbearable burlesque pity for a femininity that is not even guilty, just handicapped from the start by its inescapable ecstatic masochism. It remains only for shrieking heroines to shout out the truth of their morbid jouissance, in the face of the impostures of the nihilistic males, who consider them superfluous and often succeed in fiercely exterminating them.

"The Meek One," or "There Is No Sexual Relation"

"The Meek One" (1876) (*krotkaia*, "tender, fragile, humiliated, abased, appeased"—even "inner peace") presents as the "fantastic" narrative of a man ruminating his pride, as cruel as it is debased, such that from dream to fantasy he fantasizes it "realistic in the highest degree." The wordless solitude of the couple in "The Meek One" recalls the earlier *Adolescent* (1875) and the passion of Versilov for Sofia, the wife of the serf Makar, from which Arkady is the fruit: "The twenty years your mother and I have lived together have been spent in silence." But the naïve ardor of that deist father idealizes feminine humility and submission while venerating firmness: "Humility, meekness, self-deprecation, combined with firmness, strength—yes, real strength—all these make up your mother's character."

In this phantomatic tale, on the contrary, a veritable anatomy of hatred gnaws at the couple. *He*: disastrous retired officer, about fifty, who has become a pawnbroker; *she*: poor, meek young girl of sixteen who deposits at his pawnshop little trinkets as well as the icon of the Virgin and Child, to pay for an offer of employment. She possesses nothing, an ideal situation for him to marry her and establish her dowry in the form of a loan. Married, in debt, she becomes his principal pawned object, in sum. *He*: hypochondriac, miserly, silent as a stone. *She* throws herself at him, exalted, in love. *He* receives her infantile babbling with a cold shower. *She* remains silent. *He* demands total respect, besides she isn't worth a penny, "there's no originality in women." Her sweet face defies and disgusts him. When the Meek One takes the liberty of being generous with a female client, he sees "rebellion and independence." *She* ends up leaving home, returns, privately encounters a former friend from *his* regiment. The suspicious spouse joins the cohort of husbands who are jealous because they are in "hatelove" with the man, the third person (yet another). *She* now appears to him like "an unbearable tyrant," "a coquette in a French comedy," "the coquetry of a depraved but witty being." The obsessional male, steeped in inferiority, meticulously plots his suspicions and projections. *He* attributes to *her* his own abasements and tortures, which awaken and definitively aggravate those of the wife.

She lies down beside him fully dressed. *He* takes out his revolver and puts it on the table. There emerges "this terrible memory," meteoric destructive desires from *him* projected onto *her* in a hallucination-reverie. Unless it is an act actually committed, but by *her*? The polyphonic *vague*, Dostoyevsky's trembling meaning, is at its high point in this unfortunately little-known narrative. *He* has his eyes closed; *she* poses the revolver against her husband's temple, he lets her do it; seconds pass; *he* opens his eyes; *she* is not there. *He* believes that *she* has understood that *he* knows *she* wanted to kill him. *He* puts her in a different bed, the marriage is destroyed. *She* falls ill. The sicker *she* becomes, the more *he* enjoys distilling his hatred to the point of turning it into his pleasure, yielding to an ultimate humiliation that makes him scream and taking pleasure in placing himself on both sides: destroying-destroyed. "I sometimes decidedly liked the idea of her humiliation. It was the idea of our inequality that I liked."

The perversity of this passive/active narcissism becomes a pitiful vaudeville when, observing how tuberculosis causes her collapse, *he* kisses "the ground on which her feet stood," ecstatic at the idea of leaving like lovers for Bologna! And he asks his Dulcinea to "turn me into a thing of yours, into a little dog." But *she* has already forgotten, *she* is absent, laughs shamefully and just sings a romance "in a half voice." *He* goes away, as if by chance, to prepare their trip. While *she* jumps out of the window, clutching the icon of the Virgin with Child . . . And *he* continues to intone, "Why, for what reason, did this woman die?"

Inalterable solitude wipes out the dream of *Her* and *Him*. Death carries off yet another woman, while the man continues to reassess, a tragicomic version of suffering virility. They hardly realize that the war of the sexes it in the process of taking the path of the emancipation of the "second" sex. As for the author, who says "I" in place of *He*, the tender and eternal accomplice to suicidal feminine melancholy, he pours his carnivalesque poison onto *him*. Whereas the torments and commotions of the narrative aiming to be "realistic in the highest degree" leave the inevitable question without an answer: "Who I was and who she was." Ultimate *doubling* "in the highest degree."

Grushenka: A "Bitchy" Shame

Dignified, suffering, dominating, murdered, Dostoyevsky's women are not just "a function of the man," as Berdyaev writes, keen observer. They reveal to men their own little-known and repressed abysmal depths, they also inspire their irreconcilable eroticism, their solitude in the feminine—to be shared later, or never. Women beaten by the vortex of the male "I"s, they're isles.

Grushenka (*The Brothers Karamazov*, 1881) stands out in the archipelago of feminine voices in unveiling the unbeatable secret of feminine narcissism (even when it is damaged or a failure): "She was as if in love with herself." Mistress of the father and the son, she takes her distance from Fyodor, approaches Alyosha, and is taken with a passion for Dmitri Karamazov. This depraved and candid woman participates in the *murder of the father* that structures *The Brothers Karamazov*. In effect, in desiring "his father's woman," the son injects himself into the paternal desire, but very differently from the other "trios" in which Dostoyevsky's eroticism deploys. Dmitri castrates his genitor, because the woman he appropriates for himself is in the "maternal" position, and she becomes the stake in the explicitly sexual, lubricious jealousy between the two men. However, Grushenka does not stop at stoking the rivalry in this "amorous dualism," in these "double loves." With her "bold and determined character," she is the one who spurs the *initiative* and expedites the *vitality* of the Karamazovs. They would have been only a clan excited and adrift without this "fresh" "businesswoman," this "Russian beauty," a "Venus de Milo . . .—though the proportions . . . were somewhat exaggerated," who keeps reinventing herself as she transforms her men.

Even though she is a typical Dostoyevsky woman, a sensitive orphan, seduced and abandoned five years before by a Polish officer, Grushenka, whose "joy was like a child's," breaks the mold. Innocently using "the feline inaudibility of her movements" and the "drawn-out and too-sugary enunciation of sounds and syllables," she has found, for four years, a "protector" in the person of the merchant Kuzma Samsonov. Without an education—no connection to the "new woman" and a far cry from "new ideas"—she can only wait "frenetically" for the return to a "virtuous life." It's not for nothing that Agrafena bears the name of Nero's mother: she has "an extraordinary taste for business" (at the time, this was said in German: *Geschäft*); speculating without scruples, she succeeds in accumulating a little capital, like "a real Jew." The narrator's anti-Semitism becomes more upbeat and amused here than it was around Liza. He's envious, but almost admiring—all the more since by buying up debts at low prices our audacious trader brings ten times their value to her "associate," who is none other than Fyodor Karamazov, the patriarch, and who "ended quite unexpectedly to himself by falling head over heels in love with her." An expert in the art of torturing the father as well as the son, who remains dazzled by the single hour of love spent with her, it is not by chance that this winning and sensual young woman lives in the busiest place in the city, near the cathedral. For the incalculable energy of her "beauty of the moment" plunges its roots in her shame, a quite moral feeling, but a special shame, an insolent shame, a "bitchy" shame.

In contrast to *guilt* which arises from the *fear* one feels at the intimidation and punishment coming from a paternal authority (the "guilty" Cripple considers her handicap a divine punishment, augmented by anxiety and a need for self-punishment), *shame* is accompanied by an extraordinary investment of *excitation* and by a loss of mastery over it. Desire, uncontrollable, feels miserable and unworthy, open to the sarcasms of a world with a globalized, all-powerful gaze, debasing and defamatory. (Dostoyevsky, from *dostoinyi*, "worthy," passionately explores the unworthy labyrinths of shame.)

The abreaction of *guilt* culminates in the identification with the aggressor through the demolition of the self by pride (Nastasya Filippovna), or through delirious collapse (the Cripple) or the suicide of the hunted (the Meek One). Whereas *shame* can be revenged by returning the sarcasm: the other's gaze, feared for causing debasement, reveals its own misery, and the dominator seems only suited to be dominated. The narrator excels in these reversals, inexhaustible source of "dialogic" eroticism.

"Bitchy" shame or "sorceress" shame? Yet the total dominion of this "beauty of the moment" has its roots in her shame: a truly moral sentiment, but a special shame. Insolent shame, "bitchy" shame when the unworthy Grusha so successfully seduces her rival, the "worthy" Katerina Ivanovna Verkhovtseva, who greedily kisses the "swollen lip" of the vulgar winner, until the latter projects her shame onto her pretentious competitor by refusing to kiss "her lovely little hand": "I'm just not going to kiss your hand." One could hardly be more villainous. "You slut! Get out!" The proudful woman thus defied explodes.

Emphatic shame, "sorceress" shame: the seducer flirts with Alyosha, the purest of the pure; she senses his *shame*, which rises with the excitation brooding under the unmasterable sensuality of the Karamazovs. Unstable Grushenka and timid Alyosha, their pleasures both in suspension yield to each other, an angelic osmosis: "I found a true sister . . . You restored my soul just now," Alyosha reassures himself.

But the achievement of the Russian woman's triumph must wait for the unbelievable encounter in Mokroye: Agrafena-Grusha drops her Polish officer who has come to marry her; then, "animal" and "wild," she promises herself without giving herself to the ardent Mitya, who in the meantime has almost killed his father, Fyodor. The trial will follow, the son will be condemned. Mistress, mother-mistress, Grushenka induces and accompanies the resurrection of the "new man" in the condemned man. She knows how to go about it by nullifying herself, in a fullness of hysterical intoxication: "I'll be your slave now, your lifelong slave! It's sweet to be a slave! . . . Beat me, torment me, do something to me." Mitya can leave Katerina Ivanovna to her haughty love. He dreams of escaping from prison, fleeing to America with his voluptuous captive—implausible mach-ination. There, the man will till the soil alongside the country bumpkins, the beautiful woman will work too and even learn gram-mar with the last of the Mohicans, they will end up returning to Russia to die, acting like Americans . . . "So Grusha will be with me, but look at her: is she an American woman?"

Does this final Dostoyevsky carnival prophesy the improbable destiny of an incredible couple, globalized citizens of President Putin, having settled the universal fantasy of parricide? In any case, it sketches the amusing possibility of a life for two, submissive to the libertarian whims of a man starting over because reconciled, thanks to the sinuous, submissive, faithful sensuality of a woman. The aging novelist remains a stranger to the feminist ardors already beginning in this fin-de-siècle. But his archipelago of feminine solitudes is completed with a complicit wink at the inexhaustible ruses of femi-nine sexuality.

5.3 Children, Loves, and Cruelties

THE "ONES THIRSTY FOR FLESH"

Ultimate threshold of pathetic humanity, the infantile in Dos-toyevsky embodies the purity that saves—when it doesn't unleash delirium, acting out, or suicide. The orphans and poor children are headed for decline, like the Marmeladov children (*Crime and Punishment*, 1866). The eldest, Sonya, prostitutes herself and will "intuit" and support Raskolnikov, but she will be unable to keep her brother and sister from mendicity, the implacable ransom of their mother's madness, of their father's ruin. The debauchery and debacle of the adults make their children frenetically sensitive, compulsive, and wild. Offering herself to the narrator, the little Lenochka says her name is Nellie (*The Insulted and Injured*, 1861), the name her demi-mondaine mother gave her, which she attempts to fulfill by misbehaving like her. Kolya (*The Brothers Karamazov*, 1881) claims he is a "socialist" but scorns the "cretins" everywhere ("There's no one stupider than a stupid Frenchman"), not forgetting the muzhik simpletons. His maniacal fever has him on the rails, despairing and amorphous. Such a gesture of defiance continues today in the Russian adolescents who run away, lying on top of the French TGVs at the risk of their lives, a jouissance to the death available for transfixed internauts to stream. Others, uncurable old children, caress, deplore, and console their lost maternal containers, far from the Baudelairian "green paradise." Nothing but an absolute pain; innocent plenitude, however, irremediable destiny of the unfinished *neotenes*, dependent, badly loved, worse, without love. Thus Mitya Karamazov, dumbfounded by Grushenka's confused deposition in the trial for the murder of his father, dreams of the "little one": he sees himself as a deprived child hanging on to the dried-up breast of his mother. His "sinuous" mistress is not a mother, could she be a good breast? As for the Idiot, desiring "confidence" and "happiness," mocked at first by the "little folk" of the Swiss village, he "tell[s] them everything, keeping nothing back," to the point that his "little birds" "couldn't do without [him] in the end." "I have always been drawn to children," his soul sinking under "many troubles," and always "on account of the children."

The interminable anthropology lesson given by Ivan Karamazov about the mistreatment of children throughout the ages likewise attains the "concupiscence of thought" when he details the tortures of *Bulgarian children*. Tortured and burned by the Turks, they are added to the long list of other acts of barbarism: children forced to eat their excrements or whipped by parents enraged to the point of orgasm. Ivan, the most reasonable nihilist, the most exigent and the coldest of intellectuals—even if he cannot avoid the visit of the Devil, and no doubt precisely because he doesn't avoid it—reveals himself to be subjugated by the vehement libido that invades and torments the infantile universe. He insists on it, revealing to Alyosha that they both love children: "Do you love children, Alyosha? I know you love them . . . I, too, love children terribly. And observe, that cruel people—passionate, carnivorous, Karamazovian—sometimes love children very much."

After the inventory of the " 'beastly' cruelty of man," there comes the famous tirade by Ivan about the *innocence of children*. Shielded from the sins of the fathers, indeed from original sin, their innocence embodies the essence of human existence and is the only thing that is worth the trouble to protect—in the eventual building of "the edifice of human destiny" dear to the "architect" Alyosha. The Christian accents of this indictment, which is addressed to nihilistic indifference and beyond that to the crime of Stavrogin that haunts the novel until its explosion in Tikhon's cell, take on the appearance of a humanistic warning as universal as it is irrevocable. We are all potentially criminal through ideological blindness: "While there's still time, I hasten to defend myself against it, and therefore I absolutely renounce all higher harmony. It is not worth one little tear of even that one tormented child who beat her chest with her little fist and prayed to 'dear God' in a stinking outhouse with her unredeemed tears!" When Jean-Paul Sartre's existentialism affirms its humanism—"I have been apprenticed to reality. I have seen children die of hunger. In the face of a dying child, ideas mean nothing"—the engagement of the atheistic philosopher resounds in unison with Ivan Karamazov's sobs. It is on this affective basis, and sneering in its wake, that Ivan recites a poem he "made . . . up in great fervor" and memorized: the "Grand Inquisitor," his alarming reading of the sectarian excesses that threaten Christian and post-Christian humanism.[11]

Between a stormy discussion with his father and a high-voltage rendezvous with the worldly Madame Khokhlakova, Alyosha Karamazov makes a connection with some young boys. A band of rascals bombard one of their number—weak and undersized—with stones and call him a "scoundrel" and a "squealer." Alyosha, young monk with "pants of coarse cloth," intervenes and tries to protect the victim, who takes it badly, doesn't trust him, attacks, and ends up biting the middle finger of his unexpected defender, "near the nail, deeply, to the bone; blood began to flow." The furious eroticism confessed by Vlas (in A Writer's Diary), when he blasphemed the Eucharist,[12] is replayed here as a parody: the monk's middle finger replaces the stick in the scene in "Vlas," and the bite recalls the host placed on it to be pulverized with gunshots. Alyosha goes to find the gourmand rascal, Iliousha Snegiryov, who, misunderstood by his buddies because he was passionately defending the flouted honor of his father, had the whole gang on his back. Later, accompanying him from his illness to his burial and reconciling adolescent passions surrounding the father and the son united by death, the narrator wants to make us believe that "the love of children" can survive the libido of faith. With the example of Alyosha who lives his religion "unrepressibly": "we go like this now, hand in hand" with his "loving boys." This final effusion of The Brothers Karamazov (1881) doesn't hold up against Dostoyevsky's immersion in the rape of little girls, which had constituted the (too?) black matter of Demons (1872), the complete text of which, with the rediscovery of the chapter "At Tikhon's," wasn't published until 1922.[13]

AN EXTRAORDINARY APTITUDE FOR CRIME: PEDOPHILIA

After having attempted to rape Dunya, Raskolnikov's sister (Crime and Punishment, 1866), Svidrigaylov realizes this drive comes "more for my own zeal," and that "Raskolnikov had guessed" it. He dreams of Dunechka, "more dead than alive," followed by a mouse that slips "underneath the blanket" of the sleeper. Then he attends the burial of a girl who killed herself by drowning, whose distress the dreamer feels as if it were his: "a last cry of despair, unregarded, but boldly shrieked into the dark night, into the blackness, the cold, damp thaw, when the wind was howling." Soon he comes upon a little girl in tears in the corridor of his hotel, takes her to his bed and notices, in the redness of her fever, "a flush from wine," obscene, satanic, a "somehow unchildlike eye," "debauchery," "the impudent face of a mercenary French harlot."

With clinical precision, the narrator minutely follows the trajectory of the rape: the delirious phantasm of the abuser has another man in mind (Raskolnikov); he freezes and stagnates in a plaintive impotence projected onto the passive role of a little girl flooded with shame who kills herself; and ends up inverting this feminized, infantile, and tormented image of himself ("an unloved child whose mother . . . was in the habit of frightening and beating the child") into a depraved little girl, insolent and seductive, which he could never have been, which he desires and abhors, which intoxicates and terrifies him. But petrified in his agitation and excitation, Svidrigaylov does not actually rape or kill her. His lubricious phantasms depress him and lead him to suicide, haunted by Dunya armed with a revolver (like the Meek One) and by the little lady of the camelias.

Quite different is Stavrogin (*Demons*,1872). In the printed sheets he reads to Tikhon, the libertarian and libertine nobleman scrupulously details the "unbelievable pleasure" "moments of crime, or . . . moments threatening to life" procure for him, the baseness he sees in himself; the "shameful and violent sensation" "waiting for my adversary to shoot" in a duel, for example, and especially in being slapped. The consciousness of the transgression ("and it was all based on consciousness!") tortures him, but the shame blanketing this split is "light," at best just useful for perfect self-control and to better sharpen his "animal sensuality" without ever "stopping it." To Kirillov, his likeness and his opposite, Stavrogin specifies: "the burden is light for me because of my nature . . . Nothing to be much ashamed of, only a little." Stavrogin projects himself to the point of fusing with the couple formed by Matryosha (is she fourteen or ten?

The confession at Tikhon's hesitates) and her mother, and he minutely retraces their sadomasochistic torment, placing himself on the side of the scolded and beaten child. Tears and punishments, shame again, but "shame a lot," shame made into a little girl. He drinks in the shame in turn, coldly, contains and retains it; a sort of ennui takes hold of him, implacable symptom of bridled excitation: *indifference* is his armor.

Ennui and indifference take the place of ecstasy, for him: Stavrogin ignores and scorns the agitation of a Pyotr Verkhovensky; he fascinates and dominates the dispossession of his clandestine followers, febrile dreamers of revolution, by freezing his piercing sensuality. But the drive doesn't cool off. Body contact of adult and child. Ephemeral loves, blazing with fear and shame. The transgression transforms the desire of the rapist into anger, repulsion on the brink of laughter: "her face suddenly seemed stupid to me." *She*, prey to her dizzying self, brandishes her impotent hatred, threatening him with her little raised fist; fever, nausea, mortal sickness follow: "I killed God." *He*, on the contrary, "was [fully] in possession of [his] mental faculties." He knows she is going to kill herself, coldly keeps watch and lets her do it, listening to the deathly silence of the little flies, his eye on the red spider on a geranium petal. A photograph of a little girl who resembles Matryosha, bought in Switzerland, will embellish his existence, on the mantle.

When he deposits his debauchery at Tikhon's (*tikhii*, "the silent one"), Stavrogin compares himself to Rousseau: "Giving myself with extraordinary immoderation, until the age of sixteen, to the vice confessed by Jean-Jacques Rousseau, I stopped it the moment I decided I wanted to, in my seventeenth year." Through these solitary and forbidden pleasures passes the phantom of the "divine marquis," brought to him by the intransigent Shatov struggling with the "extraordinary capacity for crime" of his leader.

Beyond the debauchery, Stavrogin's sensual indifference "frees him from all his possessions and all his duties." It recalls the "diabolic inner laughter," "its secrecy and the audacity of the deception," of a certain French lady, whose "thirst for sexual gratification was such that even the Marquis de Sade might have taken lessons from her," mentioned in passing by Prince Valkovsky in *The Insulted and Injured* (1861).

A few hours before killing himself, Kirillov plays ball with a little girl.[14] He loves children just as he loves life, a leaf, or a spider. "Have you seen a leaf, a leaf from a tree? . . . I saw one recently, a yellow one, with some green, decayed on the edges. Blown about by the wind. When I was ten years old, I'd close my eyes on purpose, in winter, and imagine a leaf—green, bright, with veins, and the sun shining. I'd open my eyes and not believe it, because it was so good, then I'd close them again." He prays, but "to everything." Everything that's alive, perhaps even nature in its entirety, in any case "all those who know that everything is good." His epileptic aura, an infinite plenitude of senses lost and found again in consciousness at each recovery from the seizure, will have convinced him that happiness exists, that it's the *good*, and man is part of it. The God-man who will return was crucified for knowing it, "but as long as [men] don't know it's good with them, it will not be good with them."

Kirillov is playing ball with a little girl whose mother is dying. He acts like a child: life is a children's game. The little girl is life: "Life is, and death is not at all." The engineer talks to this child in a halting, ungrammatical language, which names only the essential, fields of meaning and life composed and recomposed at will. A sort of childhood of the mind, on the other side of childhood and language: the innocence of the Idiot coded in compact reasonings, elliptical scientific tremors. Kirillov doesn't kill himself to defy life and the living; on the contrary, to bear witness that there exists a Life, a child's game and cosmic jouissance. A grandiose solipsism, the fatal act of suicide defies the God-man, the Creator, by reversing onto Him the freedom He has given to men. Just an example of extreme freedom, not a model to imitate, so that everyone will know that *all is good*.

The psychosexuality of this man of Technology is obstinately opposed to the muzzled sensuality of the aristocratic Stavrogin, but *right beside* it. Without rape or profanation of marriage, and in acquiescing to the cycle of life and death, Kirillov *feels* a "completely new idea," a newly terrifying one. His justification of the cycle of life, deprived of the Creator and lacking eternal life, imposes a *leveling* without distinction between *good* and *evil*. When everything has the same value, there is no crime. "And if someone dies of hunger, or someone offends and dishonors the girl—is that good?" Stavrogin is asking. Kirillov does not hesitate: "Good. And if someone's head gets smashed in for the child's sake, that's good, too; and if it doesn't get smashed in, that's good, too." This palliative serenity could have sunk into total indifference, if Kirillov weren't killing himself precisely to "light the icon lamp," in an attempt to convince us that being alive is the supreme good and that to feel "quite a new thought" is the only rampart against rape. "When they find out, they won't violate the girl."

Stavrogin doesn't listen to him, but like an echo to his lunatic colleague's phrasing, he follows the broken thread of his own thinking, of his ridiculous dirty thoughts. The shame of his transgressions becomes heavy with guilt, bringing greater pleasure yet by imagining the reprobation, rejections, and revenge of "people and how they'll be spitting for a thousand years, right?" His very syntax is pawing the ground with confused impatience, closely savoring his resemblance-difference with Kirillov, as well as, from a distance, the punishment that posterity will—and must—inflict on him.

Stavrogin will also put an end to his life, but without having felt Kirillov's absolute harmony. Perhaps because life with a comprehending woman like Daria bored him; because the pardon from the "cursed psychologist" Tikhon, who had identified the split in the confessor and guessed his suicidal temptation, put a fissure in his pride; because there is no crime more appalling than the rape of a child; and no punishment can equal its pleasure. Unless it's the strangling of solitude in the impotence of hanging.

Violence of the trauma, indelible phantasms, obsessing drives? The writing slips into these and promotes them. It refines them, is heightened and takes delight in them, with Svidrigaylov and Stavrogin. It fills them out with the muzhik Marey and Vlas the penitent.

The brutality of the prison had made the nagging impact of sexual torture real, also *viable*. The man condemned to death, prisoner and gambler, literally sur-vived by overflowing "literature" with his writing dedicated to the torments of the underground. To attest his particular truth. And invite humans to hear within themselves the gravitational pulses of his dark matter. Or did he sense or provoke *opinion*, the consumer of scandals, abjections, and crimes, to excite himself to the death? Was Stavrogin with his *crime of crimes* conceived as an unforgivable admission, guaranteeing a glorious posterity only at such a price, a "ticket for the future"? Like an assurance of celebrity, necessarily scandalous, among the transhumans or what might remain of the directionless herd, without laws and without resurrection?

The *carnival* does not exclude it, but the *polyphony* of the work is not reduced to it either. Jouissance is written in the composition of unavowable passions and dismantled ideas—surprising rebounds, infinite expansion.

6

THE PURLOINED LETTER

The entire mistake, on the "feminine" question, consists in dividing the indivisible, man and woman are taken separately, whereas it consists of a single organism, homogeneous. "He" created them man and woman.

—Dostoyevsky, *Notebooks* (1880)

6.1 Jouissance

On the scaffold, in the caesura of the "grand mal," and even in the low sound of swoons, tremors, absences, short circuits losing contact with the self and the exterior, death cannot be stared in the face unless a hypersynchronous overexcitation manages to seize it, in the *no-thought* of a tortured and triumphant narrative.

The text: martyred, ridiculous, adjusted. This sur-vival bears a name that readers of Dostoyevsky took some time to pin onto his work: *jouissance* (in Russian *naslajdienie*, with declinations *sladostrastie*, *prelubodiestvie, slastolubie*) is a psychosexual experience that mobilizes "limit states." Different from pleasure, and bearing on the suffering, violence, torture, and shame induced by the psychic apparatus, canalized and instrumentalized by religious or ideological codes, *jouissance* is inevitably *ontological* in Dostoyevsky.[1] Supported by the gnostic substrate of Orthodoxy, it proves to be constitutive of the moral conscience of the writer.

The "artistic point of view," a sublimation consubstantial with sin, a jouissance torn between the life drive and the death drive, would be capable of transposing these paroxysmic states into a "truthful" and "pure" dimension, as a double of the sexual discharge and carnal effraction breaking social constraints and values. However, the author does not fail to accuse himself of original criminality, an unforgiveable, mysterious, sinful act, which he perhaps not only imagined but actually observed and committed.

On one side, the defense of Pushkin's art (and the character of Cleopatra in his *Egyptian Nights*), which according to the author of *Demons* (1872) has nothing to do with "something licentious in the manner of the Marquis de Sade." But it produces an impression of "horrible terror," not "improper, but overwhelming," for someone "capable of feeling poetry and submitting to the enchantment of art." Or the claim of his right to the "artistic" exception to defend the grotesque saintliness of Zosima, his Elder with the stinking cadaver in *The Brothers Karamazov* (1881), in the face of the reserves of the General Prosecutor of the Holy Synod.

On the other, various contemporaries of Dostoyevsky, including numerous "notable and respected personalities" (Tolstoy, Turgenev, Grigorievich, Sofia Kovalevskaya), report memories in agreement with the rumor started by Nicolas Strakhov dwelling on his irritable sensitivity and his violent sexuality, going as far as the rape of a little girl.[2] For the last twenty years, with the help of the removal of Soviet censorship, literary criticism, especially Russian, and then English and American, has opened and reinterpreted the delicate file on the sexuality of the man and the text. Employing a few "tools" borrowed from contemporary philosophy and sexology, these studies speak volumes about the moral and sexual presuppositions of their authors. But without resolving Dostoyevsky's secret, they renew the reception of the monumental body of work while inviting the reader to reread, starting with this "purloined letter" that has always been there, but henceforth makes meaning anew: the rape of a child.

In one of the last pre-Siberian texts, "White Nights" (December 1848), the dreamer, "a creature of an intermediate sort," pours out his perpetual tension and his "inexhaustible fantasy" in his dreamlike encounter with Nastenka (the family diminutive of Anastasia, "the resuscitated one"). The poor young girl in tears, a little kitten martyred and humiliated, lives "pinned" to her blind grandmother's dress, surrounded by a deaf maid and an old mute renter. The specter of Matryosha, raped by Stavrogin in *Demons* (1872), is already prowling: the landlady in these white reveries is called Matrona, and the spider of Stavrogin's guilt decorates the ceiling. The seeds of the "sensuality of insects" (*The Brothers Karamazov*, 1881) will blossom in the works to come.

The sleepless dreamer projects himself as much in the potential aggressor as in the future fiancé of the young girl. Farewell to the clammy loss of all sensation of reality, which threatens with madness the "white nights" of the one who believes his life is a crime. The "trio" formula replaces them, a tad sarcastic, but a magical compression all the same, which promotes enjoyment: "feeling is not destroyed but concentrated." About twenty years later, *The Eternal Husband* (1870) will pierce the triumphal autoeroticism of these "dreams without flesh," subjecting the passions of the two rivals to derision until their passions explode in the hope they will be rid of them. As in *The Brothers Karamazov* through the murder of the father, presumed to emancipate Mitya's desire for Grushenka.

But it is above all his absence of desire that the dreamer discreetly reveals. He palpates and cultivates *indifference*, the psychic fracture where denial and the split lodge. This shameful scar is nonetheless a precious singularity, indispensable for purging sentimental romanticism beyond the laughter without flesh of the white nights, to bind the death-dealing emptiness of Stavrogin (*Demons*, 1872), and be finally free of the "casket language" the *ridiculous man* is fond of. The morbid obsession of the violated and abused infantile feminine will have been the "purloined letter" of this deep self-analysis. Over the course of many years, Dostoyevsky will pursue, through *writing*, this indispensable interpretive process. While making fun of all the postures and ideals that writing calls into question and shatters "into fragments, into dust." So as to "build" and to "struggle to survive" through this laboratory, ultimate expression of the "soul that longs and craves for something else." With an inexhaustible *perseverance*.

The two Russian terms for *jouissance—naslajdienie* and *sladostrastie—* associate the root *strast* for "passion" with the root of *slad*, "delight, savor," which evokes gustatory pleasure and anchors jouissance in *taste*. The oldest of meanings, contact of the mouth with the nipple, nourishment and respiration, feminine dawn of life for both sexes. Doesn't aesthetic experience call for the judgment of taste? The jouissance of the white nights, satisfied, lazy, inexhaustible passage of the dream toward the flesh, is consonant with this etymology, which harks back to the original infantile fusions and separations. The *fruitio Dei* of the Catholic mystics also understands this savor, this carnal degustation, though privileging the proud rigor of a logical and symbolic assumption, beyond the torture of the senses.

6.2 The Ravished Young Girl

Varenka, the ravished young girl, appears in the early *Poor Folk* (1846), received as a social protest. Dostoyevsky evokes rape in "A Christmas Tree and a Wedding" (*Notebooks of an Unknown*, 1848) and adolescent sexuality in *Netochka Nezvanova* (1849).

With *The Insulted and Injured* (1861), the theme of the violated young girl takes on a larger role at the repressed heart of the plot. Nellie, thirteen, is delivered over to the director of a brothel who has her deflowered to sell her to a debauched merchant. Whether dream or reality, like in a "white night," a threshold separates her from the rape that the young writer Vanya (Ivan Petrovich), the narrator in the novel, describes like this: "Suddenly the door was violently flung open and Elena [Nellie]—pale, with dazed eyes, in a white muslin dress that was completely crumpled and torn, with her hair, which had been nicely combed, disheveled as though by a struggle—burst into the room. I stood facing the door, and she rushed straight to me and flung her arms around me." Who is seducing (or raping) whom? "Charming little girl" and "disheveled victim," the breathless narrative voice instills sexual excitation in the words of love and the feverish embraces of the young people. Vanya will save Nellie from dishonor, but the adolescent girl, brutally awakened to her unavowable sexuality, rapidly succumbs to tuberculosis. Between thresholds and irruptions, through walls and confessions, enthusiastic loves and melancholy abnegations, the vibrant narration by Vanya does its best to protect social morality, his own modesty, and that of the ravished one. All the while letting it be understood that the rape of a child is the tragic unthought of this sentimental melodrama that the insulted and injured feast on. And that the villainous Prince Valkovsky dominates, on whom the narrator complacently accumulates and tears off the masks.

The narrative strategy changes with *Crime and Punishment* (1866): a narration with a narrator takes over from the earlier monologues. The fantasies and attempts at ravishing Dunya, insidiously addressed to her brother Rodion, are resolved in a lubricious nightmare. The violator undresses and puts into his bed the little five-year-old girl who excites him with her appearance of a depraved prostitute, with her shameless "camelia" laughs.[3] The libidinous bundle of desire and hatred is distanced by third-person narration and by the dream-work. Obscene and miserable, sordid pleasures cannot be spoken in full. They ravage the intimacy of sleep, obscure secret guilt, which leads to suicide.

In *The Idiot* (1868), the violated girl is not a child. Totsky had waited for the "sexual maturity" of Nastasya Filippovna to "offend, enflame, and debauch her"—after her first period. From then on, a triple distance, otherwise unmaintainable and with abject consequences, is sketched now with regard to this infamy done to the woman: the distances kept by Totsky, the Idiot, and Nastasya. They open the way for Rogozhin's crime.[4]

To rid himself of Nastasya, and concerned about respectability, Totsky requires her to marry the suitor making the best offer, whom he bribes. Furious, devastated, she throws the money into the fire. Myshkin participates in the hypocrisy of repression by offering her the "idiotic" illusion of an ennoblement by marriage. Contrary to Jesus who forgives the sinner and asks everyone to see themselves in her, the naïve prince prefers to ignore the sexual life of the "creature" and her capacity to "destroy herself entirely", "in a monstrous fashion and with no going back . . . as long as she could laugh at that man for whom she holds an inhuman revulsion," as Totsky likes to say. While Ferdishchenko awkwardly recalls people to their "lewd little games."

For body language, Nastasya has only her trenchant pride, a veritable time-delayed bomb that comes to light precisely as a result of Myshkin's generous blindness. He upsets her mind so deeply that, from the time of the marriage project, this prideful reader throws herself into extravagances approaching madness. She shouts, sneers, calls herself "cheeky" when it's not "girl of the street," "Rogozhin's girl" who in short only deserves to "do the laundry" to wash off her defilement. And lets herself be carried away by the death drive, which her participation in debauchery revealed in herself, yielding herself to Rogozhin's knife in all consciousness. Nastasya's confession to Myshkin, gaping infantile solitude tensed in the expectation of an imaginary father, reveals the melancholy power that durably closes off feminine jouissance. And the jouissance of the feminine in the Dostoyevskian man. The Idiot's sermon comes to an end with Rogozhin, his criminal double, whose head he caresses before plunging again into dementia. Unsolvable female distress?

The murderous libido of Rogozhin; the perverse hypocrisy of Totsky; the ontological guilt of Nastasya Filippovna revulsed against her tortuous procurer, but incapable of accepting and forgiving herself for her own pleasures and weaknesses; and the illusory disincarnate holiness of Myshkin: so many impasses of imposed and incommunicable pleasure, for which The Idiot (1868) has no answers. Beyond and through the carnivalesque poetics of the work, Dostoyevsky's troubling art diffuses the jouissance of these impasses themselves: underhanded and toxic, veritable "sexual poison," this double turn bewilders the reader. The author could say, with the narrator of the "Dream of a Ridiculous Man" (1877): "But how to set up paradise—I don't know, because I'm unable to put it into words. After my dream,

I lost words ... I can't recount what I saw." Masochistic hallucination, this jouissance of the impossible? "And is our life not a dream? ... Well, but I will preach all the same."

The rape of the little girl is no longer a "purloined letter" in *Demons* (1872). The absolute demoniacal that closes the novel is none other than the confession by Nikolai Vsevolodovich Stavrogin, at the bizarre *starets* Tikhon's, of his rape of little Matryosha, followed by the little girl hanging herself and, at the end, the abuser hanging himself too.[5]

The nihilist Stavrogin reads to Tikhon a text he published abroad, a sort of "secret proclamation" of political liberalism and obscene literature, as if it could take its place in the library of this rather special spiritual master, which contains theatrical writings and "maybe even worse."

Tenant of a room in the home of "middle-class Russians," the mysterious libertarian encounters little Matryosha, whose mother beats and humiliates her savagely. This torture having augmented his excitement and his controlled masturbation, taught him by his tutor Stepan Trofimovich, the man undertakes physical contact with the little girl. The matter culminates in an embrace, the narrative of which retains only lips, hands, and legs, touches, laughter and convulsive spasms. But for all its compact and laconic tone, the narrative makes penetration wildly manifest. Voluptuousness belongs to the victim. A destitute and distraught child who has escaped from her mother, Matryosha "began kissing me terribly," like an adult conscious of her shame. For Stavrogin, on the other hand, who keeps his composure and controls his will, the action he takes leaves an "unpleasant" feeling of "pity."

Far from the theatrical "indifference" of the dandy, this postcoital weakness points rather to dementia, the blank psychosis of the aggressor confused with the annihilation of his "object." Until he returns to the scene of the crime with the detached curiosity of a murderer, as if to assure himself that it did indeed take place. And he confronts the feverish victim threatening him as she "raised her little fist," then lets her hang herself. In a rearranged version of the chapter "At Tikhon's," the abuser maintains his "Nothing happened. Nothing."

Rape? Or "simple" action, pedophilic to be sure, but with a little girl possibly in love with her inaccessible, idealized lord? From this ambivalence Nabokov was to draw a tantalizing Lolita, while Dostoyevsky's terebrant nervousness struggles to expiate the action by doubling himself. Heads and tails, masculine and feminine, Matryosha and Nikolai, the one and the other, neither the one nor the other, the writing oscillates and *frees itself* from it.

At bottom, any "point of view being false," jouissance escapes from the point of view, whatever it may be. It pulls back (purloined, Poe wrote in "The Purloined Letter") and colors the floating sensuality of the detective-artist. In the emulsion of the writing. If Stavrogin is also Dostoyevsky, the "ridiculous man" who wants "suffering, in order to love"; if "the feeling of shame after the meanness [he] had committed" "made no difference to [him]," he cannot keep from contemplating himself in Matryosha's insulted and assassinated, jubilant and dying femininity. Blended with the childhood of each man and woman, outside sex and all the sexes. With the child in the man. With the man himself, such as he is, when he writes.

6.3 The Violence of the Trauma: Things and Words

Did young Feydia, about ten, see a little playmate die after being raped by a drunk in the courtyard of the Hospice for the Poor that his father ran? This misdeed is revealed only in the 1970s by a noble lady of the former Russian aristocracy. In her childhood, toward the end of the nineteenth century and the beginning of the twentieth, she remembered having heard her uncle say that Dostoyevsky had related this tragedy from the 1830s. "All my life this memory has haunted me as the most frightful crime.... She died, pouring out blood," the writer supposedly affirmed, adding "the most frightful, the most terrible sin—was to rape a child. To take a life—that is horrible... but to take away faith in the beauty of love—that is the most terrible crime."[6] Never narrated as such by Dostoyevsky, hardly credible for certain biographers, plausible for others. Unbearable trauma that returns, that haunts the man and the work, "explains" it?

The *Notes from a Dead House* (1862), written in parallel with *The Insulted and Injured* (1861), does not reveal any rape. *Rape* is permanent there, ravaging, exciting, annulled in this leftover from Dante that is the prison, an absolute jouissance, the only one, the ultimate one. The writer never complains about it, he replays it and overplays it—at work, in the theater, in the bath. Prisoners beaten or beating each other to death, and the stupefying tenderness of depraved, insulted bodies. Languages that take revenge, that jubilate. Except for a "monster" who stands out: A—v, "a piece of meat with teeth and a stomach, and with an unquenchable thirst for the coarsest, most brutish carnal pleasures, and to satisfy the least and most whimsical of these pleasures, he was capable of cold-blooded murder, cutting throats, anything so long as it left no traces . . . He was an example of what the carnal side of man can come to, unrestrained by any inner norm, any lawfulness . . . I recall this nasty creature as a phenomenon . . . I am not exaggerating; I got to know A—v well."

Oh! What abjection of contagion in this "I got to know well"! "Monster," "a moral Quasimodo," it contains the seeds of the gallery of scoundrels swarming from Dostoyevsky's pen: villains, big and little, like Mikolka, Totsky, Pyotr Verkhovensky; seductive scumbags like Raskolnikov, Stavrogin (whom Berdyaev admitted liking, apparently he resembled him); and those Karamazov brothers also, finally judged, analyzed, sublimated . . .

The writer's first mistress and love, Apollinaria Suslova (1862–1865), denounces in her diary the "obscure forces" and the "cruel blind passions" of her lover "implicated in sin" (*prichasten ko grehru*),[7] the "abyss of his soul" dragging him to "the dark side of sin." At this time of hyperconnection, disinhibited specialists scrutinize the writer's "erotic limits," the "disgusting vices," the way the writer "catches fire" in speaking about the "relations between the sexes" in his interviews. Could women's legs be his preferred fetish? He is an "honorable man," asserts his wife, Anna Grigoryevna, to refute rumors and malicious gossip.

Sophie Kovalevsky notes in her *Memoirs* that during a reception at her parents' home (1865), Dostoyevsky described a morning reverie around the "slant rays" on the bare shoulders of a Saint Cecilia at the Munich museum, a paragon of beauty and harmony; but it was followed by a "mysterious pain." This troubling sensation reminds him of the crazy night when, encouraged by intoxicated companions, he raped a little girl. Stavrogin's confession was not yet written, Sophie Kovalevsky could not have known it. Horrified, the mistress of the house stops the boaster.

In 1875, the writer visits a colony of adolescents with "depraved" (*porochnye*) behaviors and takes particular interest in the extreme cases of "debauchery" (homosexuality and masturbation) that develop among chaste incomers as a result of the mockery by those already there. In a long study devoted to the Kroneberg trial (*A Writer's Diary*, 1876) the chronicler protests the defense lawyer's arguments, which had succeeded in acquitting the father who was guilty of savagely beating his seven-year-old daughter Maria. The little girl reminds the former convict of the bloodied spines of the inmates "administered by a thousand blows of the stick." Dostoyevsky defends the little victim's right to intimacy, even if she is a liar, thief, and onanist (this last "deficiency," judged major, is either stressed or "elided" out of "modesty" at the trial): "Yes, the person belongs to society, but not the whole person," the writer protests. And to warn those who by an excess of "responsiveness" "pursue in others the vices that are their own from their heads to their feet," he appropriates an expression from his friend-enemy Belinsky, the "concupiscence" (*bludodeistvie*) of *talent*. He will use it for the title of the chapter on the trial of Mitya Karamazov, "The Concupiscence of Thought"—a charge against verbal masturbation, hollow words that Mitya's lawyer Fetyukovich uses during his plea for the defense. For the moment, Dostoyevsky opposes a soul able to "keep the responsiveness under control, even in the most ardent poetic frame of mind," to the prudishness of opinion and justice in Russia. Like his soul, which he locates and defends in "depraved" and "martyrized" childhood and adolescence?

In an important interview with Evgenyi Opochinine, Dostoyevsky points out that it is impossible to guess what a child is thinking: he speaks "for you" but, without lying, keeps the "authentic truth" "for himself." "Even adults are often ashamed to open their souls . . . but the child opens his world for no one. Only God hears his truth."

This radical innocence is not exempt from "a sort of depraved habit"—like the frenetic masturbation of Maria and so many others . . . But in children innocence is sheltered by "their lack of responsibility and their touching defensive attitude," which draw visitors to the court.

In a letter from 1883, Nicolas Strakhov writes a vitriolic portrait of his former friend, saying "he was drawn to base actions and boasted of having raped (*sobludíl*) a little girl brought to him in his bath by a governess." In reply to these rumors, Anna Grigoryevna Snitkina writes: "My dear husband represented the ideal of a man."

Dostoyevsky goes to the office of Turgenev, who personifies for him the hollow Occidentalist, a figure he caricatured in the worldly writer Karmazinov in *Demons* (1872), to confess "an action of the most infamous sort": he raped a little girl. "Why did you tell me this?" Turgenev asks. "To prove to you how much I scorn you." The provocation ended there, but the anecdote continues to intrigue biographers.

6.4 Writing and For-giveness

Fragments of memories, vague reminiscences, fleeting impressions, even intimate confessions . . . could these be the "atomic facts" that formal logic speaks of, the original constituents formed by a particular and a predicate, whose purpose is to construct stable propositions and more complex relations? The pleasurable states of polyphony are not "facts," but *quantum states*, impossible to rein in, to localize, to know through an act of memory, an avowal, a declaration, a provocation. Trans-identitarians, interfaces of feelings and signs, drives and language, meaning and signification: the "facts" evaporate there. Organic and signifying, sensitive conflagrations with death to oneself, union-disunion with the other, linked by the navel to desired and forbidden creation-procreation: these are the bounds and rebounds of *jouissance*. They put thought and the sentence into motion, accumulate appositions and contradictions, tremble with the so-frequent adverbs of Dostoyevskian hesitation: *almost, can he, it would seem, approximately*, that pierce the pathos of the sentence and the narrative. The underlying, explosive jouissance *is the center* of Dostoyevsky's writing, which is consumed in loves, hatred, and crimes. And it is in the last of the great novels, *The Brothers Karamazov* (1881), that the author explicitly makes claims for it by inscribing the *traversal of death by jouissance* as the ultimate condition of the *parlêtre*.

Having noted that "In your family sensuality is carried to the point of fever," the seminarist Rakitin, agitated and spiteful, defines jouissance (*sladostrastie*) as a human capacity to "[fall] in love with some beautiful thing" (*kakuiu nibud*). "It's that a man falls in love with some beautiful thing, with a woman's body, or even with just one part of a woman's body (a sensualist will understand that), and is ready to give his own children for it, to sell his father and mother, Russia and his native land, and though he's honest, he'll go and steal; though he's meek, he'll kill, though he's faithful, he'll betray." Love-fall, into what *beauty*?

That of the body, even of a "part" of the fragmented body, foot or lip, some sort of fetish for extenuating and perverse rituals? Or the beauty that "saves the world" according to Myshkin in *The Idiot* (1868) and repeated by Stepan Trofimovich Verkhovensky in *Demons* (1872)? But the impotent prince does not manage to save Nastasya Filippovna, and the writer (or failed father) collapses in tears, admitting he has lied his entire life. Or rather Dmitri Karamazov, who nearly killed his father in "just" wanting to steal his money, but not having done so expiates his parricidal desires and savors a *beauty* in which there cohabit, side by side, "the ideal of the Madonna and ... the ideal of Sodom"? Alyosha himself, the virginal boy with his novitiate's habit, though nevertheless a "sensual insect," he too seized by trembling in Grushenka's lap, discovers his aptitude for certain not solely solitary pleasures, in the end. Liza Khokhlakova, for her part, consumes her stewed pineapple while imagining she's crucifying a little boy of four (*The Brothers Karamazov*, 1881). And Arkady, in *The Adolescent* (1875), rivaling in voluptuousness his debauched progenitor, the freethinker Versilov, obsessed with the inaccessible Katerina Nikolaevna whom this biological papa accuses of sexually abusing his son: "As depraved as you may be by nature and as expert as you may be in your depravity, I still thought you would restrain your passions and not deploy your wiles on mere children." Since it "surpasses all limits," jouissance is a flower of evil, in Baudelaire as in Dostoyevsky.

To fully acquiesce to jouissance, demonic or bridled if not impossible in this world with God or without God, it's into infantile eroticism that the narrator projects himself. Because the infant takes pleasure as soon as it lives and speaks—nature, society, and conscience posing laws and limits from the start—the pleasures of the innocent and irresponsible child-adolescent participate in the risks of its free flowering. They are inherent to the fulfillment and future of the human. As a result, the priority is to protect children and adolescents, says the writer, and he has the abusers Svidrigaylov and Stavrogin kill themselves. While the journalist Dostoyevsky revolts against the mistreatment of the child, even within the family, and also rages against the new legislation when it yields to the patterns of enlightened Western rationalism. As a defender of the rights of children, what the writer basically reveals is the irresistible voluptuousness of humans, of speaking *neotenes*, pleasures that, not content to be "polymorphous" like infantile sexuality according to Freud, prove to be, and assert themselves as, frankly perverse.

Masochism or sadism? Homosexuality under cover of the little-girl-object, does it not accuse the spectral image of the envied-abjected feminine of the mistreater, the abuser? The categories are too trenchant for this mixed zone of excitation-repulsion where the aggressor, inspired by the aggressee, takes revenge on her for not being her himself; where the imperious sexual push of the pedophile satisfies his wounded narcissism through the possession of the little boy in himself erected into a fetish. All as erotic scenarios that the split superego must keep hidden, secret, without a trace. And which the *indifference* of the split forces to degenerate into blank madness, into the anguish of annihilation.

It is indeed with this infantile intimacy that Mitya remains in contact throughout his errant febrility. He tries to connect this intimacy—excited, exciting, threatened and threatening—with Grushenka's sensuality, another sinner also abused, though insidiously a winner, proud to sin and without repentance. I perceive Mitya's moves as a lucid transfiguration, a little too optimistic, of the "Ridiculous Man" (1877). Having fled the Stavrogin sin but also having conquered his father's mistress, he ends up recovering the "little girl" in his mistress; he could have cried "I'm hale, I'm fresh, I'm going, going."

He moves ahead, Mitya Karamazov does, with the parricide, the trial, the prison, and "burning dreams." He moves forward for Dostoyevskian children, for their jouissance, for the infantile aflame in all humans. "Because everyone is guilty for everyone else. For all the 'wee ones,' because there are little children and big children. All people are 'wee ones.' And I'll go for all of them, because there must be someone who will go for all of them."

Dostoyevsky is not the master of tragic humanism. The melancholy voices of ontological pain-expiation, essentially religious, or its moral version, humanist and secularized, which resonate throughout his oeuvre, do not hold back but reignite the triumphal or calamitous *carnival of jouissances* in the *jouissance of the writing*. It runs alongside them and transcends them. An exorbitant ambition, informing humanity, which has let go of the reins of its drives and its languages, that there is no other way of dying on this earth while "overcoming the limits" than to bring transgressions to fruition through the abundance of the speaking: "Fruitio,"[8] *proliferating jouissance*. The gospel of John preaches (12:24): "Except a corn of wheat fall into the ground and die, it abideth alone: but if it die, it bringeth forth much fruit," quoted in the epigraph to *The Brothers Karamazov* (1881).

When the rape of a child is the last sexual transgression, a condemnable one, *fiction* claims to displace it into a *different jouissance*, spoken and thought, the jouissance of the writing-reading. It calls for *interpretation*, that ultimate form of forgiveness without consequence: "endless" for-giveness from meaning to the senseless. Are our explosive solitudes still capable of it, so as not to die of hypocrisies or crimes in the surreptitiously totalitarian framework of the hyperconnection we have programmed for ourselves to eternity?

On a sunny day, with a salty wind on an island in the Atlantic, I believed I had detected and perceived—the way one sometimes comes upon a folded letter inside hundreds of millions of pages—that Saint Dosty wrote in the face of death, obsessed with sexuality that kills. Since then, I've kept this "purloined letter" in mind, it's my compass. I no longer fear drowning in the vast thrusts of his vocal meditation, inscribed in the hiccups of his universal Russian.

I go, I reread, I run, I swim in it, accompanied by this fever of a man who cries and who laughs, and I don't forget the impossible.

7

EVERYTHING IS PERMITTED

And now it's to be expected that the other of the two "Heavenly Powers,"
eternal Eros, will make an effort to assert himself in the struggle with his
equally immortal adversary. But who can foresee with what success & with
what result?

—Freud, *Civilization and Its Discontents* (1930)

7.1 From the Dead Father to the
Murder of the Father

The paternal voice is hardly absent from the Dostoyevskian polyphony. Often buried among secondary bit-players, pitiable pathetic
specters, the father dwells behind the scenes of polyphony and participates in the Dostoyevskian doubling from the young author's
first novel. In *Poor Folk* (1846), a palimpsest, the father of Varenka,
whose "troubles and failures tortured him," dies suddenly, the creditors take everything, mama is shaken, they fear she'll lose her
mind. But along with the two letter-writers/narrators (Makar Alex-
eievich and his cousin Varenka Alexeievna), the two fathers of
Varenka's teacher provide an early sketch of the son's torment, which
Dostoyevsky will return to with *The Adolescent* (1875): old Zakar
Petrovich Pokrovsky, the legal father, is much taken with his son,
who "was the spitting image of his dead mother," but who scorns

him openly; and the biological father, the rich Bykov. Miserable but inevitable, insurmountable papa Pokrovsky! It's out of the question to get rid of him—it's the son who dies, while Zakar (*sakhar*, "sugar"), sugary and numb, piteously follows the funeral procession in the mud, letting fall from his pockets the volumes of Pushkin he had given his son.

Could this deplorable carnival father be a compassionate inversion of the Oedipus complex—have the son die rather than risk confronting the unpassable paternal obstacle? Or, more profoundly, is it a masochistic identification with the suffering-castration captured by the hatelove with the father and perceived in him and in itself as a primary jouissance, foundational and unavowable source of the eventual phallic pose, itself reparative of the fault/failure of the father? Conceived as such from the beginning, the father will be posed as the principal *focus* of the writing only with The Adolescent (1875) and definitively as an *obstacle* or an occurrence to suppress—as the threshold to transgress—in The Brothers Karamazov (1881).

Netochka Nezvanova (1849) doesn't have a father but a stepfather, a fascinating violinist who lives like a "foreigner" in a house where only mama works for everyone, while "eternal hatred" maintains the couple. That's before the mama-wife dies. The daughter, finally liberated, freely daydreams about living with step-papa in a "magical home," "eternal beatitude" that the madness of the tragic maestro does not fail to annihilate.

Paternal figures occur in multiple versions in The Insulted and Injured (1861) (Prince Pyotr Alexandrovich Valkovsky, the landowner Ikhmeniev, the rich English manufacturer Smith) who impose checks and interdictions on the desires of their adolescent boys and girls, especially on the girls (Alexei, Natasha, the mother of Nellie), and disrupt their lives. Not without ending up forgiving everything in scenes of effusion, tears, and convulsions, like the one between Natasha and her father. Guilty of having abused of his repressive power outstripped by his supposedly feminine sensitivity, the father falls apart, and goodness as well as the paternal function itself become comical.

In a different social context, it's the sinuous phrasing of his monologue, stretched to the point of the loss of breath and meaning, punctuated by rare suspension points or exclamations, that the "drunken" paternity of the civil servant Marmeladov imposes (*Crime and Punishment*, 1866). Serious, a drunkard but a "man of Enlightenment," the functionary devastated by the poverty of his "accidental" family (*sluchainoie semeistvo*, according to the term in *The Adolescent*, 1875) dies because of the anger of his second wife and the prostitution of his daughter Sonya, her prostitution imposed by the stepmother out of resources and at the end of her rope.

As for Rodion Raskolnikov's father, absent throughout the novel, he appears only as a powerless voyeur in little Rodion's nightmare, in which the father and son observe the putting to death of the light brown mare, whipped up to the eyes by drunken peasants. "Papa! Why did they"; "it's none of our business," refuses the impotent spectator father, while "the boy puts his arms around him, but his chest feels tight," and he awakens with a cry. The nihilist student needs only to abreact this "primal scene" to murder the old moneylender.

The figure of the *general* lends itself ideally to this dismantling of paternal virility and authority. Thus, General Zagoryansky, supposedly chief of his colorful family (*The Gambler*, 1866), is swept aside by his mother, the ancestor of the clan: "Upon seeing Grandmother, the General just stood there dumbfounded, his mouth wide open, unable to finish the word he was going to say. He stared at her, his eyes bulging, as though spellbound by a basilisk." The narrator and the author—former engineering student and ex-convict—like to make fun of generals. In *The Idiot* (1868), General Yepanchin, a loving father, is pitilessly dominated by his wife Lizaveta Fyodorovna, the true "general" of the tribe and cousin of Prince Myshkin whose intermittent and hilarious bizarreries she shares with naivete or finesse. His homologue, General Ivolgin, inveterate drunkard, he too, and responsible for the downgrading of his family, draws our attention less. A great prevaricator, hated by his son Gania, the unlucky suitor of Nastasya Filippovna, Ivolgin's aspiration is to make people believe he met Napoleon during the occupation of

Moscow in 1812. He dies of a heart attack while chanting the name of the "king of Rome," not without his son Kolya kissing his hands and crying. So ridiculous, bothersome fathers, as a backdrop.

But it's the specter of the dead father, sketched in the earlier works, that is insinuated in the chiaroscuro of the central couple, Myshkin-Rogozhin, as if to make their spectral passions plausible. The prince is an orphan, his education had fallen to an old friend of his dead father's, who entrusted him to aged relatives seconded by a governess and a majordomo. This original uncertainty discredits his princely rank, an empty shell that holds the strangeness of the character without "explaining" it: "he could explain little satisfactorily."

Without a father or a mother, without a family, but not without a name, his saintliness disincarnated and not of this world, any allusion to social paternity is incomprehensible to him. Even more when the pretention for it comes from General Ivolgin. Retired and softheaded, he presents himself as a childhood friend of the deceased father of the prince, though he confuses his patronymic, having carried baby Lev in his arms like a double of his father: "I was still passionately in love with your mother." "'Really?' said the prince. 'My father died all of twenty years ago.'" The misunderstanding is complete. It makes you wonder who the idiot is, the one who hallucinates being a father (the general) or the one for whom there is no father except dead (the infantile "saint").

A victim of this unthinkable "paternal function" differently, Rogozhin inherits the lugubrious paternal house, a lot of rather dirty money, Holbein's *Dead Christ*, and the sinister sensuality, haunted by eunuchs, of his genitor.

Stavrogin also has only a dead father (*Demons*, 1872)—general (yet another!) of a brigade, "a frivolous old man who had died of a stomach disorder on his way to the Crimea, where he was hastening on assignment to active duty." Separated for four years from his wife, Varvara Petrovna Stavrogina, for reasons of incompatibility, he was sending alimony to this only daughter of a rich farmer, majestic patroness around whom the demons gravitate. "This was a woman-classic, a woman-Maecenas, whose acts presupposed only the loftiest considerations." Obstinately, necessarily, she fulfills all the possible and imaginable functions of parenthood underlying a destiny as demonic as that of her son in the company of her encumbering and indispensable friend, or who seems to be one, the antifather par excellence, the most complete figure of Dostoyevskian carnival, the highly respected Stepan Trofimovich Verkhovensky. This man plays the part of the preceptor (but young Stavrogin pays no attention to him and does his schoolwork by himself) and is apparently the progenitor of a little "nestling," "the fruit of a first, joyful, and still unclouded love," left him by his wife, from whom he had been separated for three years, after she died in Paris, when the little boy was only five. Like the progenitor, the reader quickly forgets this detail, which slips like a youthful error into the hazy, dark personality of this father in spite of himself. Until the unexpected irruption of the "nestling," Pyotr Stepanovich Verkhovensky, who has become the overexcited leader of a secret society of revolutionary nihilists and the fervent admirer of Stavrogin, the son. Nikolai Vsevolodovich Stavrogin, whom the modern reader knows as the violator of the little Matryosha, had been entrusted to the care—to be sure not really paternal, but "of a supreme pedagogical quality" according to his mother—of Stepan Trofimovich, this fake whom she had stuck in the vacant place of the father—and more generally of *sense*, in all the meanings of this word.

First central character representing the humiliated, lying father, Stepan Trofimovich Verkhovensky is a "liberal idealist," a failed academic, a "reproach incarnate" to his fatherland, "this most innocent of all fifty-year-old infants." He "loved writing to distraction, wrote to [Varvara] even while living in the same house, and on hysterical occasions even two letters a day." Author, moreover, of a "revolutionary poem" for which he has hopes—but in vain!—and claims to fear being persecuted by the reactionary powers. Pathetically endearing, this modernist paranoiac, who later admits having lied for his whole existence, accomplishes his last voyage as an unintended pilgrimage, called by "the immeasurable and infinite." The carnival of the father reaches its heights here, tender derision of the monotheistic axis, of its irremediable decomposition.

His two virtual sons notice his unreal existence so little that Nikolai Stavrogin ignores him royally and Pyotr Verkhovensky repulses him with a "hasty and all too naked rudeness": "What have you got there, Spanish history or something?" "You've been flirting with her [Varvara Petrovna] for twenty years and have got her used to the funniest ways...Just a mutual outpouring of slops...Pah, what a lackey position you've been in all this time. Even I blushed for you." Further: "sponger" off a "capitalist," "sentimental clown," "I advised her yesterday to send you to an almshouse." "Generally, your letters are quite dull; your style is terrible."

"But tell me finally, monster, are you my son or not?"

"Of course, fathers always tend to be blind in such cases..."

Pyotr specifies that he found his mother's "note to that little Polack," "there's nothing certain." Before adding that Stepan Trofimovich "didn't spend a ruble on me all his life, he didn't know me at all till I was sixteen...and now he shouts that his heart has ached for me all his life, and poses in front of me like an actor."

In counterpoint to this uncertain paternity, Shatov, "also a revolutionary," but a man of the people, exults in the symbolic paternity that his wife Marie (heavy reference to the mother of Jesus) brings him when she gives birth to a child certainly conceived with Stavrogin. Without an ounce of comedy, and on the path toward Christ that he has already taken with Stavrogin himself, Shatov recognizes the baby as his son. While the midwife doesn't take a cent and declares that the two of them "have made me laugh for the rest of my life," and Marie affirms "Nikolai Stavrogin is a scoundrel!" the group of conspirators prepares the murder of this Christlike father, a sacrifice designed to give the signal that unleashes the revolution...

Thus lit in stages, the brasier that burns in the last two great novels by Dostoyevsky will be the father. Inaccessible, evasive, fickle. To be recognized and created-recovered. His stupefying vitality is indispensable for the son when the foundations crumble. *The Adolescent* (1875) exposes this vision. It will be necessary to confront him, surpass him, kill him, truly or in fantasy, so the sons can reinvent—as the writing does—"beautiful forms to convey the chaos and disorder of the past." *The Brothers Karamazov* (1881) traces this path.

The Adolescent was to be a novel solely on children and "a child hero," while reprising the theme that obsesses Dostoyevsky, left cruelly in suspension, for the time being, by the suppression of Stavrogin's confession: "The Atheist," or "The Life of a Great Sinner, Written by Himself." But in the fever of the writing, punctuated by violent epileptic seizures, it's the implausible paternity that persists and comes to occupy the central position, initially intended to be Arkady.

Dostoyevsky's adolescent lacks a father only because he has too many! To begin with, there are two. His legal father, the old gardener Makar Ivanovich Dolgoruky ("with long arms"), clothed in the famous princely patronymic which he transmits to his son, carnivalesque complement, if one were needed, to his evanescent paternity. And his biological father, Andrei Petrovich Versilov, landed proprietor and "man of the Enlightenment," who had conceived Arkady with the wife of Makar, the young and pretty peasant Sofia. This "pity love," docile, sensual, and fulfilling, attaches a voluptuous atheistic side to the mystique of maternal Eternity, Russian Earth, and divine Wisdom—which he shares with the author. While Makar respectfully embraces his wife's infidelity, takes up the pilgrim's walking stick, and heads out on the highways.

Versilov's torments multiply these doublings and infect Arkady, exasperating the communion of father and son. This modern papa had thought to believe in Christ, the Jesuits had converted him to Catholicism, he broke the icon the dying Makar had left to Sofia, Arkady's mother, his faith had shattered. Definitive atheist, then, and "only European there," Versilov professes a lyrical humanism and, haunted nonetheless by the "Yiddish kingdom,"[1] poses as a pioneer of Russian European thought.

It's all over for the nihilists of *Demons* (1872). Populist Saint-Simonian socialists replace them who refuse, among other things, the "lordly" image of Tolstoy's characters and wager on the "good" (*blago*) that all humanity will be capable of and of which Russians could be the predestined initiator. Versilov is its herald, trumpeting in the novel the accents of the ideology that Dostoyevsky develops in many pages of his *Writer's Diary*. The golden age of *Acis and Galathea* as seen by Claude Lorrain, which Stavrogin describes to Tikhon, omitting the rape of the little girl, results in the recognition of the irremediable solitude of humans, as Versilov's sentimental education has it. This stoical, if not disabused, humanism leads the deist father and his natural son to the contemplation of Christ on the Baltic, inspired by Heinrich Heine's Christian socialism in his poem "Frieden," Peace:

> And, like a heart in his breast,
> He carried the sun,
> The great, red, burning sun.
> And that flaming heart, that fiery splendor.

The "conniving" orphan men meet and unite through "love and renunciation": "how could you have forgotten it?" The father borrows the lyrical accents of the poet which announce Christ's last resurrection, the ultimate mirage in the "wide-opened eyes" of Versilov-Dostoyevsky.

The affective doubling of the deist genitor—structural schizophrenia, acted, imposed, accepted—underlies his spiritual wandering and gives the rhythm of his limit states. On the one hand, pity-love stabilizes and roots Versilov in and with Sofia; on the other, his voluptuous passion for Katerina leads him to madness, to murder, and to suicide. And for the first time in Dostoyevsky, the two men who desire and share a woman—such a recurring trait of his novelistic psycho-personality—are father and son. The rival *is* the father, the rival *is* the son—impossible lovers struck by the fatal beauty of Katerina Nikolaevna Akhmakova.

In this universe where doublings, clonings, and breakups pile up, Arkady, the son of a former serf and bastard of a former master, has just one idea: "become a Rothschild." Vast program!

Grotesque solution, consecrated nonetheless in the universal imagery of the capital-F Father, who summarizes the social and religious need for *constancy* and *continuity*. (Naming him in German, *Vater*, emphasizes his imposing and ridiculous character, a wink in the direction of German finance now becoming universal.) Moreover, and by a most advantageous paradox to which his distress aspires, Arkady calculates that "Rothschild's millions" will place him outside society and shield him from the common banality while exacerbating at the same time his need for solitude and his desire for power. "I'm not afraid of money—money will never crush me or force me to crush anybody," the adolescent proclaims. His own *Vater*, the biological one, is not opposed; to the win-win Rothschild "idea," with which the adolescent deceives himself, he also adds the irresistible excitability of the male, his unchecked sexuality sweeping away ideals and arousing an animal vitality: "I'm immensely strong . . . There is nothing that can destroy me, wipe me out or for that matter, surprise me. I have the survival capacity of a mongrel dog."

In his commentary on the French translation of *The Adolescent* (1875), always in tune with the amplitude of the Russian language, André Markowicz maintains that one can read it as the novel of two words: *blago* (the good) and *obraz* (from the root *ob-raz*, "environment," and by derivation "contour" and "text," inside-out interiority, hence "image" but also definitively "holy image," icon).[2] Every adolescent, in fact, and Arkady in his singular fashion, aspires to invest in an ideal, *value* or *Good*, to construct his *image of the Good*, his own idea, to construct *himself*. Neither the nobility of birth, *blagorodstvo* (from *blago* and *rodstvo*, "relation, consanguinity") of his genetic father Versilov; nor the *blagoobrazie* (from *blago* and *obraz*, in the image of the Good, reflection of God), which designates the mystical experience of his adoptive father Makar Dolgoruky, "tall and straight," "just," and as "vagabond" as possible, suffice for this child who grows up in a "baseless" society in which "everything is permitted" and "money is everything" (*Notebooks*, 1875). Versilov's utopia, as grandiose as it is implausible, claiming to rebuild the two paternities that are tearing the son apart, rings hollow like an ultimate return to the decentering Arkady has experienced since his birth. The "European gentleman" and "citizen of the world" condemns his son to a teetering, inaccessible identity.

To grasp the causes while seizing the benefits of "everything is permitted" and "money is everything," this modern young man in search of the ideal will want a new idea so he can take on the dominant power, henceforth concentrated in this modern Moloch that monopolizes capital (Marx's *Capital* [1867] had just been translated into Russian in 1872). Inescapable and desirable usurper, to disengage, replace, dominate. Under his skin the adolescent has an *idea* in the Dostoyevskian sense of the term.[3] It is not limited to the idea (*eidos*) of the Greek philosophers, which is already a *vision*, but is tributary to language and capable of imposing forms, then arguments, onto the previously named substances. In creating the *novel of ideas*, Dostoyevsky does not stop at refining the intelligible beyond the sensed world. He overloads writing with a fascinated revolt against galloping modernity, imposing on it at the same time a superior *reflection* of the *obraz* (image, form) that defies the seeing and the knowing and attains a hallucinatory comprehension, for better or for worse.

The Dostoyevskian *idea* comes close to radical evil (the homicide committed by Raskolnikov), suicide (with Kirillov), epilepsy (Myshkin's and Kirillov's), castration and the horror of death (like Ippolit), the condemnation to death (according to Myshkin); it emerges at the borders of the living speaking person and accompanies him in his limit states, ultimate trauma and truth.[4]

To this series of cohabitations Arkady will add his Rothschild "idea." The "consciousness of being deformed" that his "soul of a spider" grants itself begins by withdrawing from the world to devote himself to this "idea" that seized hold of him in high school.

The Rothschild idea was already circulating in the 1840s around Petrashevsky, who accused Baron James, the "king of the Jews," of manipulating the Bourse for his profit and persecuting the socialists in coalition with the liberals. It spreads during the 1870s, again on the left and notably in the writings of Herzen, who denounced the political power the banker Rothschild has over the tsar of Russia Nicholas I. Already present in the hatred for the moneylender assassinated by RRR in *Crime and Punishment* (1866), the "idea" traveled to Grushenka in *The Brothers Karamazov* (1881), this "Jewess" whose art of amassing money is not the least of the charms that bewitch the Karamazovs, father and son.

Arkady adheres to it clearly only when, at an auction where he encounters "some Jews eyeing gold items," he launches into bidding for an insignificant object. And coldly asks an exorbitant price, evoking the name of the famous banker to justify himself: "'James Rothschild . . . earned several millions in a few second. So you see, that's how some people operate!' 'So what do you think you are, a Rothschild?' [a distinguished-looking gentleman] shouted at me indignantly, probably deciding I was some sort of fool" (*The Adolescent*, 1875).

In the whirlwind of his passions, and torn by the *obrazy* of his two fathers, his "Rothschild idea" suffers metamorphoses: in a search for freedom, the adolescent's thirst for money and power and his phallic-anal excitation seek purification. A violent diatribe by Versilov about the "Jew kingdom" ends up making him completely abandon the "Rothschild idea," touting instead his "too precocious, almost vengeful thirst for clarity of the soul" (*blagoobrazie*).

The "Jewish question" constantly haunts the journalist, whereas the novelist, who does not want to become a "historiographer" (like Tolstoy) but aspires to paint the contemporary "Russian chaos," will find a sort of carnivalesque happy ending: Mitya Karamazov has no "idea of becoming Rothschild," in prison he dreams of marrying Grushenka the "capitalist" and going to American to make his fortune.

The Adolescent (1875) is not only a novel about the absolute need to believe that constitutes every adolescent. It is also a novel about the indestructible paternal ideal, frantic and fiery guardian but also *structural third party* (between the mother and the child) even in "accidental" families—ultimate "guard dog" of the aspiration for surpassing oneself. In this ideal resides the transcendence of the *parlêtre* and of the writer in passing. Whether it's in the mystical manner of the poor fellow Makar or of the passionate, lubricious deist Versilov.

Deep into his genealogy of the "great sinner," Dostoyevsky is not the dupe of these children, "a strange lot; I dream of them and see them in my fancies" ("The Boy with his Hand Out," 1876).[5] He grabs hold of them to reach the infantile sexuality that submerges the "ideas" of the fathers as well, before being diffracted by the sons. *The Adolescent* (1875) gathers these "fractals" but leaves the author dissatisfied; he judges this novel severely, "a not altogether insignificant inquiry," a "thankless work stripped of beautiful forms," and yet "I would not want to be the novelist of a hero from an accidental family!" Always in search of his great "sinner," he is also not the dupe of this "new and final resurrection," this "thirst for sickly socialism," for indefinite idealism embodied differently by Versilov and Makar. *The Adolescent* is an apology for unsustainable paternity. A wager on its uncertain rebirth, though freed of the lordly severity of the majestic Tolstoy and delivered over to polyphonic anxiety, in its very idealism. "To guess—and to be wrong" would be his formula.

A new work is needed in which the cursor aimed at the children will pass over into *parricide*, which carnal passion necessarily leads to. In order to inaugurate *for real* the recomposition of the fathers put to death by and in the transformation of the sons.

"Why is such a man alive?" Dmitri Karamazov asks—"his speech was slow and deliberate"—while pointing a finger at his father. The father and the son (*The Brothers Karamazov*, 1881) are "infected" with the same "rage" for Grushenka; the "wheel has come full circle." "Parricide!" cries Fyodor Karamazov. And the Elder Zosima, anticipating the crime, bows down before Mitya. The murder of the father is under way. Its target is a "despicable comedian," a "depraved sensualist," a blasphemer, enjoying his shame and his degradation. At the trial brought against the sons, Ivan Karamazov proclaims with "an ardent scorn," "Who doesn't wish for his father's death?"

Oedipus had killed Laius without knowing he was his father, and Sophocles tells us nothing about the sexuality of the king of Thebes. Hamlet kills his paternal uncle Claudius, the assassin of his father (also named Hamlet) whom he wants to avenge, but Shakespeare doesn't dwell on the carnal links between his mother and his uncle, nor on the desire of Hamlet for his mother or his father. Dostoyevsky portrays the character of a *father to be killed*, which provides "sensuality," "lubricity," "concupiscence"—the terms to name the father-son relation vary, charged with fascination, horror, and derision. But Grushenka is not just a pretext for this passion between men, she also introduces feminine pleasure as such into the heart of the Dostoyevskian polyphony. Although Dmitri confers a maternal role on Agrafena during the trial and in his daydreams, it's the father's mistress who clearly excites the son's desire. Incestual desire is not *repressed*—repression is not a Karamazovian "value." The son doubly desires Grushenka: he desires her the way his father desires her, and because of it; and he desires his father's desire itself, with which he constructs himself, the "pattern" that constitutes him, repulses him, and excites him to the death. In this way, Mitya's desire, totally mobilized by its object (the woman, object of jouissance) and by the wave bearing the drive (identification-disidentification with the father in the family triangle), attains its paroxysm: it rejoins its inner lining, the *desire for death*.

The earlier novels had concentrated this destructivity on the maternal feminine object: woe to the women victims and shriekers, condemned to death by the novel's plot. But writing is an analytical process that proceeds by new developments, each of which is embodied in a new narrative structure. Different from the sinister Dr. Mikhail Andreyevich Dostoyevsky, the author's father, and from the inexistent spectral father of the earlier novels, Fyodor Pavlovich Karamazov is "a great sensualist all his days, always ready to hang onto any skirt that merely beckoned to him." His first wife, the beautiful Adelaide Ivanovna Miusova, from a rich aristocratic family, asserts her feminist independence and defies her family by letting herself be captivated by such a "worthless runt." No "mutual love," the husband filches the totality of her cash, the wife beats him, giving him shameful pleasure; she abandons the conjugal domicile for a seminarian and dies "somehow suddenly" from typhus or hunger, leaving little Mitya, aged three, with her husband. Papa Fyodor forgets the kid and, after "the first son [was] sent packing," "set up a regular harem . . . and gave himself to the most unbridled drinking." Then he contracts a second marriage, with Sonya Ivanovna; the depraved man is transported by the razor-blue gaze of the little orphan from the provinces who, because of her "phenomenal humility and meekness," terrorized since childhood, falls into one of those nervous illnesses of peasant girls who are called "shriekers," who sometimes end up mad. Sofia gives him Ivan and Alexei. Smerdyakov (*smerdít*, "to stink") is the fourth, the son of alcoholic chance and the village idiot, Liza, the stinking epileptic. A marginal creature, the disgusting bastard Smerdyakov is "a pail and manure," "avant-garde meat," and a "broth-maker." As for Fyodor, he carries his depravity on his face: prominent Adam's apple, aquiline nose, pagan patrician, but Russian by the shame that makes him take pleasure-pain to the death. This is the father who will be killed, who must be killed.

Zosima warns: "And above all do not be ashamed of yourself, for that is the cause of everything." The masochistic pleasures of debauchery are not enough for Fyodor Karamazov, one of those fathers who "resemble their misfortunes," about which the pleading of Fetyukovich will speak in seeking to acquit Mitya, in vain: "Oh! To kill the father—well that's even impossible to think of." If the four sons do think about it all through the story, it's above all because Fyodor Karamazov does not speak. He proffers an overcharged oral chaos of buffooneries in snatches, driven by instantaneous pathos and reinflated by swigs of cognac. As early as the rough drafts of the novel, Dostoyevsky insists on the indecisive verbal texture in which the portrait of the character is diluted, until he altogether drowns in it: collections of sayings, puns and anecdotes, improbable bursts of Sade and Diderot, pontificating allegiances to the Devil rather than God, all puffed out between suspension points to portray the type of his inconsistency, of one who defines himself as "maybe not the father of a lie, I always get my texts mixed up; let's say the son of a lie, that will do just as well!" All while twisting himself around to "kiss the hem" of the "blessed man" Zosima.

His sons develop four strategies in attempting to appease the incandescence of desire released in the family. Alyosha returns to the Christian sources of morality, sublimating homoeroticism through a commitment to education. He will be a father-brother among brothers. Ivan denies carnal desire, which will not fail to visit him in the form of the Devil, and intellectually admits of parricide while letting Smerdyakov execute it, paying for this split with madness. Smerdyakov is the only one who dares to kill this "rotten" father and joins him in the process, killing himself by hanging. While Mitya accepts his condemnation to twenty years of prison because it answers to his desire for parricide. However, this condemnation of Mitya condemns itself because it is mistaken about his actions and punishes an innocent man. It leaves the man alone with himself, free with the consciousness of his desire for life and for death. The son considers this freedom as a *new beginning* with Grusha, in Siberia perhaps, or by escaping with the help of his family, at best, to discover America and finally immerse himself in the dream of Russia—carnivalesque replies to the impossible Golden Age by Claude Lorrain.

No solution, in short, for the murder of the father when the Oedipus complex is not suppressed by *repression* but structured by the *split*? More Freudian than Freud: good old Dostoyevsky, whose *re-splitting* immediately wins the day over *repression*, while Freud himself, having discovered the Oedipus complex (letter to Fliess, 1897), doesn't name and examine "splitting" until his last works (1927–1938)?[6]

No solution, unless it's in the writing, since it neither judges nor calculates but is satisfied with a "kind of painting," an "artistic realism," and while conceding the "vulgar meaning" when it is "truthful," develops "another meaning, the inner meaning." Dostoyevsky specifies it himself in a letter to Pobedonostsev (to whom he entrusts the role of tutor to his children after his death), when this procurator of the Holy Synod regrets the lack of "resistance," "objections," and "explanations" in the Poem of the Grand Inquisitor.[7]

7.2 The Grand Inquisitor

The four brothers are not the only ones thinking about the murder of the father. A young girl, Liza Khokhlakova,[8] summarizes the universality of the problem for Alyosha: "'Listen, your brother is on trial now for killing his father, and they all love it that he killed his father.' 'They love it that he killed his father?' . . .'Everyone says it's terrible, but secretly they all love it terribly.'"

The poem of the Grand Inquisitor emerges from this anthropological love to the death. Its author, Ivan Karamazov, calls the internal structure, the central fantasy, a "poem," which the young theologian-philosopher fabricates to connect the passions that torment him with religious and cultural memory. A "poem" that his brother Mitya's sexuality puts into play; theories that will visit him in the guise of the Devil; passions he will find in Smerdyakov and that he will let this disastrous "kitchen boy" execute in a state of half-consciousness, before sinking into madness himself.

According to the drafts of the novel, Ivan is a radical atheist who combats the "terrible argument of the crucifixion" and wants to "completely annihilate the idea of God." The only one of the brothers capable of *thinking* the murder of the father explicates a fixed idea with this grotesque fiction, an idea already conceived by Kirillov, according to which the Man-god can kill God and kill himself to demonstrate this extreme freedom.[9] More penetrating, laboriously narrative, Ivan's satirical fantasy chooses Seville in the fifteenth and sixteenth centuries, when the Inquisition ruled. Having returned to earth, Christ does some miracles and is imprisoned by the Inquisition—a literary way of showing that Catholicism begins by arresting the Christly message and the man Jesus himself, even threatening him with death. Although the Grand Inquisitor decides to let him leave, he's basically driving him out of this world and can only observe the hurdles facing the God-man's dwindling message here on earth.

Ivan Karamazov's version of Torquemada essentially preaches that, in accepting to die on the cross, Christ entirely accepts his libertarian vision of the genius of humanity. But as a result of "overestimating" this path to liberty and making it accessible, his self-proclaimed successors have denatured the meaning of the three pillars of Christian faith: the *miracle*, the *mystery*, and the *authority*. The miracle was reduced to the obligation to provide

"bread" to the "flock," a deal for material satisfactions. The freedom of conscience, which replaced the mystery of communion, of
ritual veneration in common, has proven painful and unsatisfiable.
It undermined divine authority and all sovereignty. Made for the
elect, ignoring that men are "little children" and "mean," official
Christian doctrine pushed the "rebellious and the wild" to "eliminate each other." There remain only a few bits of advice from the
"great and dread spirit [that] could at least somehow organize the
feeble rebels."

Ivan's poem denounces the dangers of the Catholic heresy as the
Inquisitor himself develops it and omits mentioning that the Spanish Inquisition also combatted "Judaizing practices." Its misdirec-
tion toward "a kind of future servitude" gangrened even the "nascent
humanism of the society of nations," a sad remainder, the poet
believes, of an "exceptional Roman clergy" and its competitor, the
Masons. Could Ivan be one, Alyosha wonders, while his brother
reveals the end of his poem.

Before getting rid of his prisoner, the Grand Inquisitor comes
into the cell and admits he doesn't know who He is: "Is it you? You?
. . . Why, then, have you come to interfere with us?" And he naturally expects the inmate to answer. "But suddenly he approaches the
old man in silence and gently kisses him on his bloodless, ninety-
year-old lips." Thunderstruck, the Inquisitor "lets him out into the
dark squares of the city." "Go and do not come again . . . do not come
at all . . . never, never!"

The old man does not give up on his accusatory, unsolvable ideas;
and he declaims his poem while the burning kiss rankles. Indestructible complicity of enemy brothers, of *self-loves*, in the interminable
declinations of monotheism, from the love to the death of the
Father.[10]

Ivan is betting on the debris of Christianism, not without envis-
aging its possible resurgences, even intermittent renascences, when
he evokes the "dark squares of the city" where Christ will find shelter. "Without a woman to love," without the carnal world of the "sticky
little leaves, and the precious graves, and the blue sky" the sensitive

Alyosha dreams of. Just to recognize "the force of Karamazov baseness," but not so that "everything can be permitted," as Ivan did say,
borrowing Rakitin's phrase.

Horrified by Ivan, the author of the Grand Inquisitor, by "such
hell in your heart and in your head," Alyosha leaves, restored to his
Christly solitude troubled just a bit by a fleeting promise of complicity with Liza, the "little demon," and carried in fact by his love of the
"boys."

The story of the Karamazov brothers ends in the prison. The
novelist chooses the fourth route, that of the *desire* for parricide,
missed but expiated, which Mitya accepts as is, with Grushenka.
Tender derision begins again through the accepted punishment, singular carnival, and time opens for *both of them*, later or never. While
finishing his book, Dostoyevsky writes his most passionate love letters to his wife: "You are my queen . . . you are my only sovereign . . .
and this after twelve years, in the most down to earth sense of the
term . . . even though you have naturally change and aged . . . you
please me in this way incomparably more yet."

7.3. Shigalyov: "Desire—We Will Kill It"

The "solution of the social formula" constructed by the sinister
Shigalyov, with the unnatural size of his ears—"long, broad, and
thick"—is somewhat more tragic and realistic than the fabulations
of the Grand Inquisitor which it precedes. Presented in *Demons*
(1872), this totalitarian theory announces the political-theological
speculations of Ivan Karamazov and reads like a premonition of
"Big Brother" from George Orwell's *1984*, of Hitler's "final solution," and of Stalin's gulags.

The dreary theoretician of "our people," a secret cell of revolutionaries tossed back and forth between despair and destruction,
sweeps away "fools" of the past: "Plato, Rousseau, Fourier . . . all this
is fit perhaps for sparrows, but not for human society." Since the
cell is "finally going to act," Shigalyov wants to "stop any further

thinking about it" (while the Grand Inquisitor is still thinking!). "With the air of a dictator," he imposes "[his] own system of world organization" in a book with ten chapters that it is out of the question to read to the brothers, who either are laughing or silent, or to have them read it in its entirety, or to extract from it any sort of conclusion that would last ten evenings. All the more so since the system is not yet finished; but he presents "the original idea from which [he starts]." Shigalyov's solution is indeed "final," the author himself recognizes that "there can be no other": "Starting from unlimited freedom, I conclude with unlimited despotism." The conspirators, who see it as a hoax, sneer; then Pyotr Verkhovensky in person summarizes and radicalizes the essence of Shigalyovism. Not hesitating to cut his fingernails in the presence of "our people," the son of Stepan Trofimovich takes a stance as the ideologue of Shigalyovism, out of love for Stavrogin, his idol or, better, king. "He suggests, as a final solution of the question, the division of mankind into two unequal parts. One tenth is granted freedom of person and unlimited rights over the remaining nine tenths. These must lose their person and turn into something like a herd, and in unlimited obedience, through a series of regenerations, attain to primeval innocence, something like the primeval paradise—though, by the way, they will have to work."

Grabbing hold of his Shigalyov ("Shigalyov is a man of genius! ... but bolder than Fourier, but stronger than Fourier ... He's invented 'equality'!"), Pyotr Verkhovensky delivers himself of a terrifying encomium to equality with respect to which the (Vatican or Freemason?) casuistry of the Grand Inquisitor seems only a naïve humanist promise. Exalted and developed as it is by the extremist, Shigalyovism institutes an equality so absolute and total that "each member of society watch[es] the others and [is] obliged to inform. Each belongs to all, and all to each. They're all slaves and equal in their slavery. Slander and murder in extreme cases, but above all— equality." This program implies that "the level of education, science, and talents is lowered." "Cicero's tongue is cut off, Copernicus's eyes are put out, Shakespeare is stoned—this is Shigalyovism!"; "As soon as there's just a tiny bit of family or love, there's a desire for property.

We'll extinguish desire... Boredom is an aristocratic sensation; in Shigalyovism there will be no desires. Desire and suffering are for us; and for the slaves—Shigalyovism."

With the father and God scorned, the government of this totalitarian leveling nevertheless supports itself with a supreme chief, according to Pyotr Verkhovensky's fervor—not yet a *führer, Duce,* or "Father of the People," but the amusingly inevitable outgrowth of the papacy: "You know, I thought of handing the whole world over to the Pope... The Pope on top, us around him, and under us— Shigalyovism. It's only necessary that the Internationale agree to the Pope; but it will. And the old codger will instantly agree."

The Shigalyovist demons confront God *religiously.* Ivan Karamazov does so too, more explicitly, troubled by parricide in his sermon on the Grand Inquisitor, which presents the debacle of Christianism. For five centuries, according to these characters and the writer-journalist himself, Christianity has supposedly failed to make freedom possible, because it imposes the State (with its Roman model) on the Gospel (unfathomable singularity of the transcendence that Christ reveals to men). This reduction of *faith* to *the political* was to lead inevitably to egalitarianism and the rush for money. Unless, on the contrary, the Church manages to diffuse itself within the State and open the horizon of the utopian fraternity of men: restoration of the golden age and dream of the ideologue Dostoyevsky, which he cradles in the ending of *Crime and Punishment* (1866) with Sonya accompanying Raskolnikov to the prison and in *The Adolescent* (1875), Versilov's formulation of a Christly humanism that also traverses Ivan and Alyosha Karamazov in *The Brothers Karamazov* (1881).

However, Shigalyov's egalitarian "philanthropy" reveals its inconsistency even in Pyotr Verkhovensky's view, because "one or two generations of depravity are necessary now... that turns men into vile, cowardly, cruel, self-loving slime" and "an aristocrat, when he goes among democrats, is captivating!" "What is there in socialism: it destroyed the old forces, but didn't bring any new ones." Besides, he himself says "I'm a crook, not a socialist," it's better to say so.

7.4 Zosima: "Life Is Paradise, and
We Are All in Paradise"

However corrosive it may be, autoanalysis by writing is supported by another paternity, mortal and outmoded, but at the antipodes of the disembodied and feeble asceticism of Myshkin (*The Idiot*, 1868), and more lively than the seductive empathy of the Elder Tikhon with Stavrogin (*Demons*, 1872). The Elder Zosima, gambler, sinner, with a scandalous body, imposes it with his stinking cadaver.

Perhaps in echo to the Elder Ambroise whom the novelist met at the Optina monastery, and in unison with his own "poem" of faith that Dostoyevsky lives by writing, Zosima will be the "Russian hermit" who incarnates this desirable paternity.

In the beginning was the older brother of the monk, Markel, a weak tubercular adolescent who dies at seventeen. Associated with a political exile, a university philosopher who fills him with the "new ideas," the young man gets angry and insults "God's church" when his mother asks him to fast and to take communion. But it is he who leaves to his younger brother Zinovy (the future Elder Zosima) the two maxims resulting from his experience that will later inspire the hermit's teaching: "life is paradise, and we are all in paradise," and "each of us is guilty in everything before everyone." Before bequeathing to him only this: "go now, play, live for me!"

Having learned to read in the book of Job (like Dostoyevsky, who was also a younger brother), Zosima spreads vitality even into death, where it rots so it can be felt; and he recites the parable from John (12:24): "Except a corn of wheat fall into the ground and die, it abideth alone; but if it die, it bringeth forth much fruit."

The first fruit of this plenitude, with and beyond death, is a story of love (and sin?) whose intensity he feels at night beside a river. During his long walks along Russia's highways, which he did with his friend Anfim some forty years earlier, "we were joined by a comely young man." "Fresh messenger of eternal Russia combined with the mystery of God," this young peasant introduces him with a "burning" heart into the "sinless world of blades of grass and insects: ...

how good and wonderful is all that is God's! He sat deep in thought, quietly and sweetly . . . And he fell into an easy, sinless sleep beside me." The scene recalls the ecstasy of little Fyodor hidden in the bushes and fleeing to Marey for fear of the wolf.[11] Thus is spun the uninterrupted thread of fraternal love, in spite of the age difference, the erotic spirituality of "self-loves," which comes to its culmination in the passion of the monk for the novice Alyosha: "Alexei seemed to me to resemble him so much spiritually that many times I have actually taken him . . . for that youth, my brother."

Explicitly carnal encounters are also added to the "mysterious route" of the holy man. In the cadet corps, "I transformed into an almost wild, cruel, and absurd creature" when "we were all but proud of our drunkenness, debauchery, and bravado." The future monk even "formed an attachment to a young and wonderful girl, intelligent and worthy," who later marries a rich landowner, "a very amiable man," but undeniable jealousy reappears. Doubling once again opens its tortuous labyrinth. First the humiliated cadet Zinovy strikes his valet in the face with a "beastly cruelty," not without asking for his forgiveness; then, overexcited, he goes to a duel with his rival; then he refuses to shoot, because Markel having appeared to him in the meantime makes his brother understand "what a crime it is to kill a man"; finally, the witnesses to the duel as well as his comrades in the regiment accuse him of sullying the uniform by evading the encounter, and they require him to resign; but he has already done so to don the frock. "Here comes our monk!" the regiment spouts.

The 150 pages of the Zosima dossier, written by Alexei Fyodorovich Karamazov, interrupt and impede the saga of the Karamazovian parricide. To keep up the suspense, the saga has to advance by rebounds, and though it authorizes digressions, it doesn't tolerate one as ponderous as this one. Yet, since this hieromonk insists a great deal on transgression (necessarily that of paternal and divine laws), consubstantial to humans, his impure holiness can *also* be read as a variation on parricide, an integral part of the mystery of faith.

The result is a *metaphysical detective story* determined to settle its accounts with atheism as well as with abstract, disembodied faith. Probing the intricacies of masculine homoeroticism, the author raises the stakes at the same time. He surcharges the narrative (written by Alyosha) with the long story of the "mysterious visitor" (a double of the Devil that Ivan Karamazov receives) whom Zinovy-Zosima regularly welcomes and for whom he plays the part of a "shrink," before he became an elder, to liberate the intruder from remorse for his crime. This very special, unexpected "patient" apparently killed a married woman out of jealousy (return of the pathetic love trio), and with the help of the analysis-confession (like Raskolnikov in *Crime and Punishment*, 1866), he ends up denouncing himself. Not without making the improvised analyst himself appear suspect, since the opinion is that, by his complacency, he certainly caused the torments of his patient and even the madness that submerges him after his "confession." A capital detail among all: the unfortunate man, no doubt overcome by his murderous tendencies which the conversations have liberated, admits to the therapist that he has considered killing him as well! Alas, Zosima doesn't advance his analytical lucidity to the point of revealing his countertransference as a future hermit having heavily participated in all innocence in the awakening of the death drive as well as the somnolent desire of his visitor. If the latter did not kill him, it was because he could not break away from their pitiless *sameness*. Prey to the hatelove that carries him off, the man kisses his "shrink" with a kiss of death, in effect, admitting: "Know, however, that you have never been closer to death." And he—the visitor, murderous patient—dies a week later. Leaving the elder to take his own measure of death, which is to say of holiness.

A sober Zosima merely emphasizes that the whole city rose up against him after the burial of his visitor (his double?). People stopped inviting him, although at the same time a (perverse?) minority began to frequent him with much curiosity and joy: "for men love the fall of the righteous man and his disgrace. But I kept silent and soon quit the town altogether"—to devote himself to God. All that remains of the analysand with the mortiferous drives is a first name,

Mikhail (like Dostoyevsky's father and brother), to be mentioned in the monk's prayers.

What is a monk? Isolation and mystical solitude, liberation from the tyranny of objects ("They have succeeded in amassing more and more things, but have less and less joy"). Fervor with the "theophorous" people—it's from the Russian people that salvation will come, from their faith, their "humility," their "dignity," "even in spite of the rank sins," Zosima preaches. Communion of sinners "with the other worlds." "Do not be afraid of men's sin," "ask gladness from God ... Flee from such despondency." "[Hell?] The suffering of being no longer able to love." "Christ will not be angered by love." Moral exegesis, spiritual teaching, and holy maxims raise the picture of a mediation: the monk is the mystical *hyphen* between believers and God. And a dedication "without repose" to "love man also in his sin for this likeness of God's love is the height of love on earth."

The last conversation of the elder with his visitors, transcribed by Alexei, ends suddenly on an ellipsis ...

The elder's body remains a man's body, however saintly his experience may have been. He is neither sublimated nor entirely transcended in "spirit" (*doukh*). His remains stink (*zapakh*, "odor"). Dostoyevsky does not separate these two universes: *odor* and *spirit*. He even replaces the usual word for *odor* (*zapakh*) with one that more frequently means *spirit* (*doukh*) to signify that in Zosima's holiness the *body* and the *spirit* are inseparable: praying spirit and sublimated stink. Waste, putrefaction, anality, death itself are of the nature of spirituality. The stink that the narrative attributes to the cadaver of Zosima is the most irreverent account ever of the wild delicacy inherent in inner experience. At this precise point, the body along with the spirit and all identity, me and you, the same and the other, lose their beings, dissemination and concretion, nucleus and flare. Thanks to his extravagant sensuality, his maximum, available concentration, between quivering narratives and edifying precepts, Zosima's holiness is in external inclusion, in internal exclusion in the dogmas, as it should be among mystics, Catholic or Orthodox. The extreme freedom of the drives, filtered by the strict observance of the reinvested religious code, does not destroy but literally pulverizes the *identity laid bare*, that of the Ego, of sex, or of language.

"Of the vaporization and centralization of the Ego. Everything is there. Of a certain sensual pleasure in the society of extravagants," wrote Baudelaire (*My Heart Laid Bare*, 1897). A contemporary of Dostoyevsky, the French poet translated this experience for which "God is a living scandal" in perfumed terms: some are "fresh as children's flesh," "others, corrupt, rich, and triumphant" ("Correspondences," 1857); "flares" that "dig into the sky," the "infinite void," always.

Outrageously nauseating, the vaporization and centralization of Zosima-Dostoyevsky only spread emanations of the "carcass." Warnings of death in love, rape of the interdictions and limits, rotten sign that "neither I, nor you, nor any man is capable of understanding" (Father Paissy diagnoses), the emanations do not sing, they nauseate and interrogate. It's Alyosha who becomes "ecstatic" after having wept extensively for this carnal deflagration. But he's only a beginner, and his brothers Ivan and Mitya are otherwise immersed in the foul "truth." No triumph in the "odor of corruption," just "an opportune moment": the puff of abjection shakes up the essential beliefs of the youngest Karamazov, who after his transition through Grusha's beauty lets his exaltation drop "to the ground" and "the celestial vault . . . into his heart." There is no other way to "stay in the world" than to feel with all your heart how this *novel about the death of God* questions the "transports of the spirits and the senses." A great insolent question mark, in place of the greatest seriousness.

The sexuality that Dostoyevsky's writing calls *sensuality* is not "immediate and global," like that sought by "certain gentlemen of the good old days in their restless activity," says the author of *Demons* (1872), with irony. The "nervous, tormented, and divided nature of people in our time" is like Stavrogin's rage: "cold, calm, and, if one may put it so, *reasonable*, and therefore the most repulsive and terrible that can be." In such a way, in Dostoyevsky, drives and desires snake endlessly between thresholds and effractions: fleeting shocks, encounters and surprises, implausible rebounds.

7.5 The Serpent, a Mother Alone, and Shakespeare

The encounter between Stavrogin's mother Varvara Petrovna and the Cripple, whom her son has secretly married, breaks all the social conventions; it is actually unimaginable. The narrator describes the return from the church like an irruption prepared far in advance by strange noises: the racket made by the carriage at the entrance, the scathing speed of footsteps "with a strange quickness, almost running, a way in which Varvara Petrovna could not have entered." All at once the gaze is struck by an apparition: "suddenly [Varvara Petrovna] all but flew into the room, breathless and extremely excited." Lizaveta Nikolaevna, a young noblewoman who is supposed to be Nicolas's fiancée, is standing there, holding hands with Marya Timofeevna Lebyadkina.[12] A "dream of a scene," the narrator admits, only too happy with his find, and he gives himself a few dozen pages to rejoin reality itself, no less stupefying and implausible. Avalanche of entrances, irruptions, and penetrations.

Let's go back and enter the church with him, while the Cripple Marya Timofeevna, during the sermon, comes to the cathedral square, passes through mockeries and astonishment, falls to the ground, cries and laughs. Varvara Petrovna crosses the threshold of the cathedral, doesn't notice anyone outside, then stops a moment in front of this "strange being" kneeling in front of her. There under the entrance begins the subtle erotic ballet between the mother and the secret spouse: "You are unfortunate," "I've come just to kiss your hand," "You're shivering." The noble lady "with her own hands wrapped [her shawl] around the bare neck of the still kneeling petitioner." She is called Lebyadkina, Liza takes part, Varvara Petrovna takes them both "home." The unfortunate woman runs joyfully to the doors of the carriage. And Varvara Petrovna, terrorized, notices then that the young woman limps.

Inside or outside? Where are we? What has she guessed? Attraction-aspiration, limits have been surpassed, because the boundaries of social classes and conventions have been transgressed, they are melting away before their very eyes. Overcome with this "magnetic sleep," we suddenly return to the Stavrogins' manor. Did we leave it? After the rapid footsteps, we saw no bodies go through the door, and now she suddenly collapses, preceded by the ringing of a little bell: "Varvara Petrovna rang the bell and threw herself into an armchair by the window." The parlor is a prolongation of the cathedral square, of the inner core to the outside.

Improbable guests who could never have met: Lebyadkin the brother, poet and drunkard, and Prascovia Touchina, the general's wife and mother of Liza, among others. The mistress of the house tells them about an absurd anonymous letter which says that Nicolas, her son, is going crazy and that she herself will be afraid of a cripple... Lebyadkin insinuates an incomprehensible story about money, rather sordid... Coup de théâtre, the completely unexpected arrival of Nicolai Vsevolodovich himself is announced, preceded by the no less astonishing arrival of Pyotr Verkhovensky. He's a loopy nut, endowed moreover with an extremely long pointed tongue, whose "constantly and involuntarily wriggling tip" is disgusting and from which a "string of ever ready words" rolls out and puts his father into an aggravated state of stupor. The major surprise, finally: from stupefactions to reciprocal adjustments, no one realizes that Nicolai Vsevolodovich is already in the room! Surely he had never left it, he was already there from the start, ultimate and unique pole anchoring maternal desire as well as the secret society that Stavrogin ceaselessly galvanizes. He is there without being there, inside and outside, he too, a revolutionary who "resembled a mask," but perhaps with a new thought in his eyes. "Quantities of things" are going to happen in this "concentration" of "totally wild," undecidable desires.

Varvara Petrovna is on the crest, in a fashion: totally abandoned to the "prism of her life," at one with "her" question, she finally formulates it for her son like a threatening challenge: "Is it true that this unfortunate lame woman—there she is, over there, look at her!—is it true that she is ... your lawful wife?"

There were laws, limits, thresholds. The semantic field preceding this voicing of opinions, the situation itself, and the shuddering of the voices suggest that all this is already outmoded, traversed, transgressed. It remains to say it, truly. But the mother's speech stammers.

And Nicolas takes a dodge, "gravely," he acts a stranger and refuses all sorts of familiarity with the Cripple.

The Russian word *porog*, "threshold," also designates the whirlpool of water when contrary but equal forces combat, cancel each other out, and remain immobilized, while also generating the start of a new whirlpool. Nicolas's face resembling a mask evokes none of the plasticity of an actor with multiple facets, only a mask on the *void*—the whirlpool frozen into a threshold, explosive scar. Liza, who loves him and knows how to pierce the pasteboard of the domino mask, thinks she has just touched "a sort of serpent."

Maternal penetration is of a different magnitude. The serpent leaves the stage with the Cripple, with the help of Pyotr's complacent chatting that goes on and on about the "scandal," the "whim" or the "sarcasm" Nicolas imposes on them, and Varvara Petrovna regains control of her parlor to announce her intention to "adopt" this "unfortunate organism" that is the Limper. But the lady does not stop at this somewhat wacky demonstration of Christian charity. In a process that is as carnivalesque, but that participates in the "realism in the high sense" that Dostoyevsky claims for himself, "Mama" becomes a Shakespearean. She is no longer satisfied with the divagations of her friend Stepan Trofimovich, who saw in Nicolas a Henry IV dragged along by his Falstaff (Lebyadkin, today) into frenetic acts of wantonness and duels. "Stupid, stupid": she merely swept them away, while still seeking particular protections for her son, a degraded officer. Now she climbs alone to the heights of the tragic sublime, but it's to evoke Hamlet without naming him. Her "singsong voice" indulges in a lightning *proniknovenie* ("penetration, effraction, shock"): "And if Nicolas had always had at his side . . . a gentle Horatio, great in his humility . . . But Nicolas never had a Horatio, or an Ophelia. He had only his mother, but what can a mother do alone and in such circumstances?" The Shakespearean Mama is the second coup de théâtre in this chapter (book I, chapter 5) of *Demons* (1872), with a promising title: "The Wise Serpent."

An implicit intertext thus opens between *Hamlet* and *Demons*, digging into the abysses and accumulating the thresholds of the demonic according to Dostoyevsky, which spins when "everything is permitted."

Contrary to Sophocles's *Oedipus the King*, read by Freud, Hamlet, prince of Denmark, does not kill his father. Not only is King Hamlet (a significant homonym) already dead, killed by his own brother Claudius, the usurper of the throne and new incestuous spouse of Hamlet's mother, greedy Gertrude; it's also the paternal Specter himself (though the prince doesn't really believe in him) who gives him the idea for paternal vengeance, seconded by his friends Marcellus and Horatio. Hamlet's spectral "belief" in this paternal "thing" is a while coming, and procrastination becomes the principal trait of his dubitative character.

Love or murder, Hamlet recoils in the face of the reality of action. He plays the fool and acts the artist *by staging* the murder of his father, in which the guilty Claudius recognizes himself. But finding the latter in prayer, the son renounces. He will kill this father substitute only after having dismantled the machination contrived by Claudius to have him killed in a duel with Laertes (Ophelia's brother), whom Hamlet accidentally kills. Mortally wounded himself, the prince makes his mother drink the poison destined for him, then kills the king and dies.

Freudians assume he has a repressed desire for parricide all the same, which, precisely because it is repressed, leads Hamlet to hold back and avoid it; desire transforms into revenge, and from accident to accident kills off the entire lineage. But Freud did not write a specific study of Hamlet-and-Oedipus; he leaves the task of elucidating the relation between the two tragic figures to "other adepts of psychoanalysis" (*Summary of Psychoanalysis*, 1938). Hamlet kills only one secondary character of his own free will, the chancellor Polonius, a father, actually, but of the fragile Ophelia ("fragility, your name is woman"), and this murder of a father can be considered as a variant of "oedipal" murder: revenge displaced against a father who is opposed to the passion of the young prince for his daughter.

Mother-son incest, an unbearable identitarian threat, remains the unavowable focus of desire and appears in the pantomime that Hamlet directs representing "the Queen embracing him, and he her." The repressed parricide doesn't avoid the primal scene, then, but plugs the gaps in it: the "sexual question" really is the motor of the assassination. Although it doesn't seem to invade Hamlet's love for his young dulcinea, to whom he is content to address overacted tirades, along with the scrutinizing looks of a painter and aggravated gestures of rejection.

Ophelia's drowning tears from Hamlet his immortal, nostalgic meditation, "To be or not to be, that is the question." Without complaining or accusing. Neither guilt nor revolt, Hamlet denounces the political malady ("Something is rotten in the state of Denmark," I, 5) only to call for reflection on the state of permanent war, which makes the killing of humans banal, even mortality itself ("Why the man dies," IV, 4). Revealers of ineluctable Evil, these preoccupations torment the Elizabethan age. "Undeniable existence of evil," Freud insists, probing the discontents of civilization.

Was the "death of God" already ongoing, as always, though more inescapable with the Renaissance of technology, the surge of money and markets, the blossoming of the arts and spectacles that Shakespeare stages and questions? Well before Nietzsche deepened our consciousness of the nothingness at the back of being, like evil at the back of good, and before the pre-Bolshevik nihilists took action— Hamlet opened the still ongoing series of orphan sons lacking fathers, of sons without fathers.

Varvara Petrovna Stavrogina recognized herself in this tragedy, with the desperate, grandiose flair of mothers who try to inscribe their sons in it. She already knows, during this reception at her "home," that Nicolas is lost. But she is wrong to attribute all the responsibility for the coming disaster only to the fact of having been a "mother alone" overcome by "circumstances," and not to accept that her *Nicolas* could not have known either Ophelia or Horatio. Stavrogin *is* and *isn't* Hamlet, for Dostoyevsky reveals an "undeniable existence of evil" more radical in his holy Russia in the process of acceding to the industrial age than that revealed in Shakespeare's sixteenth-century play.

Without the constriction of paternity which by legislating defers the life and death drives, the homonymous son Hamlet is subject to his own melancholic violence-impotence. His revenge is at bottom a sacrifice: in killing the usurping uncle—the man who possesses the mother and embodies a false sovereignty, this substitute for Hamlet's father whom Hamlet the son echoes—he runs the risk or the chance of being executed too. He accepts it after Ophelia's death, kissing a skull. Could the fate of a woman (of his own femininity-fragility) reduced to madness and to drowning, after having been deprived of her desires by the family conspiracy and the conspiracy of the males, have forced the prince of Denmark to "feminine castration" (as Lacan interprets it)? Beyond his own? To leave free rein, even more deeply, to the work of unlinking within oneself, to madness performed for real. The madness of Ophelia: "She hears / There's tricks i' the world" (IV, 5), like Hamlet himself feeling there's "something rotten."

Shakespeare's hero yields to the omnipotence of the desire for death that corrupts beings. But he is Shakespearean only when he insists on a sole singular and sharable sovereignty: the sovereignty of the *desire to play*. In putting into play the meaning of others, the words having become sublime acts let it be understood that in playing with madness, Hamlet is playing his cohabitation with death. With the lightness of one who accepts *not to be*, only thus to be able to *say* and *transmit* his manner of living with the work of death in oneself and outside oneself: "I am dead; / Thou livest . . . what a wounded name, / Things standing thus unknown" (V, 2).

A foreign king, Fortinbras, will take over the kingdom of Hamlet the father, but the warriors' spectacles will continue, Prince Hamlet's cadaver will be exhibited on a podium, and Horatio as his testamentary heir takes on the task of telling his story, the dying man insists on it: "So tell him, with th'occurrents, more and less / Which have solicited. The rest is silence." In all "humility," the faithful friend turns his back to incest, to hatelove, and to death, he has only to . . . organize the spectacle: "Bear Hamlet, like a soldier, to the stage" (V, 2).

Another play is being prepared within the play. There will be no end to the staging. His performances immortalize the playwright soldier, William Shakespeare . . . who names his own son Hamnet.

Mama Stavrogina, who does her Shakespeare on departing the Orthodox mass, is not really a *Précieuse ridicule*, even if Moliere's breath does penetrate Dostoyevsky's voice as he struggles with his doubles. After the debasement of the misalliance and the downfall of *Nicolas* with the Cripple, Varvara Petrovna needed Hamlet's higher stature to return "home" and realize that this matrimonial tempest comes from the absence of the father, no more nor less. Nicolai Vsevolodovich was raised by his tutor, the infantile Stepan Trofimovich Verkhovensky, who not only didn't take care of his own son Pyotr, but also played the child with his little student, two devastated children hugging in tears, and worse: "the friends wept, throwing themselves into their mutual embrace at night," provoking in the very depths of the boy "the first, still uncertain sensation . . . which the chosen soul . . . will never exchange for any cheap satisfaction." Mama only sees a quasi-father, "devoured all his life" by "the sad and 'sudden demon of irony.'" She imagines nothing further.

Enough so that through Shakespeare Dostoyevsky can moor his "Russian Hamlet" to the universal memory. So as to better invest this new degree of Western consciousness, nihilism, where the tragic no longer questions (*To be or not to be, that is the question*) but feels "the being as the abysmal basis of nothingness" (Heidegger, *Inaugural Lecture*, 1929).[13]

Raised on emptiness, Nicolas can only explode or extinguish passion. Of the man there remains only the unsustainable mask, "faux self" or "as-if personality," under which there suffers an unbridled impotence, violated since childhood, suppressing the slaps, and ready to rape. He doesn't know how to speak it, write it, play it, play it out. Even if his mother is right to prefer the faithful Horatio to the agitated Pyotr Verkhovensky, what Nikolai Stavrogin is really missing is the sense of pantomime, the art of composing the *being* with the *nothingness*, even if one must die from it. Since dying is inevitable—but knowing that "There are more things in heaven and earth, Horatio, /

Than are dreamt of in your philosophy," as the very theatrical Hamlet meditated. To be sure, the son of his mother dared to write a confession admitting his rape of Matryosha. But Tikhon, "cursed psychologist," did not like his style, and the confessor himself only drew more shame from it, no verbal intoxication. He succumbs, voiceless: "Blame no one; it was I." Hanged in the attic, in Mama's home.

Dostoyevsky's dialogism invites us to carry over and amplify Varvara Petrovna's inroads into the underground of the Danish prince. To imagine, for example, a Hamlet who knows there is no father except dead and also knows, before his time, that God is dead, as the faithful realize, crying over the *kenosis* of the God-man who died on Good Friday, more in Orthodoxy than elsewhere, before resuscitating. Could he have become a Stavrogin—handsome, depraved, brilliant, murderous, beyond limits, abusing—had he not had Ophelia and Horatio and if he had not killed—by mistake, to be sure, but without regrets— his almost-step-father-uncle Claudius and his mother Gertrude? Certainly not. Giving in to death with the enthusiasm of a gambler, Hamlet believes that jouissance is possible. He displaced the satisfaction of the drives from the *scene of power*, where desires to the death are depleted, to the *scene of language*, where he secured for himself the sovereignty of sublimation. A certain glory, but beyond the specter of the father, and without killing the "paternal function." The imaginary legitimacy of Hamlet, evasive and risky, still fascinates.

In *Hamlet*, the undeniable evil, the *serpent*, is Claudius the usurper, the false father envious of his brother and his brother's son: "The serpent that did sting thy father's life / Now wears his crown" (I, 5). Quite different from this imposter, Nicolai Stavrogin is only a "wise serpent." A factitious countenance pasted onto his toxic wickedness, the violator of Matryosha is convinced God doesn't exist. Without necessarily believing in the Devil, the way Ivan can let himself be tempted to in *The Brothers Karamazov* (1881), Stavrogin is "devoured" by his drives, which come together and accumulate, leaving under the mask of indifference only the ravages of the unlinking. The man emptied of emotion is the impotent eye of the demonic cyclone.

From threshold to threshold, when everything is permitted, nihilists can't cope, they are possessed by nothingness.

Varvara Petrovna doesn't want to know that the son's love to the death for the father is a jouissance whose vicissitudes will provide the deep rhythm of innovations in the technical age. She is intrigued by the melancholy joyfulness of the Hamlet spectacle, struck down by Stavrogin's sordid pedophilia; the "sexuality of insects" is advancing, it animates the "new men," the Karamazovians, who have all the time in the world, after madness and the prison.

A spectator in the convulsing crowd no less exalted by the trial of the parricidal brothers, Dostoyevsky returns to the comparison in a mocking tone: "They have their Hamlets, but so far we have only Karamazovs."

7.6 The Madonna, Sodom, and the "Ode to Joy"

The Karamazovs are "jouisseurs." The word *naslajdienie* (jouissance) is scattered throughout Dostoyevsky's writing, but Alyosha folds his ecstasies into pedagogical projects, and only Dmitri's purifying torture gives it its full voice without bringing death. Jouissance is a mystical operation paid for by a "pound of flesh" (Lacan); it is closest to us and escapes us the most; it is heard in French in the verbal expression "J'ouie" ("I hear," approximately), and in all languages when a body takes pleasure from another to no avail.

In the ruins of a gazebo at the back of a garden, after going through courtyards "almost without a path"—crossing fences, hedges, and borders of all sorts—Alexei and Mitya have one of those encounters which the writer indulges in to structure his implausible plots, "overflowing the limits" like the writer himself. An encounter as impossible as it is inevitable, absurd and essential. On the table, a bottle of cognac, the favorite pick-me-up of their father Fyodor, the drunken buffoon. The same back courtyards, lanes, and bridges in which Lizaveta the stinking one wandered and slept, whom the insatiably lubricious papa had probably raped, and who had climbed over the fence of their garden to give birth to their half-brother Smerdyakov. This dreamlike décor muddies the waters, and time opens like a funnel when Dmitri relates the villainous pleasures of the father who transmitted to them the imperious Karamazovian sensuality.

For Mitya with the ardent heart is the son who resembles him the most. Ivan protects himself from him as a philosopher accusing God in his poem on the Grand Inquisitor, while also receiving the visit of the Devil and ending up sinking into madness; Alyosha becomes an educator and seeks to pacify boys' passions by remitting his to Heaven or to a later time; Smerdyakov gets rid of them by killing the pleasure-seeking father and killing himself in the process—ultimate fusion with the impossible. Only Mitya follows a transgressive labyrinth in his father's footsteps. "I loved depravity, I also loved the shame of depravity. I loved cruelty: am I not a bedbug, an evil insect? In short—a Karamazov!"

To take pleasure in everything: the pervert's mirage deludes him with this definitively unsatisfying, unsatisfied totality. A Karamazov succeeds where a Stavrogin fails? The eldest son of the horrid clown casually admits the rape of a little girl of his acquaintance, plus other anonymous ones, "just Paul de Kock's little flowers . . . album of memories." And better than his desire to the death (under a comical appearance) for Alyosha himself ("I'll throw myself on his neck! . . . I'll give him a scare . . . 'Your money!'"), it's in fanning the flame of the rivalry between two women, Grushenka and Katerina Ivanovna, that Dmitri's lust is at a maximum. A challenge or a ruse? More than that, and frankly, "she [Katerina Ivanovna] really and truly fell in love with Grushenka—that is, not with Grushenka but with her own dream, her own delusion—because it was *her* dream, *her* delusion!" Absorbed in the dream-delirium of the other, tributary of the other's phantasm. Not just any other: Katerina and Grushenka, two women alone together who supposedly take pleasure through him but without him—if one can believe Alyosha's narrative (or delirium) when he explains the details to a "tetanized" Dmitri. Gratified by such a power, perhaps, but losing mastery and identity, Mitya poses as the fortunate pivot of feminine jouissance, projecting himself into the one as well as the other. Definitive "object of exchange" between two "self-loves," happy about the humiliation of Katerina (the girl who wants to save his father) when Grushenka (the kept woman) removes his handcuffs.[14] Exalted by the impudence of Grushenka, the daughter of hell, the queen of all sorceresses, Mitya the sensual son of his father is simultaneously fulfilled and repulsed, neither subject nor object: abject ("as though the dishonor was lying and being kept precisely there on his chest") and insatiable, jubilant that another "horrible dishonor is being prepared": "but I will not stop." "Insect," like Kafka's Samsa, who judges himself "less than nothing," but a "sensual insect," the Karamazov son feasts on the jouissance of the two lovers who inhale his secret masochism. Implacable Dostoyevsky never tires of dissecting the amorous trio, this time between two women and a man—which he had already sketched between Myshkin, Aglaya, and Nastasya Filippovna (*The Idiot*, 1868)—nor of probing masculine jouissance down to the depths of the maternal ascendency that accompanies the phantasm of a mother who is also doubled: daughter of the father (Katerina) and sorceress indulging her devouring drives (Grushenka).

There is nothing cheerful about this male exuberance. The bad-smelling streets recall the father's stinking Liza, "death and darkness." The sense of horror, keeping permanent watch for the narrator but also for the Karamazovs, judges this sexuality as "criminal." As the object desired by two rival women, Mitya gains a narcissistic inflation that reassures both his moves for domination and his sacrificial thrusts. From transgression to transgression, this destiny was already entirely spelled out, from the start of the novel, in the strange first encounter at the monastery, when the blow of the fist from the beloved son makes the father's blood flow. The idea of parricide matures, is prepared, and fails, in parallel with the man's desires as they drive him, heat up, and focus on the women. To the point of distracting him (in the strong sense of the term) from his rivalry with the patriarch's jouissance. Fyodor is no longer a target of desire, he is nothing but a means (he has the money!). The *obstacle-father* to be confronted becomes a *passage* to be traversed while putting into play one's own monstrosity in headlong fashion, a "pound of flesh."

Henceforth, wrongly condemned for a murder he didn't commit, Dmitri is capable of "enhancing" even the prison sentence: knowing he is not guilty in the face of the law (since the judgment of men is fallible and unjust), the unconscious guilt of wanting to take pleasure like the father in the father's place also attenuates. And the legal error turns into an alleviation of the moral conscience, a certain liberty. How comical!

Living one's desires for parricide like an exhausting fantasy without actually committing it nevertheless leaves open the unsolvable question: "but who killed my father, gentlemen, who killed him? Who could have killed him *if not I*?" cries the condemned man at the end of the trial. For all that, Mitya is not a reconciled man. This "sufferer for nobility," this "humiliated soul and not guilty of anything" continues his search for dignity (*dostoínstvo*) through the "dirty things." *Dostoínstvo*, indeed: honor and gravity, like *Dostoyevsky*. A modern Diogenes, he thanks the Lord for having revealed to him that he is a "monster of a sinner," while not preventing him from leaving his father alive. "I did not kill him ... But I meant to kill him."

A jouissance-like twist from the biblical and evangelical man, the weepy exaltation of the character is too affected to be convincing. Mitya is a muddle of commiseration approaching ridiculous sarcasm, a mixture of Christly moralism and carnivalesque excess. Dostoyevsky never forgets to overload all these spokespersons with a tragicomical tonality.

I hear him, but I prefer to keep Mitya in the gazebo, squeezed into his contradictions, having no issue in sight, not even prison, and delivering to Alyosha a conviction whose prophetic intensity reaches down to us.

This survivor of nihilism, this sinner before God, posed only enigmas, and like a celibate of art, without an answer, he retains only the most mysterious, the enigma of *beauty*: "I can't bear it that some man ... should start from the ideal of the Madonna and end with the ideal of Sodom."

Sodom: depravity, anality, passivity, femininity, insatiable homo-eroticism? Or the Hebrew Sodom, the archetype of universal evil, focus of immorality and vice, insatiable killing desire? "No, man is broad, even too broad, I would narrow him down . . . What's shame for the mind is beauty all over for the heart . . . Believe me, for the vast majority of people, [Sodom is] just where beauty lies."

So it's the Karamazovian beauty, "terrifying thing," secret bat-tlefield between the Devil and the good Lord. But Dmitri is not sat-isfied with his narrations, his stammered confessions. For "man to rise from his abasement," though "fully in his shame," he ends up relying on the European literary memory. So, "in an exalted voice," he recites Schiller's "Ode to Joy"!

To each his poem. Ivan, the son of his father and the shrieker, composes his Grand Inquisitor. Alyosha, the youngest, stops dis-coursing like a pedagogue and becomes a walking educator for the "boys." Mitya, the oldest brother, son of the same buffoon and the independent aristocratic woman who used to beat him, a feminist before her time, burns for an odd sort of romantic humanism. He declaims for Alexis some verses celebrating the orgy of deism with mother earth: "The brimming cup, love's loyalty / Joy gives to us; beneath the sod, / To insects—sensuality; / In heaven the cherub looks on God!"

Much more irreverential, however, than the German idealist he cites—his mentor, it happens—Dmitri rushes into debauchery, "head down and heels up," and finds beauty in this "humiliating position." Beyond sarcasm, is it the demoniacal he is mocking, while trying to "kiss the hem of that garment in which my God is clothed" and to achieve a new stage of sensuality? This absurd condemned man no longer complains about "not knowing how to say it with words," and he doesn't "preach" anymore either. Having found the formula for *beauty*, he puts it into action and sketches a future with Grusha as his wife: together, they will traverse prison and America.

A version of Schiller's ode inspires the last movement of Beethoven's Ninth Symphony. This theme, without the words, has become the anthem of the European Union. Today, romanticism and sarcasm maintain globalized marketing, and the Karamazovian jouissance is being diluted or radicalized in the "everything is permitted" of the Web. The ideal of the Madonna is posted entirely without shame beside the ideal of Sodom. In appearance. It is not certain if men and women are "broad" enough (as Mitya wanted) to grasp its "terrifying beauty."

When the repercussions of this battlefield escape us, let us reread Dostoyevsky. Proliferating dialogues that are not a means, but THE goal of the writing. The only remaining possible goal?

PART II

A CARNIVALESQUE THEOLOGIAN

I am not considering a substitute for religion; that need should be sublimated.

—Freud, Letter to Jung, February 19, 1910

8

THE RUSSIAN VIRUS

I took off again through the air, having isolated in my mind like a virus
under the microscope.

—J. Brodsky, *Flight from Byzantium*

8.1 Duties of Memory

Dostoyevsky would not be Dostoyevsky if he were not Russian: poet
of the Orthodox peoples, of the "Russian Christ," of the "Russian
idea," all "infinitely above the West" by their "vocation" to bring about
the "great renewal that is being prepared for the entire universe."[1]

I am not Russian, and I admit that I have not read the thirty-
three volumes of Dostoyevsky's writing in the magnificent edition
by the Soviet Academy of Sciences. As Russian language and literature have accompanied me since my Bulgarian childhood, I am
incapable of calculating the exact extent of the bearing supporting
what is called my personality—which has always been, and still is, in
movement.

My father, more fluent in Slavonic than Russian (because of his
experience as a seminarist and student of theology), was enamored
of the Russian novelists who maintained the Orthodox flame of the
"true God." Although he had abandoned the idea of transmitting

the faith to his daughters, he absolutely insisted (and it hit home) that "failing immersion in the Immortal, we should learn the Unperishable": the Russian language. My sister, perfecting her violinist skills at the Moscow Conservatory, became a perfect Russophone. Bulgarians dedicated a sincere and obligatory cult to the Russian big brother, who had freed us from the Turkish yoke. In Sofia, a devotional fear and trembling seized anyone crossing the imposing square of the tsar liberator Alexander II, conqueror of the Ottoman army. For five centuries, the Sublime Porte had reduced us to the status of *ra'ya*, a herd of infidels subjected to the Muslim tax. Indebted to the blood lost by thousands of Russian soldiers, we were supposed to attain autonomy, and the national narrative was reborn in this movement with the restoration of the medieval Bulgarian State whose borders abutted Charlemagne's empire, though shrunk by the Treaty of Berlin of 1878 (oh well!). The second liberation of the country came in 1944: the Red Army, having driven out the Nazis our government had compacted with, initiated pro-Russian and pro-Soviet communism. This new equality for all gave rise to an enthusiasm as blatant as it was mitigated, though a few shining moments of national pride persist in my childhood memories. Mockeries behind the backs of Stalin's officers (sandals with socks to midcalf) and their spouses in evening dress in the middle of the day. Plus the unsinkable duty to remember that the Russian alphabet is nothing but the Bulgarian alphabet invented in the ninth century by the saintly Byzantine brothers Cyril and Methodius. Granted; but because the Slavic language was their native tongue, they were and still are Bulgarian for us. The Russians stole this genial invention from us at least a century later. The proof, if it were needed, whether or not *batiushka* ("papa," "little brother," "brother," or "dear parent"), *we* were civilization!

All the same, for adolescents seeking objects of unconditional admiration, of which I was one, there was no literature on earth other than the great Soviet and (in passing, after all) *Russian* literature. More and more Russian, with the softening of Stalinism and the "thaw." Every self-respecting person knew about Pushkin, Gogol, Chekhov. Not to forget, of course, Gorky, Sholokhov, or even

Fadeev and other stars of Soviet socialist realism one had to have read, and whose names I've forgotten. I reserved my fervor for the theater. So many sighs and tears at *The Seagull* and *The Three Sisters*, for example, to be read in the original. And at famous recitals of *poems*, the versification supposedly consubstantial to the Slavic soul had become the prayer of *Homo sovieticus* and his satellites, translated into Bulgarian for communion. But true fans sniffed out their roots in the original Russian.

My mother was a gentle presence at these literary masses, and at first I attributed her reserve and mutism to the innate scientific mind of this former biology student. She had abandoned the idea of becoming a scholar to devote herself to her husband and her two daughters. In fact, she helped me decipher and solve the complicated exercises that were to prepare me for the Math Olympiads, and I have her to thank that I had some success in this ritual of communist education—to the extent that I coddled the dream of reaching astrophysics heaven in a closed Soviet sanctuary in Siberia to which only children of the nomenklatura had access. More down to earth than her contemplative daughter, this perfect wife of her Christian-focused spouse had slipped me a few Darwinian reflections from biology as learned at university, which made sense of the materialism taught against religious obscurantism as early as elementary school. But which had the inestimable advantage of watering down my father's flights of fancy for both religion and literature, indistinctly. My father who grew red with anger . . . against me, the rebel, never against her, a clandestine feminist, clever and devious, who let me enter the fray. An incredible offering to paternal passion.

I was twelve when the generalissimo Little Father of the People, Josef Vissarionovich Jughashvili Stalin, died in 1953. I was to stand watch before the plaster bust of the deceased mounted on a column draped in black crepe, along with other "top schoolgirls," all pioneers. White shirt, black pants or skirt, red tie knotted around the neck. Was the rifle on our shoulders charged? "No one is irreplaceable" (except him!), Jughashvili had declared during the Great Terror. This rejection of the idea that human life is sacred because unique turned the funeral ceremonial devoted to the Superman into a disturbing simulacrum: did it not in some way foresee other terrifying, en masse disappearances? The icy celebrations of this passing weigh heavily on my mind now, when I envision myself as an adolescent with my back against the demise of the Russian Titan, of titanic Russia. But at the instant I was plunked in front of the death of the Other, I wasn't thinking of anything. I was laughing hysterically. Irresistible relief of my thunderstruck horror and convulsive excitation. My terrorized teachers glared at me, the police officer in service, not daring to break the silence, shook a menacing finger, nothing could be done, blasphemy had desecrated the political communion. One of the organizers took it upon herself to grab me, the next "top student" was hastily brought to replace me, and my parents summoned to take me home for rectification.

We didn't know what was being planned in secret, and I have no recollection of what happened next. Other than the fact that, shortly after this sinister incident, each student was required to inscribe for all time her sorrow, love, and glory for the lost leader by writing a poem. (I remind you that poems were our prayers.) Dry-eyed and hard-hearted, I couldn't think of a single word. Was I also going to fail this pensum after my insolent laugh? It was my father who tackled this job. He composed in my name the one and only poem of his life, which won me I don't remember what prize created for the occasion!

The burlesque cynicism of this episode came to mind only very recently because of the film by Armando Iannucci, *The Death of Stalin* (2017). For those who are still interested, this film reveals, in spite of the viral war at our heels, the frantic struggles of the bodyguards to seize the phantom and his powers. Was this already the beginning of the end of communism? We had to wait for its "thaw," with Khrushchev banging his shoe on the rostrum at the United Nations, the Cold War, the Berlin Wall, and the Cuban Missile Crisis. Stalinism was dissolving without disappearing, but the "thaw," by definition uncertain, loosened the totalitarian vise while perpetuating and perfecting its vices, the roots of which Solzhenitsyn denounced: lying. More pernicious than the suppression of freedom, lying impregnates and perverts the entire social compact: conspiring, denouncing, defaming to the point of abolishing the very existence of a person. Those ten years of Destalinization (1956–1966) definitively detached me from any devotion, belonging, or cult, and, with no hope of sublimating the collapse that threatened me because of the inaccessible scientific ascetic at Dubno, the city of the emerging Soviet nuclear research (this illusion had cradled me during high school), literature became my freshwater.

The noose of Stalinism seemed to loosen. Alongside the great, indomitable names—Boris Pasternak, Mikhail Bulgakov, Ilya Ehrenburg, Anna Akhmatova, Maria Tsvetaeva—there arose authors till then clandestine, rebellious, and dissident, now accessible. They were the *refuseniks* and their *samizdats*, "social parasites" who had experienced prison and camps. They said, in substance, that *we can say things differently*, otherwise, justly, truthfully, it's always been done, they are doing it again, it's done here and now, let's dare, let's speak of it ... And we were seized with the desire to rediscover we were *Russian*![2]

8.2 A Disruptive Language

Glaciation-deglaciation, then *perestroika*, Brezhnev, Gorbachev, Yeltsin ... In counterpoint, poetry and music allowed truth to filter through.

The undisciplined Yevgeny Yevtushenko caused a scandal in hailing Vladimir Dudintsev's *Not by Bread Alone* (1956); but he became the youngest member of the Union of Soviet Writers, while also shaking up its system. "Hebrew is me ... it seems to me I am Dreyfus," he claimed in his *Babi Yar* (1961), which denounced the Nazi atrocities that exterminated the Jewish population of Kyiv, just as he denounced Soviet atrocities. The text inspired the thirteenth symphony by the "contestatory" Shostakovich, who succeeded in not getting arrested although he was judged "formalist" and "enemy of the people." In 1964 the composer wrote a rebellious cantata, Op. 119, on Yevtushenko's poem "The Execution of Stepan Razin." Razin was a Cossack chief and legendary hero, leader of a peasant rebellion against the feudal system. The abject Pyotr Verkhovensky in *Demons*

(1872) cultivated his memory while attributing his role to Stavrogin. Readings and recitals by Bella Akhmadulina, Yevtushenko's wife, attracted thousands of girls to the Luzhniki Stadium. The word was being liberated. We were all bluffed by the imposing Khrushchev's attack on the uncontrollable Andrei Voznesensky. But I had a weakness for Joseph Brodsky.

Indifferent and demanding, because he was discontented with himself, Brodsky was stunned by the vulgarity of the anti-Semitism that pursued him, and he fought tooth and nail in his Byzantine Russia. I can picture him hastily trying to hide behind a column in Saint Mark's square in Venice to shake off the KGB agents who had infiltrated the self-proclaimed "dissident milieu" of late Gorbachevism. He received the Nobel Prize for literature in 1975. "What is a metaphor?" the honorable jury of the Nobel committee had wanted to know. And I am still wondering which of us was more abstruse in reply. Was it the enigmatic examples by Brodsky, "real rebuses," like his poems, according to Solzhenitsyn, who didn't like them, distilled with the air of boredom he affected to keep the curious—and the Russian language itself—at bay? That language which was nothing but ambivalence and lie, if you believed him: "verbs and nouns change places as freely as you wish." And whose school education "developed as much will as an alga's." Or rather my Freudian-inspired explanations, which invited our hosts, worthy Lutheran evangelists, to immerse themselves in "the flesh of words"? We concluded that metaphors are not made for juries! Brodsky's Elizabethan poetry is in perfect harmony with the island cemetery of San Michele in Venice, across from the Cannaregio and the Jewish ghetto, where he is buried.

The children, grandchildren, and great-grandchildren of Pushkin, Gogol, Tolstoy, and Dostoyevsky compressed their anger and their anxiety in strangled cries, despairing. Did these *refuseniks* and their *samizdats* bear witness to the vitality of an "eternal Russia," at last free from the manifestations of Jacobin Terror and the abysses of nihilism? Or rather, in undermining totalitarian communism, did they invent (inflexible freedom of the human spirit) a *disruptive language* calling into question the identity, the nation, the language itself, and that "ancient trinity" before which Solzhenitsyn yet bowed when he too received the Nobel (1970): *truth, goodness, beauty?*

Conveyed in Russian, this intimate-extimate experience, which people took for a political subversion of a concentration-camp regime (which it was), turned the social pact inside out like a glove and seized its religious substrate—implicitly or with a roar. The French Revolution had already done that, overthrowing the Throne and the Altar, by instigating the Cult of the Supreme Being like a religion, a break with the de-Christianization propagated by the militant atheism of certain revolutionary currents. "A Being supreme in evil," scoffed the Marquis de Sade. Be that as it may, ever since the Declaration of the Rights of Man and of the Citizen (1789), humanist spirituality will remain a juridical, political, and social pillar of the Republic.

8.3 The French Exception

In its process of secularization, French laicity establishes the neutrality of the State and guarantees the freedom of consciousness, imposing the equality of all before the law without distinction of religion or belief. This distance-taking from the religious continent does not bring into play the "break with Tradition" that took place in Europe and nowhere else, as shown by Alexis de Tocqueville and Hannah Arendt. In globalized secularization, laicity cohabits with the diversity of beliefs and spiritualities that practice their own freedom of expression, unless they brandish fundamentalism and prophesy the "great replacement" of "feminized" democracies at bay (which is how the enemies of democracy regally express themselves).

French laicity remains hard to understand outside the Hexagon. It is badly explained, insufficiently conscious of itself, and even less proud of the advances it has nurtured and continues to support in the face of the globalized return of fundamentalist radicalizations. Nevertheless there remains a "new idea" in counterpoint to certain people's denial of the "need to believe" and the "make no waves" resignation of others, in the face of interconnected explosions and abstentionist indifference. It is the "transvaluation of all values" (*Umwertung aller Werte*) dear to Nietzsche: "And time is reckoned from the *dies nefastus* with which this calamity began—after the *first* day of Christianity! *Why not rather after its last day? After today?* Revaluation of all values!" (*The Antichrist*, 1896).

The human and social sciences, emerging from the Enlightenment and the decomposition then resurgence of the radicalized religious continent, approach the "need to believe" and "religious facts" as *objects of knowledge*, interpretation, and debate. Phenomenology and existentialism accompany them, defying *being* and *nothingness* to the point of nausea and the words, while the structuralist reformulation of anthropology and literary criticism desacralizes *myths* and *belles-lettres*...

In the same spirit, psychoanalysis participating in the deconstruction of consciousness and its philosophy opens another avenue: perlaboration and sublimation. The arts and literature, in the meantime, add their *turnabout* (*Verwindung* or overcoming), according to Heidegger, to the *transvaluation* seeking its role in the *narratives of nations* now in the process of reformulation among globalized undercurrents. These experiences have composed and continue to recompose a *European narrative* of transcendence as the surpassing of self, synonymous with freedom—before crossing the Atlantic and diversifying in the novel (from Faulkner to Philip Roth), in "radical" sociology, in *underground* art and poetry...

To return only to the end of the nineteenth century— Dostoyevsky's time—these existential and symbolic turnabouts and appropriations were inscribed in the gothic Catholicism of Baudelaire;[3] in the death throes of Christianism encrypted in hermetic formulations by Mallarmé; in the indignation of Proust and Rodin at the closing of the cathedrals; in the Rimbaud illuminations and in *Maldoror* by the impossible Communard Lautréamont; in the surrealistic immersion into dreams and the "transubstantiation of every thing into miracles"; by Alfred Jarry calculating the surface of God, following Rabelais, arriving at zero, and "laughing at the sacred"; and even in the dying Proust's recovered memory initiating Albertine into Dostoyevsky....[4] And closer to us, Simone de Beauvoir who teaches women that "we are free to transcend all transcendence.

We can always escape toward an 'elsewhere,' but this elsewhere is still somewhere, in the heart of our human condition ... It alone makes language [*la parole*] possible" (*Pyrrhus and Cineas*, 141).

Dostoyevsky's writing and his existential journey participate in this European narrative. But his narrative is quite different from the transvaluation that has taken place in the Catholic memory in France, for example, which was snuffed out by the Enlightenment and the Revolution.

In mobilizing the "religious pathetic" of Orthodoxy,[5] seduced by the post-Socratic carnival, and overcome by the vocal flourishes of Job, Dostoyevsky resonates with our fractures, our diverse and tumultuous "genders," and our postmodern "wokisms."

Don't say it's only literature. In *in-presence* psychoanalytical sessions during the lockdown, but also in *virtual* sessions where iPhones ceased to be an obstacle and became an "in-between" *membrane*, I heard *inner experiences* being revealed. The ones Georges Bataille, blasphemer and explorer of mysticism, defines as an "approval of life in death," "contestation" of the withdrawal into oneself, of limits, of links. In ordinary times the analytical process recognizes them, but the pandemic let me hear that the transference-countertransference can also make them appear in internauts' physical distance, in the desocialization of work-from-home, and the phobic anxiety about death among the consumers of the spectacle.

Am I proposing a utopian antidote to the ongoing transhumanism? The pandemic spread by viruses and the decapitation that radicals practice, neither pathetic, comical, nor poetic, reveal to me the heartbreak of the *cleavage*. But after the age of suspicion, in the age of uncertainty, I wager on the capacity of the Self to welcome the question, on the conversation that problematizes, with infinite adjustments. And once again I hear Dostoyevsky's grating laugh crying for his stinking saint Zosima and obstinately unmasking the Unnamable by linking up his Proustian sentences, with trembling adverbs and digressions ... timidly, cruelly, precisely ... endlessly ...[6]

To each historical era pertain possibilities of survival. Political, social, spiritual, religious, ethical, psychosexual. Inner experience operates underground and *duplicates* the "order of things," the social consensus with its pacts and laws, monarchies and republics. First and Second World Wars; Cold War; *perestroika*, fall of the Berlin Wall, and creation of the European Union; globalization and *vaccino-dromes*. *Soixante-huitards*, beatniks, refuseniks, and dissidents . . . Could *inner experience*, escaping from the *control* of calculated thought, be the blind spot in today's anthropological acceleration? A sensitive point, but also a lever; the revolt of inner experience is the condition that guarantees, through innovative modalities of questioning, the possibility for speaking beings to revive.[7] Viral time, suspended, invites us to an interpretive return to the founding texts of the religions and spiritualities of the world, to the metaphysical dichotomies (body-soul, good-evil, etc.) that also govern sexual difference. Opening up binary identities loosens toxic anger. What has functioned as unreflected thought allows an opening, and there is a hint of a new beginning. If the end of history is not already programmed by Silicon Valley, and no new Renaissance is visible in the disarray that corrodes the authority of science and of the judicial and the political—let us admit that we are in the fourteenth century! With Duns Scot (1266–1308), who taught that truth is neither in opaque matter nor in abstract ideas but in *this* man, *that* woman: the foundational *singularity, haecceitas* from the demonstrative *haec, hic, ecce*. And with Meister Eckhart (1260–1328) who asked God to leave him "free from God." The *overturning of values* by the *turn* of language: a sur-vival, the only one that remains for digital humanity after "neither God nor master."

8.4 Orthodoxy and the West's Uncertainties of Identity

At the crossroads of the East and the West, Orthodox Christianity grafted its reading of late Hellenism onto the biblical text. The stoic principle of "interior touch" (*oikeiosis*), *universal incarnation* and vital dynamism, as well as the *anthropomorphic figurability* of the cosmos, which dialectical philosophy had applied to the diversity of the cosmos, served to put the believer in agreement with his affects and passions. The fervor of Emperor Constantine (272–337) for the Cross (*In this sign thou shalt conquer!* was his motto), which displaced Rome to Byzantium, brought Roman jurisdiction—caesaropapism—to this oriental expansion of Europe. It instilled the *sacredness of suffering* and the *reality of evil* in the spiritual quest; the annihilation of the Christ-God is more accentuated in it, but the illuminated celebrations of its Easter (the most important Orthodox celebration) never led to the launching of gothic cathedrals or the spectacular sumptuousness of the Renaissance and the Baroque.

After the Fathers of the Church monopolized the Old Testament, translated into the Greek of the Septuagint, patristic dogmatism (virulent against the Jews, who refused Jesus as the Messiah) did not recognize the "chosen people" and saw Christians as the "true" Israel. Along with that, the eventual union of the Orthodox Church with the State promulgated measures of rigor against the Jews, considered as the enemies of Christianity.

At the same time, Orthodox Christianism, far from suffering an erosion of faith, tightened its concentration, on the contrary, by extending to a chaos of ethnicities and the bazaar of beliefs— toward the extreme north and to the east as far as Persia. The anti-individualist energy of Islam—abstract weave of sabers, minarets, and rugs—and the anti-figurative bent of its decorative calligraphy failed to replace the Cross with the Crescent. They pushed the Orthodox soul into the shell of the rounded domes, into the retroactive prophecy of its devoutly kissed icons. There exist various so-called autocephalous versions of the independent Orthodox churches with their nationalistic colorations (Russian, Greek, Bulgarian, Georgian, Armenian . . .), but Orthodox faith, especially the Russian version, considers itself as the faith of its "origins." It is as likely to sacrifice itself savagely crossing swords with the conqueror as to abase itself in all humility under the yoke of the tyrant. But it remains always, and proudly, opposed to the Roman church and its ramifications, its ethical and political modulations in the so-called Western models of the State and the person. Persuaded, also, of the incomprehension, even the hostility, of the Roman Catholic Church and the West as a whole in whatever guise as regards the *orientalized* Christianity of that "third Rome" that Russia became.

Russian Christian Orthodoxy must be taken into consideration as the atavistic identitarian substrate, because both national and religious, of what is conventionally called post-Soviet *dissidence* and its cultural expression, notably its literary form. This observation is equally valid as concerns the upheavals of the domestic and international politics of Russia in the twenty-first century.

Today, Orthodoxy occupies an ambiguous place: opium of the people massacred by a bureaucracy that took its place or identitarian refuge easily instrumentalized by the political powers. Orthodoxy struggles to articulate its quest of the absolute with its tendency to retreat substantially into the local community of "suffering servers," where it finds sovereigntists of all sorts whom it can claim to seduce. However, drawing on the identitarian underground that Dostoyevsky novelized, Orthodox structure and history resonate with the identitarian uncertainties and catastrophes of being, consonant with geographical and historical crossroads and interstices, past and present. The language and the writing that come from that experience, far from being regressive or backward leaning, and in spite of their national diversity, necessarily and paradoxically echo the now viral, hypermodern contingencies of democracies. Under their economic-social surface, these recent shakeups undermine the very *tradition* that held for two thousand years in Europe. The Renaissance, the Revolution, and European humanism have constantly rebuilt the permanent foundation of tradition in the face of technical hype, whose benefits and horrors we recognize and which globalization attacks, with unpredictable consequences. With its limits and its advances, the Orthodox experience of subjectivity and freedom questions, stimulates, and completes Western experience. And reciprocally: Orthodox faith benefits from the West's achievements, which it defies. With unequaled ardor, Dostoyevsky's polyphony probes the promises and the threats of this composite civilization.[8]

8.5 What Freedom? Digressions on the "Religious Pathetic" (*pafos stihii*)

In 1789, the French Revolution had just proclaimed the principles of the republican trilogy *Liberty, Equality, Fraternity* when the Terror, in 1793, bloodied the country in the name of freedom. At the same time, the Declaration of the Rights of Man and of the Citizen, also 1793, radicalizing the English *Habeas corpus* (1679, reinforced by the *Bill of Rights* in 1789), guaranteed for the first time in the world the rights of man as a supreme obligation of the social contract.

In 1781, Kant had published his *Critique of Pure Reason*, completed in 1789 by his *Critique of Practical Reason*, lucid meditations on the libertarian essence of the human Self, defined as a *free* soul endowed with an autonomous will with regard to external constraints and the weightiness of his sensitivity.

In spite of the Terror and the excesses that mark the growing pains of the Western democracies to come, the deployment of freedom sets fire to the national liberation movements in the Old Continent. It won't be until the middle of the nineteenth century that the Balkans, for the most part Orthodox, reject Ottoman domination.

In 1793 in Russia, there was a return to the hesychast tradition with the monk Paisius Velichkovsky (1722–1794).[9] Known since the eleventh century, hesychasm propounded the intimate union of spirituality and knowledge. Velichkovsky translated the *Philokalia* (literally, "love of beauty") into Russian. The *Philokalia* is an anthology of contemplative Christian Hellenist texts, which inspired the renascence of Russian Orthodoxy, notably with the *startsy* (the "Ancients" or "Elders") of Optina, venerated and frequented by Dostoyevsky. A certain *freedom* of the believer is affirmed in it: *silence of the Ego* and displacement of the intelligence and reasoning reason toward the heart, understood as the pole of an *unrepresentable infinite*, as well as the intuitive source of the *ineffable* divinity.

Kant and understanding on one side, the *Philokalia* on the other: two opposed or complementary foci of freedom?

Rousseau's *Social Contract* (1762) had proclaimed the intrinsically free nature of the free individual, capable of self-conquest against the intrinsically alienating *socius*, to initiate new links and contracts. In contrast to freedom conceived negatively as man's independence with regard to nature and God, Kant proposes a positive definition: freedom is an absolute auto-activity, an initiative and potential of man for self-determination. From Plato's dialogues to St. Augustine's questioning (the Ego is a questioning: *se quaerere, quaesto mihi factus sum*), the West's valorization of questioning leads to Kant's affirmation of a spontaneous understanding, a sovereign and in that sense liberating self-beginning. The genealogy of this elevation of the reasoning, initiating, and autonomous Self harks back to St. Paul and St. Augustine followed by Luther and Protestantism. Human liberty, "caused" by *a transcendental cause* that surpasses it and on which it depends, may deploy to become a "practical liberty." Created by a causality, it can also be created as produced by the "cosmological" causality of natural and economic forces. Thus Max Weber, in *The Protestant Ethic and the Spirit of Capitalism* (1904–1905), was able to demonstrate the reformulation of transcendental choice into salvation by free enterprise, by production and accumulation of social goods. A teleology (causality-goal) governs freedom; adapting to it, freedom attains its fruition when understanding dominates all sensuality, structurally and in the last instance morally.

As of 1930, Martin Heidegger, although compromised with Nazism during his directorship of the Rectorate of Fribourg, denounces the danger Europe and the world face in being subordinate to productivism and technical reason, and he operates a reversal (*Kehre*).[10] Freedom, assimilated to *the essence of philosophy*, does not derive from a cause but is introduced at the beginning of the *Dasein*. Freedom is in the Being as long as the Being "presents" and not because it is "cause of." Any causality could only be subsequent to this "presence/presentification" of the Being, which is delivered and freed in proximity and preoccupation, whereas the causal chain of *givens* is constructed technically and scientifically "after" this deliverance.

What Lacan called the "Copernican revolution" in the psychoanalysis founded by Sigmund Freud was his conceptualization of Sophocles's intuition in the tragedy *Oedipus the King* (320 BCE), though it is not reduced to this. The subjacent economy of subjectivity is a *crossroads* between amorous desire for the mother and desire for the murder of the father. The subject is tragically free in his forbidden double desire of incest and parricide. It is only at the price of his perlaborated and sublimated desires that he can become a subject of knowledge, of philosophy, and of science.

This oedipal model has not disappeared. Its revisions underlie the metamorphoses of parenthood and generate various symptoms and alienations, which contemporary psychoanalysis identifies and elucidates.

The capacity to judge is disintegrating to the point of disappearing, noted Hannah Arendt, reader of Kant, apropos of the "banality of evil" in Nazified Germany; and sadomasochism is released as a result, which culminates in *radical evil.* Today, the new technologies excel in the acceleration, storage, and calculation of information, which contribute to the unprecedented spread of scientific tools and artificial intelligence. Whereas the "subscribers" to the hallucinatory toxicity of images, to the incessant flows of information that overexcite or anaesthetize, are given over to a reality show in the face of which the *free subject* has become a mirage. Numerous are the patients afflicted with "fake selves" (Winnicott), borderline personalities (Kernberg), or "as if" personalities (Helene Deutsch). Under the pressure of the drive and by the disintegration of the social framework, the fragmented psychism is expressed in psychosomatic illnesses and suicidal depressions. Drug addiction, acting out, suicide, vandalism, and various forms of cynicism are increasing. Black bloc and various contestatory anarchisms, prey to a subjective and social malaise, dissimulate the inaptitude for exercising one's freedom.[11]

Modern art—ugly, minimalist, destructive—whether it claims adherence to psychosis or not, constitutes perhaps one of the rare variants of libertarian effect capable of accompanying and supporting the deflagration of Western subjectivity. After the bankruptcy of providential ideologies, the political "great replacement" by extremists veering toward sovereignties and religious fundamentalisms seems unlikely for the moment. But the planetary pathos is holding on by an emotional "us"— ephemeral Web communities—by which digital finance manages to contain these "new maladies of the soul." "Separations," even "social wars" are everywhere fragmenting the social link of democracies, even in western Europe, which was their cradle.

Orthodox Faith Today

Are Orthodox religious traditions still full of life, in the face of apparent disaffections? According to data from research done at the Pew Research Center, the Orthodox Church in Russia enjoys a very fervent minority, beside a broad population of people partly marked by the heritage of a nonreligious education and for whom the self-designation as Orthodox stems rather from the identity and recognition of a national and cultural heritage, without any real spiritual depth.

Orthodox memory thus understood influences—in an underground, unconscious manner—the style of life, customs, mentalities, and decisive attitudes of the social actors in the political and economic organization of their society. In fact, when the dogmas of communism imposed by violence yield, what emerges to fill the void are routine behaviors, "spontaneities," as it were, "programmed" by family traditions.

In "Bulgaria, My Suffering" (1995), I evoked the deep helplessness of the Orthodox Slavic people—*liberated*, but not for all that *free*. The nations that a broadened Europe integrated after the fall of the Berlin Wall toss back and forth to each other their specific and underlying conceptions of the individual in the form of conflicts reigniting wars of religion; at best they spark nationalist claims or insurmountable incompatibilities that are weakening the indispensable European project.

In my childhood I witnessed the power of resistance that slumbers in Orthodox faith. I like its sensuality, its mystery, the retreat that makes us feel the pains and joys of another world in the liturgical celebration. Dostoyevsky experienced them in the concreteness of his oeuvre, in the trials of his thoughts irrigated by the "new ideas" but impregnated with faith and the practice of Orthodox worship. To the confined tweeters in quest of a supplementary soul who are starting to be depressed, I would like to recall some of the stations along this way: *Philokalia, per Filium,* hesychasm, the icon. If these modules speak to them, they will see that they are hardly models for our present times. But they are vibrations of the internal core, seeking to open.

PHILOKALIA

Zosima, the "stinking" and sublime elder in *The Brothers Karamazov* (1881), is the carnivalesque model of those men of God who practice *Philokalia,* the "prayer of the heart," the absolute acquiescence to the senses, emancipated from objectivation and intellection, at the antipodes of the self-active "freedom" of Kantian understanding. They live immersed in their mystery and available for unlimited compassion. The Orthodox theologians Alexei Khomiakov and Vladimir Solovyov drew from them the idea of "universal communion" (*sobornost*); Dostoyevsky and Tolstoy, the "great pneumologues" (Berdyaev), Leontiev and Rozanov, among others, also drew inspiration from them.

This mysterious and fervent enthusiasm will be transferred to the "mystical" movement of *nihilism.*[12] In fact, *atheistic* and *communistic* currents, preaching values that are meant to be liberating and critical, can easily become "religious" ideologies. The affective, noncritical belonging of their followers welds them to the dogmas of the communities that claim their membership, communities with which they merge.

In Orthodoxy, the questioning of the cause (divine or social) and deism itself, which can lead to atheism or the disabused contestation of the social link (from Voltaire's irony to Diderot's sober passion), seem structurally impossible. Dostoyevsky has Makar, the adoptive father of the young man in *The Adolescent,* say it: "It's impossible to be a man and not bow down to something; such a man could not bear the burden of himself, nor could there be such a man. If he rejects God, then he bows down to an idol—fashioned of wood, or of gold, or of thought." But Makar is not the narrator, whose laugh, insidious and permanent, unhinges characters, identities, beliefs, and values.[13]

Anton Chekhov, not really carnivalesque but amused and sure of his observation, proposes this ethnographer's diagnosis in "On the Road": "Russian life presents us with an uninterrupted succession of convictions and aspirations, and if you care to know, it has not yet the faintest notion of lack of faith or skepticism. If a Russian does not believe in God, it means he believes in something else." He transposes this total adhesion even into science: "nothing is so staggering, nothing takes a man's breath away like the beginning of any science . . . I gave myself up to science, heart and soul, passionately, as to the woman one loves. I was its slave; I found it the sun."

To generalize "national character" is to reject the unique pathways that blend in it or free themselves from it. And in the effort to explain, one accepts the comportments that the civilization of images reveals—and underhandedly glorifies. How to define the cynicism of communist or mafioso atheists? In my opinion, they are not sufficiently Dostoyevskian. But you can say, with Chekhov: even the communist or mafioso atheists *believe* in their cynicism, they believe in their disbelief, they adhere to it violently. Those who don't believe withdraw into their sorrowful isolation, they passionately embrace their vexation and abandon the competition. They sulk, and their depressive sensuality, their resigned negativity are maladies I noted in "Bulgaria, My Suffering."

It also appears, I feel, that passionate, fusional subjectivity serves as a counterweight to Western freedom's deterioration into the fake and the spectacular. Fertile latencies and burning excesses of the philocalic soul. Whether passivity or cynicism, compassionate self-perception seems struck down by its own difficulty in entering into the universe of competition, delivered over without resistance to the destruction of moral values, to the anomie of the world of marketing, to the enslavement by the spectacle. As a symmetric doubling of this resignation, the "religious pathetic" withdraws into indifference toward everything that is "public": like a rejection of the "collective" imposed as a cult by communism, a general apathy feeds the mafioso excesses of corruption and concussion. Which does not prevent the aspiration for "universal communion" (*sobornost*) from awakening the Orthodox nostalgia of the oligarchs themselves.

Likewise, I also note that Orthodoxy is susceptible to *political instrumentalization*: "For a Christian, no Church without Emperor." The oscillation between allegiance and submission, known even before the Great Schism of 1054, is detectable in the various national Churches, even into the twentieth and twenty-first centuries. The *basileus* (the Byzantine emperor) is involved in the affairs of the Church and chooses the patriarch, and in exchange the Church contributes to the social stability and the perennity of religious archaisms.

PER FILIUM

God is triple in Orthodoxy, but differently than in Catholicism: the Holy Ghost proceeds from the Father *through* the Son for the Orthodox (*per Filium*), whereas it proceeds from the Father *and* from the Son for the Catholics (*Filioque*). The Catholic "and" sets Father and Son as equals, prefiguring the autonomy and independence of the person (the person of the Son as much as of the believer) and opening the way for Western individualism and personalism. The Orthodox "through," on the other hand, suggests a delicious but pernicious annihilation of the Son and the believer. The all-powerful authority of the Father is unalienable; the Father Pantocrator remains the source divinity. The Son is the servant, the "collaborator" who, through this servitude (*per*), raises himself up and becomes a god. Both subordinate and godlike, the Son (and the believer with him) is caught in an exquisite interaction of submission and exaltation which grants him the joys and the sorrows internal to the master/slave dialectic, or, more intimately, those of masculine homoeroticism. Man is not called to "free himself" from God, but to "freely unite" with Him, and thereby to "communicate divine life to his nature and to the universe of which he constitutes the *hypostasis* (which is to say that he surpasses and englobes it in his personal existence)," writes Olivier Clément.[14]

In light of the Oedipus complex, the desire of and for the father alternating with the suffering of separation, never satisfied, amounts to an erotization of masochism and of the depressive position. Unable to become the equal of the Father or his likeness, the Son is driven either to identify with the Father as an aggressor, austere and inaccessible, source of fascination with absolute power; or to be feminized (as Alain Besançon says) in shame and guilt. Withdrawn into submission, becoming passive, the son-subject takes shelter under the protective intimacy of the *pokrov*, the "veil," in a tenderness of renunciation and retreat. Disavowing the "cut" separating from God (the biblical *Bereshit*), avoiding the separation from the absolute Other that is the Father—symbolic instance of the Law—this amorous abnegation can neither fight back nor disobey, which on the contrary the Jewish protagonists of the biblical revolt allow themselves, indefatigable rebels and interpreters of a Yahweh nevertheless unnamable and infinitely demanding! Vasily Rozanov, for whom Orthodoxy is a mysticism of "contact" and "touch," deliciously compares the infra-linguistic, infra-oedipal, and hypersensitive adoration of Orthodox faith to an intimacy "as impalpable as a brioche in a bakery."

The son in the *per Filium* is not incited to an oedipal revolt but to the occupation of the daughter's place: to being the admiring wife of the Father that he/she will never be. And since incommensurable divine authority allows neither argument, nor critique, nor negotiation, it remains for anxiety to express itself solely through *destruction* (such as an "unleashing of elements," *pafos stihii*), another consequence of the unthinkable subordination of the Son to the Father. The negativity of judgment that Kant analyzes is here submerged by the raging and annihilating affect of nihilism, which demolishes the former norm to erect an opposed value, just as absolutely unarguable and not subject to criticism. Dostoyevsky depicts the specific alchemy of the couple negating-violence-and-ecstatic-adoration which sweeps away the structural *limits* of understanding: "This is an urge for the extreme, for the fainting sensation of approaching an abyss, and half-leaning over it . . . This is an urge for negation in a man, sometimes, most believing and venerating" (*A Writer's Diary*, 1873). In a dialogue in *Demons*, he has Kirillov (a character strongly inspired by the holy Elder Tikhon of Zadonsk, whose secular name was Kirillov) say: "'Then history will be divided into two parts: from the gorilla to the destruction of God, and from the destruction of God to . . .' 'To the gorilla?' '. . . to the physical changing of the earth and man.'"

As favored by the *per Filium* configuration, this subjectivity could be interpreted as arising from an incomplete Oedipus complex (but who can boast of a resolved Oedipus complex?), which maintains the son in the fusional dyad, rather than accentuating the oedipal triangulation to which he accedes like any speaking subject. The bisexuality that results from this sensual dyad enriches the sensitivity of the orthodox man at the cost of a repression of castration anxiety, leaving free play to suffering and the anxiety of death.

In contrast, in the classical and normative Oedipus complex, castration anxiety is constructive of the *subject of desire* for *the other sex* (Rosolato) in distinguishing it from other objects, links, and alterities. The heterosexual link, thus elaborated on the "rock of castration," can become an arena for acts of prowess, transgressions, and provocations of the father and all authority, with Don Juan as the fabled archetype.

However, the repression of castration anxiety makes possible the expression of older psychical layers: those of the pre-oedipal *masochism* and the *primitive agony* of the neotene, the unfinished human being that the *parlêtre* is. Composed in the depressive narcissistic mode, this subjectivity exalts passion, complaint, and death, with gothic or romantic accents. The *strastoterptsy* ("those who endure the Passion," without necessarily being martyrs) of the eleventh century practice absolute obedience to the ways of Providence and accept violent death. The experience of *metanoia*—a process of "deep transformation," "change of spirit," or "repentance" by a descent into the "memory of death" ("Keep your wits in hell and do not despair")—has been legitimately compared to certain depressive aspects of the existentialist experience, notably to the feeling of the absurd that pervades Sartre's *Nausea* (Olivier Clément).

Such masochistic excesses can only fascinate the contemporary Western subject, especially when the seduction of eroticism collapses, henceforth banalized and commercialized in a more and more permissive society submissive to GAFA.[15] As a consequence, I note the return to what the Greeks called the *kakon*, the "bad," in other words the catastrophic and in particular depressive dimension of the psychism, internal to oedipal elaboration and liberation. It digs a properly speaking unnamable gap in "our" modern psyche. But it doesn't much surprise the Orthodox subject in his ritualized impasse.

In fact, depression proves to be one of the major symptoms of these "new maladies of the soul" that one cannot treat with the classic therapeutics of oedipal desire, but which require a particular attention to and interpretation of the death drive and of mortality, further reawakened by the pandemic. In this new context, "their" excesses of depressiveness and "their own" experience reflect "our" discontent, in an explicit, crude, and cruel manner.

THE HESYCHASM

In compensation for this incompletion of the Oedipus complex, mysticism proliferates in Orthodoxy. The archaic layers of the psyche animate a faith that does not *represent* them—if one understands the term "representation" here as a performance of language and images—but *welcomes* them in the preverbal register of sense experience and thereby procures an infra-linguistic, infra-personal, and infra-social pacifying consolation.

Russian theologians dwelt insistently on the humanistic qualities of Orthodoxy. Through the intervention of the Son's "collaborative" role, the Father Pantocrator *veils* or *deviates* his Jupiterian power and permits being celebrated as a "humanity-God," a "universe-God" (Solovyov). Nikolai Fyodorov drew political consequences from this in affirming that "the Trinity is our social program." This sensorial humanization of the divine is not without its effects; nor is it innocent. The unknowability of the Father leads to a *theology of the lived*—not of *knowledge*—since the believing subject is invited to an ontological ravishment, a sensual communion that remains this side of enlightenment. In taking leave of philosophical questioning and hermeneutics, the affective participation in the divinity withdraws from the *eidos* and definitively from thought itself: God is neither this nor that, neither affirmation nor negation, not even "God," according to Gregory Palamas. Orthodox faith makes a glorious divinity tower over the universe, a divinity reabsorbed into the unrepresentable and paradoxically inaccessible but "touching"; and in so doing, it takes the risk of evacuating God from human reality.

Coupled with man and nevertheless unthinkable by him, God is not dead. He implodes *inside* man. As a result, man participating in an unknowable divinity is a *microtheos* and a microcosm just as unconceptualizable, shapeless and unfathomable. "Concepts create idols of God, only the shock anticipates something," affirms Gregory of Nyssa. The glorification of the Father is seen outside the concept and outside negation in an intuitive revelation, the opposite of the Augustinian interrogation that prolongs the questioning of ancient philosophy, differently in Protestantism than in Catholicism.

Cult of silence, tenderness of the welcome, philocaly, Isaac the Syrian's "*feel everything* in God" becomes a cult of the "sensation of God" that recuses *words* and departs from the logic of Catholic and Protestant theology. *Apophasis* is the summit of this *negative theology* that denies any conceptual limitation of God: not value, concept, or representation, God is the inaccessible participated and participant, the bottomless mystery, the unobjectifiable.

The *maniakos eros*, according to Maximus the Confessor's expression, the mad love that God dispenses, as well as Mary's *Fiat*, "do not resolve the tragedy of freedom," as Vladimir Lossky envisages it,[16] but, quite the contrary, they constitute it. Thus is achieved the unknowable of the *Deus absconditus*, which makes of man adjoining Him a *homo absconditus*: undefinable, impossible to conceptualize. Isn't this central ineffability a trap in which the Dostoyevskian nihilist is caught in annulling it ("God is dead") the better to restore its absolute—but in reverse—in an All, an exterminating totality . . .

where *everything is permitted*? Well before this closing nineteenth century, which considered itself deicidal, and in the face of the very fate of Orthodoxy, we are right to wonder if the Orthodox mystique doesn't reveal more frankly than other currents do that nihilism is structurally inherent to ontotheology.[17]

And what if it's because God is unrepresentable, unknowable, and incontestable that everything is permitted—in the order of representation? Some have interpreted this prevalence of sensitivity over reason—or ratiocination—in Orthodoxy as a fidelity to Jewish spirituality. Rather, in my opinion, it is a matter of kabbalistic or gnostic grafts,[18] which lodge in the *separation* where the Jewish God is, to fill it "tenderly," passionately, madly. Orthodoxy felt no connection to the biblical separation, which provoked revolts and interpretations, nor to the Greek dialectic of the *philosophia*, nor even to the slow pre-Socratic emergence of Being into the Logos. Distrustful, without joining these pathways of freedom, it holds back and insists on its rising sensorial power.

The anthropology of Orthodoxy contrasts the excess fullness of the soul with the "new maladies of the soul" plaguing the Western subject, who manages today's globalized world. Heidegger, in a contemplative retreat at an Orthodox monastery in Kaisariani (*Aufenthalte*), had perceived the unique presence of a "consonance" which does not deny the difficult blossoming of Being. A "spirit that doesn't bend" remains protected here by Orthodoxy, in the invisible depth of this precipitation toward the factitious independence that engages us and in which the technological civilization productive of "goods" prefers to remain.

The experience of hesychasm makes apparent, *a contrario*, the pitfalls of "our" freedom when it is reduced to being nothing but an atomization of solitary egoisms in distress, of masks without subjects, bogged down in the competition that alienates them. Hesychasm removes the guilt of the need for *sobornost* (universal communication). A person who takes inspiration from it is not a successful subject, nor even a Self, but a constitutive reliance, a communion. And that person rediscovers the taste for life.

We may wonder if creating links among free individuals is still a possible objective for the globalized individual. To manage it, one would definitely have to rehabilitate the "integral, superindividual, and communitarian character" of the person (Trubetskoy), interpreted by Florensky, Berdyaev, and S. Bulgakov. Restoring the need for belonging by means of the senses would in sum amount to opening up understanding, to re-equilibrating freedom. "They" have remained longer than "us" in these "superessential" states (Gregory of Nyssa).

THE ICON IS NOT AN IMAGE

With the triumph of the "iconodules" over the "iconoclasts," Byzantium accomplished the first revolution in the modern realization of the spectacle. Thanks to the patriarch Nicephorus's theory (end of the ninth century), the image made by the human hand is justified: it is an *economy* of divine presence.[19] With this approach to the divinity, one can understand its disposition, its course, its advent, but also its management, its ruse, its dialectic. This negotiation of the image between the invisible and the visible that the *icon* is does not dissociate Being from appearance but *inscribes* it rather than making it be seen. The icon is a *graphein*, a *writing* that *paints*. The dialectic of the incarnation inseparable from the *kenosis* (the void, the emptying out, the annulment) underlies and disturbs simple evidence: it insists, it cuts into it. The icon is a sensed trace, not at all a spectacle.

On the other hand, the Latin conception of the *figura*—in the sense of a "prophecy in action" as defined by Auerbach—prevailed as a more fruitful and freer means of guaranteeing the rapid rise of representation.[20] The figure takes up the real events of a history (Jewish, but also Greek) to interpret them as the promise of an open signification to come, and it commands the entire fate of Western representation: Eve prefiguring Mary, Moses prefiguring Christ, the Synagogue prefiguring the Church, and so on. From displacement to displacement until the source-meaning is lost, then the passage through realistic figuration, up to its indefinite purification, which is modern art. In this dynamic, what was already a given of Greek and Latin figuration becomes maximally *personalized*, the face and psychology choosing precisely the universe of images to impose their empire on the work of thinking.

In the sham of the generalized spectacle today, we experience the extinction of this pathway of the icon underlying the freedom of representation. We need to rethink the implicit logic of Orthodoxy to dismantle its lures of passivity but also to extract from it the antidotes for postmoderns consumed by their screens, too sure of their freedoms and not always conscious of their downfalls. We will find there the need for reliance, the abandonment of the link, the opening of the sensed. And the unknown that calls to us in the *icon*, in the flowering of the visible.

8.6 Encounters?

We are lacking an anthropology of national and, more broadly, religious psychology. If it existed, it would clarify the undercurrents of a civilization, beyond its indispensable economic reconstruction. Such an anthropology would proceed with a reevaluation of the advantages as well as the difficulties of Orthodoxy in the face of the necessities of technology and freedom. In this respect, Eurasianism, which celebrates Russia as the union (*splav*) of the East and the West within ecclesial reason, reemerged in 1990–1991 as an attempt to rethink both Orthodoxy and a centaur Russia, carrying Mongol as well as Byzantine heritages. A *métissage*, a hyphen between Europe and Asia? Or an identitarian supremacism, an isolationist inflation? Like a new messianism, Eurasia is experienced as a variant of "Moscow, Third Rome," concentrated in a limited national space but nonetheless nostalgic for the All.

Orthodox faith has so well assimilated "the Word became flesh" (John 1:1–18) that it invites the believer to yield to a sensorial osmosis with absolute Alterity to the point of annihilation, so as to achieve unknowable hypostases. The lures of these depths, which can nurture nihilism in addition to revolution, have been only too well denounced.[21] Orthodoxy did not have its Aristotelian moment with Saint Thomas Aquinas, nor its debate with Duns Scot and the emergence of *ecceitas*, or Kant's free will and the rights of man. The Orthodox link wins out over kenosis, but free singularity remains a dead letter. The materialistic revolution that succeeded it and accompanies it today was done "in a heathen way," aspiring only to accede to the market economy, whereas the emancipation movements stemming from Christian humanism aim for the resurrection of the Unique through the infinite diversity of rebels. . . .

8.7 Something of Dostoyevsky

These dissidents—I listened to them, I read how they threw out the "system" and its meaningless "order," how they roughed up the bureaucratic voices and the supposedly cosmopolitan scholarly vocabularies, how they rose up against the confiscated speech that had succeeded in reducing the avant-gardism of Mayakovsky and even Yesenin to cant. I heard how the biblical prophecies, the sobs of John Donne, the grimaces of the symbolists, the surrealist liberation highlighted their expressivist brutality, revised and scarified by deceptive consumerist promises and the harshness of the Gulag. What could they truly relate of their tragic experience? What had they lived?

Shalamov's *Kolyma Tales* (1978) and *The Gulag Archipelago* (1973) by Solzhenitsyn unfolded on Soviet soil and in the Slavic soul. But they opened deluded eyes everywhere and emphasized the tribute paid to the ideology that the "austere prophet" (Solzhenitsyn) branded "the most terrible in human experience." Published in French at the Éditions du Seuil by Claude Durand (who will be my editor at Fayard, the publishing house he directed starting in 1980), his documented narrative of abjection swept away the Bolshevik Revolution along with the universalist spirit of the Enlightenment, which endures only because it is constantly reestablished. This literature, collecting 227 victim testimonies—"nothing is invented"—did not have the tragicomic force of Dostoyevsky's language. But what brought

Solzhenitsyn's *The Trail* closer to Dostoyevsky's *Demons* (1872) was the insurgence of Orthodox faith against the police state's rape of "ineffable intimacy," as well as the Russian language reinvented by the ex-prisoner of the Gulag—harsh, rough, playing with dialectical neologisms, forging others—and the syncopated syntax of this "language fantastic" (Georges Nivat) resonating with the hidden, sing-song orality of the popular *skaz*, along with proverbs and neo-Russianisms.

When the author of *One Day in the Life of Ivan Denisovich*, in his speech not given in Sweden, repeats the enigmatic sentence of the convict of Omsk: "Beauty will save the world," he claims that neither politics nor abstract thought can do so. In placing himself under such a patronage, the henceforth official, not to say crowned writer Solzhenitsyn is not only giving proof of his attachment to Dostoyevsky's national Christocentrism. He is making it known that another dimension transcends it, namely the beauty (the philocaly?) of art, leaving the effort to do better to those who will come after him. But does this mean beauty as Dostoyevsky understands it?

Not really. The formula for salvation in *The Idiot* (1868) is not lodged within the classical trinity of *truth, goodness, beauty*. Evoked by Myshkin, proclaimed by Verkhovensky the father, it is definitively Mitya Karamazov, in his fever, who develops and imposes it. Not without specifying, however, that beauty, "a fearful and terrible thing!" "should start from the ideal of the Madonna and end with the ideal of Sodom."[22] "Sodom" to be understood in the broad sense of vice, sin, even crime. Carnivalesque from one end to the other, the peregrinations of beauty in the writing invite scanning and rebuilding all the supports of the speaking subject, sublimation and the sublime included.

But first, and above all, these aesthetic ambivalences made me think—still make me think—that all these voices in the archipelago of Russian dissidence had *something of Dostoyevsky*. Why?

Because, like them and before them, the experience of human destructivity radicalized their works—works determined to dissect the totalitarian system while they too were intoxicated by its intemporal, omnipresent virality. But without projecting themselves into the Carnival of the incarnate Word, unfathomable, incurable Karamazovian jouissance. As for the Siberian convict, bearded in the nineteenth century manner, orthodox and epileptic, the rejected, sorrowful lover, the serious husband, the devoted father, the scrupulous journalist, the repented gambler, the possibly innocent pervert, the disappointed European, the Dantesque Shakespearian . . . neither the one nor the other . . . the Slavophile, former believer or not believer at all, antipapist, anti-French, anti-Semitic, anti-everything, although in love with this everything, children above all, in love with life at the edges of life, with the most nonsensical, idiotic, always double, winning-losing, tuberculous, fresh, demoniacal, divine, proud, ridiculous, insolent, maternal life "firm like a saint" . . . *That* Dostoyevsky, in the face of death, nothing remained for him to do but to track the only virus worth the name: God. As a result of which Fyodor Mikhailovich lived and survived only by inventing an oral, contagious, and immunizing writing.

I might as well tell you I am not one of those "souls in some sense related to Dostoyevsky's" required by Berdyaev to be able to "incorporate oneself" into the "high spiritual phenomenon" that is the "great Russian." Nor have I frequented the resistant Soviet thinkers, with their prophet-like airs, who piled into modest apartments stuffed with icons and Russian literary classics for nights at a time to perfect the future of the world through Orthodoxy. Coming after May '68 and the Anglo underground, the new-wave dissidents, resourceful hooligans adored at L'Idiot International and the Palace Club where the golden youth of the French bourgeoisie gravitated, held their alcohol, liked fighting, seduced all sorts of girls, and in all seriousness sang the praises of Stalin (Carrère). I tended to see them as characters stemming from a wacky skit on *Demons* (1872) but lacking any sort of connection with the "thought banquet" that is Dostoyevsky's *gnosis*.

Forty years later, these *dissidents* of a not really thawed Sovietism, these "under" pseudo-Dostoyevsky-ites, took risks with the consumer society and their own lives, but without the frosty fire of Solzhenitsyn or the pneumatic philosophy of Dostoyevsky. Missing was a disruptive language. With their devastating "excesses," these "Russian boys" (as Dostoyevsky liked to put it), with whom the "Russian girls," the *Femen*, were to join, remain still today as patented disturbers who seduce extremists of all stripes while defying the false honesty of the universal bourgeois with its "French quintessence" (another expression of Dostoyevsky's). Their apocalyptic nihilism—break, injure, kill; nothing before, nothing after—now spreads even to municipal elections in the Republic of France. It also deforms the "terrible bad questions" and the "final things" that tortured the voices of Myshkin and Stavrogin, of Nastasya Filippovna and the Cripple, of Rogozhin and Karamazov in polyphonic and fatal narratives, by turning them into "black comedies" for Netflix series.

Whatever their obscurantist, sovereigntist, or totalitarian instrumentalizations, national characteristics are not mere fantasies, as some politically correct thinkers suggest. The social and human sciences seek to identify and analyze their constituted historical components, their emergence, endurance, and evolution.

The "Russian soul," so celebrated for its "exalted dimension," its "apocalyptic revolt against Greek antiquity" (Spengler), is supposedly a Dionysian nucleus coupled with a "metaphysical nihilism" having "revolutionary faculties"; it is, according to Berdyaev, "holy and dishonest because it is anti-bourgeois." These are only some of the enigmas that glorify it, as it is complacently elevated to mystical heights and made to confront the "obstacles" of Western materialism. These intrepid essentialists do not try to clarify, even less to analyze, the myths, points of reference, or foils by which they might elucidate the permeability, the explosions, but also the adaptability of this Russian "ideality," an ideality that is borderline from the start and modulates its original constitution by ingesting ambient deflagrations and revolutions.

Russianness does not disappear in Russian totalitarianism, nor does it justify it completely, no more than Sinicism has (yet) let itself be dissolved into dis-localized marketing or British fully absorbed into the Globish City. Dostoyevsky, a refractory but persistent

European nourished by "new ideas," "thinks" in novels, or rather in an open narrativity, incomplete and constantly reinvented.

At first, his religious convictions do not seem to be in contradiction with the new humanism of the West that accompanied the rise of socialism. But in delving more deeply into his own underground, under the sway of the prison and guided by the compass of Orthodox kenosis, he develops his self-analysis by attacking the parricidal nihilism that deeply undermines the individualistic flattening of the post-Christian West. Confronting this scourge of humanistic civilization, the survivor of prison, of "French ideas," and of Orthodoxy itself does not shut himself up in an aesthetic religion. Neither judgment nor revelation. For him, "divine inspiration" is revealed as an indefatigable requestioning of the self and the world through the jouissance of writing.

The multiple facets of his psychosexuality are embodied in protagonists from the surrounding Russian society, an undecidable, tragicomic polyphony that orients and prolongs the self-analyses of his male and female readers wherever they may be, whatever their native language. From yesterday and today. When he discourses about the Man-God or the God-Man and tortures himself like Kirillov, he will seek Him and find Him within the hidden universality of the need to believe and the desire to know, always unfailingly *singular*. With his double, the Devil, who is consubstantial with Him, as is the cadaver stink of the otherwise saintly Elder Zosima. If he never loses Him, it is because as a true Christian and a "child of doubt" and an epileptic—the very worst, deprived of language and thought—he knows how to find Him again. And it is in the writing that they—Dostoyevsky and the Other—take hold of each other, a love to the death, an orgasm trying to *speak* without end.

Let me invite you to take one further step. Through the characters Myshkin, Raskolnikov, Nastasya, or Stavrogin, this writing interrogates each person's own post-, pre-, anti-, or non-Christian intimate thoughts. It is not the supposedly Vatican theology (the Grand Inquisitor) nor even Orthodoxy (the *starets* Tikhon) that the writer defies. But what, and whom? The demise of humanistic universalism? Emptiness draped in faith, which prompts jouissance?

Our wishing to go beyond ourselves? The attempts to eliminate us and replace us?

I am writing these lines while all the inhabitants of the Earth have put themselves in lockdown, or have emerged from lockdown, to escape the COVID-19 virus and its variants. Uncertainty about science and governments, suspension of economies and time, eclipse of thought. The win-win ideology broke down in the face of the pandemic, revealing the vulnerability inherent in the human condition. Far from the Spectacle and blatant nihilism, my analysands represent a new humanity, which commits to making the modest but demanding wager to rebound. Each person discovers their intimate/extimate or inside/outside drawn from the fragile zones of their lives, thus calling on the vitality of the analyst. There develops a real psychosomatic immunity, repelling the despondency fomented by the viral attack and the confining desocialization. We rediscover the flesh of words, in it and by it we sur-vive.

Is this so far from Dostoyevsky? This writer was never confined: not in the courtyard of the hospital his doctor father ran, which also held the family home; nor in the vocational school in Saint Petersburg where he "annihilated himself with fluidity" while drawing his blueprints; nor in the Fourierist Petrashevsky Circle, which wanted to abolish serfdom in Russia; nor even in the Siberian jail; nor in the casinos the gambler sampled across Europe; nor in his family, protected by the faithful stenographer and "groupie" spouse Anna Snitkina; nor in his novels, diaries, or notebooks overflowing with sentences, passions, and *deistvitelnie* ideas: always in action. Never confined, or the opposite: everywhere and always confined by the humanity he knew to be inevitably *viral*— like a concentrated plankton bloom on the oceans. And that was well before informatics, which disseminated this metaphor to give a name to the seduction, the explosion, the infinite memory that precedes us, the cosmic gravitation that will succeed us, the political mobilization, the mutual assistance of social media, and so on—*at the same time as* the destruction of links and people. Dostoyevsky incorporated this virality into his polyphonies. He let his words float so their meanings would be defined indefinitely, choosing them so they would clash with each other, exhausting them, delivering us from them. Terrifying and jubilating contagions and immunities.

The virus called Myshkin, Stavrogin, Ivan and Mitya Karamazov insinuates itself into you (remember the neologism *stushievatsia*),[23] gives you a fever, hampers your breathing, muddles your mind; you hold on, by dint of reading, you find it less absurd, strangely attractive, rather, you tame it well, it makes you more lucid. In the human body, there are a hundred times more viruses (10^{15}) than human cells (10^{12}). How many of the viruses treated by Dostoyevsky are already absorbed-resorbed by the proteins of our readings? Who knows?

9

CHRISTOCENTRISM

O my friend, I would gladly go into penal servitude again . . . just so as to
pay off the debts . . .
    Out of the whole stock of my powers and energy all that's left in my
soul is something disturbing and vague, something close to despair . . .
And meanwhile I keep thinking that I am only just preparing to live. It's
funny, isn't it? Feline vitality.

—Dostoyevsky, Letter to Vrangel, March 31–April 14, 1865

9.1 "Remain with Christ Rather
Than with the Truth"

Dostoyevsky's faith is an ardent Christocentrism, febrile and cosmic.
Kneeling in front of icons, the child prays: "Oh mother of God, keep
me under your protection!" From the start, Jesus is not alone, and his
protection requires *care* in the feminine: a mother or a wet nurse. But
the genius of Christianity has no defense against "new ideas"; as a
result, religious exaltation alternates with torturous atheism. Fyodor
can stand mathematics at the engineering school only by projecting
the essence of Christ, as he sees it, into literary genius: "Homer (a
legendary person incarnated as God, perhaps like Christ, and sent
to us) can be a parallel only to Christ . . . In *The Iliad* Homer gave to
the entire classical world an organization for both spiritual and
earthly life, with absolutely as much force as Christ did for the new
world" (letter to Mikhail, January 1, 1840). Immersed in romanticism, reader of George Sand and Cabet, of Goethe and Schiller, of

Balzac and Hugo, of Helvetius and Proudhon, not forgetting the *Life of Jesus* by David Strauss (1855), the young man sees in socialism only a sort of complement to and a perfecting of Christianism adapted to social and historical transformations.

That is how he justifies to the investigative commission his participation in the Petrashevsky Circle, where he had read, "a total of three times," the *Letter to Gogol* by Vissarion Grigoryevich Belinsky. This great literary critic, while casting no onus on Christ, attacked autocracy, serfdom, and in particular the Church. Recalling Feuerbach, he proclaimed that "atheism is the religion of humanity." He had abruptly made the budding novelist famous by hailing his first book, *Poor Folk*, as "the first Russian social novel." Remembering his youth, Dostoyevsky admits he would have changed and "lost Christ" under the critic's influence. "There remained, however, the radiant personality of Christ himself, which was the most difficult to contend with," he would editorialize many years later in his 1873 *A Writer's Diary* ("Old People").

In fact, incarcerated in the Peter and Paul Fortress, Dostoyevsky asks his brother for "a Bible (both testaments). I need it. But if it's possible to send it, send it in a French translation. And if you'll add a Slavonic one, that will be the height of perfection" (letter to Mikhail, August 27, 1849). This Bible will be stolen from him. And it's the convicts' religion that will return Christ to him. Is it a Christ recovered *as is*, never really lost since childhood and adolescent idealism? Or rather a Christ *re-created* in the abjection of the prison:

> I remembered how, in my childhood, standing in the church, I sometimes looked at the simple folk thickly crowding by the entrance and obsequiously parting before a pair of thick epaulettes, before a fat squire or a spruced-up but extremely pious lady, who unfailingly went to the first places and were ready every moment to fight for them. There, by the entrance, it seemed to me then, they were not praying as we were, they were praying humbly, zealously, bowing to the ground, and with a full awareness of their own lowliness.

Now I, too, had to stand in that same place, and not even in that place; we were shackled and disgraced; everybody shunned us, everybody even seemed to fear us, we were given alms each time, and, I remember, I was somehow even pleased by that, some sort of refined, peculiar sensation told itself in that strange satisfaction. (*Notes from a Dead House*, 1862)

Prison turns into absolute destiny the writer's faith in the God-man whose suffering is consubstantial to his. This *experience* enlightens him, arouses him, and calms him. Along with the vocabulary of Christianism, it summarizes a disposition of thought and language which by adventuring to the outer limits of the speaking subject brings to consciousness the *destructive violence* that accompanies the vital processes and mutates into *jouissance*. Dostoyevsky needed—in the sense that "need" is an appeal to survival—to *invest* in the God-man, to *turn back* the threat of psychical and physical death: his, others,' the people's, and the world's. This at the very moment when libertarian ideologies, resulting from the dismantling of the religious corpus, wagered with Hegel on the dialectic of the Absolute Spirit or predicted the "end of History," of *this* History. The incarcerated writer holds onto this point of contact. Nihilists—men-Gods resulting from this Absolute—speak to him just as much; he projects himself into them, identifies with them, or rejects them. A frantic race for Meaning along with ravaging uncertainty, a revivifying decomposition-recomposition of the spiritual doctrine the writer persists in formulating, in hammering out, definitive.

Liberated, impatient to elucidate his conversion, his first letters to his brother Mikhail ask him to send "historians, economists, *Notes of the Fatherland*, the Church Fathers, and the history of the Church . . . Send me the [Koran], Kant's *Critique of Pure Reason* . . . and Hegel . . . My future is connected to that!" (letter to Mikhail, January 30, 1854). He also calls for a constellation of authors on the origins of Christianism: Plutarch, Diodorus of Sicily, Tacitus, and Flavius Josephus. Did he receive, and did he read, this copious documentation?

Born in the arms of *nyanya* [nanny or nursemaid], revealed in the flagellations of the criminals and their baths, the Dostoyevsky-style

Christ is a personal creation of unprecedented intensity. To be sure, Orthodox Christian dogma foresaw it, calling for the faithful to receive Him into the most intimate depths of the self, multiplying daily prayers and mystical magnitudes which Dostoyevsky eroticizes by breathing life into Him with humility and ardor to the point of crime and punishment in the cruelty of the absurd. Both the fervent destruction of universal human suffering and the perpetual jubilation of the absolute sexuality that writing is for man. Dostoyevsky's Christ, neither a romantic character nor a theological postulate, is an extravagant apotheosis of the inalienable human singularity.

The convict had lived it like a foundational experience in the *katorga* (the penal system) in the company of the other convicts and the Gospel. Marked by this degeneration-regeneration, Saint Dosty's Christ does not become the center of the oeuvre, as Orthodox criticism habitually asserts, and many others in its wake. More fundamentally, Christ remains and radiates in the *pre-*: the original precession, pre-Father and pre-Son or both at the same time. Endowed with interior abundance, equally discreet and capable of plural, contradictory engenderings that do not become fixed in a dominant omnipotence, He ramifies "in beauty." The human face of Christ does not disappear, on the contrary: tensed in the frantic faith of his tortured, criminal characters, it is affirmed on the contrary in the Face of Christ painted on the icons they kiss, in tears.

Because it is precisely by immersing Himself in personalized madness and crime that the Christ of Dostoyevsky becomes the culmination of Christian humanism. He defies the powerful yet in the end lenifying "humanitarism" (Berdyaev's term) that dominates the realism (even when unreal) of nineteenth-century literature, from George Sand to Hugo by way of Dickens. He inscribes into his disruptive Christianism the "metaphysical hysteria of the Russian soul," Berdyaev insists. Not without evoking the accents of Baudelaire's *Flowers of Evil*, in counterpoint to the epic characters in Tolstoy, who charms him with his *Anna Karenina* but whom he brands as "a boy who [belongs to] the placid, middle-stratum Moscow landowning family" (*A Writer's Diary*, January 1877). There remains, in Dostoyevsky, the universality of the demonic, a torturing double of the Christ, original pre-cession as well: a foundational doubling.

As soon as he recovers his liberty, Dostoyevsky explains his Christocentrism in a famous epistolary "confession":

> I have experienced and felt this myself, I'll tell you that at such moments you thirst for faith like "a withered blade of grass," and find it, precisely because the truth shines through clearly in the midst of misfortune. I'll tell you of myself that I have been a child of the age, a child of disbelief and doubt up until now and will be even (I know this) to the grave. What horrible torments this thirst to believe has cost me and continues to cost me, a thirst that is all the stronger in my soul the more negative arguments there are in me. And yet God sometimes sends me moments at which I'm absolutely at peace; at those moments I love and find that I am loved by others, and at such moments I composed for myself a credo in which everything is clear and holy for me. That credo is very simple, here it is: to believe that there is nothing more beautiful, more profound, more attractive, more wise, more courageous and more perfect than Christ, and what's more, I tell myself with jealous love, there cannot be. Moreover, if someone proved to me that Christ were outside the truth, and it *really* were that the truth lay outside Christ, I would prefer to remain with Christ rather than with the truth. (Letter to Natalya Fonvizina, after February 15, 1854)

Albert Camus, post-totalitarian humanist of a decolonization in want of support, echoes this credo, but stays with his mother, imperious call of origins.[1] Not in the least similar to the incandescence of Dostoyevsky's faith.

Never is Dostoyevsky's Jesus called God. The word *resurrection* is mentioned only rarely, and the Trinity does not appear in Dostoyevsky's faith. Could he be a deist? He does slip the name of Voltaire into an article by his friend (then enemy) Nikolai Strakhov. And Ivan Karamazov quotes (without naming him) the deliberately inflammatory author of the maxim, "If God didn't exist, one would have to invent him." Could "the child of disbelief and doubt" be invoking, as "God," a universal, primordial synthesis that humans owe it to themselves to recognize, domesticate, and analyze? All the more so, since without this indispensable presupposition of the immortality of the soul, meaningless existence is reduced to "an infinitely recurring zero," as the man of the *Underground* fumes. "What would I be without God?" Sonya asks Raskolnikov in *Crime and Punishment*.

This "necessity for God," a "felt idea" (as Stavrogin says) and a personal experience, expands and is diffracted in various singular versions throughout the oeuvre. Formulated by Ivan Karamazov as a *conviction*, it turns out to be a *rebellion*. Having decided to no longer wonder if it's man who created God or the reverse, it's the *hypothesis of the Creation* that this "Russian boy" dares to "refuse": "I accept God... It's not God that I do not accept, you understand it is this world of God's"; "I want to forgive, and I want to embrace. I don't want more suffering... Is there in the whole world a being who could and would have the right to forgive?... And where is the harmony, if there is hell?... I don't want harmony, for love of mankind I don't want it. I want to remain with unrequited suffering... It's not that I don't accept God, Alyosha. I just most respectfully return him the ticket."

To the model of the Creation, the Dostoyevsky Christianism opposes a reformulation of the dichotomy that establishes innumerable pairs of oppositions foundational to metaphysics: God-man/man-God, good-evil, joy-suffering, divine-human, God-devil, and so on. His contestation of "humanitarist" atheism is also a matter of a feverish investment into a *personal* doubling, an ardent dialogue summarized as follows in his *Notebooks*: "Even in Europe such force of atheistic *expression* does not now exist *nor did it ever*. Accordingly, it is not like a child that I believe in Christ and profess faith in him, but rather, my *hosanna* has come through the great *crucible of doubt*" (*Notebook XI*, 1880–1881).

His characters engage in mind-blowing theological theorizations about faith whose contradictions, clashes, and revisions multiply their meaning and their resonances to the point of absurdity and laughter, which do not eliminate them but add seriousness to the unnamable. And the fervor of the writing aspirates and saturates the gulf that separates the *dualities* inherent in the very idea of *Creation*. The flood of language in the novels transforms the canonical *dualism* into a cloud of emanations—characters, words, and trials. The author's Christocentrism becomes an achieved Pleroma, a multiverse pluralized from the start in and for the polyphony of the oeuvre.

My reading of Dostoyevsky receives each of its components as so many *turns* or *dispositions* of the God-man and the man-God, whose "felt ideas" structure the indefatigable verbal jousts his speaking heroes engage in, unbeatable probers of the soul.

9.2 The Valentinian Gnosis

Dostoyevsky's Orthodox Christianity, in privileging the sensitive and the unnamable and proceeding by juxtaposing antinomic thoughts which bring out the passionate in the cognitive and the non-being in the being, acts like a recollection of the *Gnosis* ("knowledge," from the Greek), notably the Gnosis of Valentinus (approximately 160 years after Jesus Christ). Even though the primary focus of this gnostic model is the creation of the world and not the creation of *Identity* through *Incarnation*, it posits a divinity putting itself into motion by the play of the contrary forces animating it, engendering an *aeonic plurality* (from *aeon*, "emanation").

The original *duality* internal to God (being and nonbeing) is at the beginning a *nonduality*, since it is internal to him and similar to the contraction/expansion called *tsimtsum* in the Jewish Kabbalah.

This self-movement, the motor of the creation of the world, doesn't imply a *différance* (Derrida, Levinas), in the sense of an *original derivation* (between "creator" and "created"), but an *antecedence*, a precondition, pre-cosmic, and pre-father, a before-beginning, which make any illusory will to coincide with the origin impossible.

In sum, the original *aftereffect* is absorbed in the *before-effect* of the Pleroma (abundance)—a structure that is fallible to begin with because it is becoming plural, and which calls for a restauration that Jesus, the "perfect son of the Pleroma," is charged with. Thus, originally pluralized, the absolute generates its *gnosis*, its knowledge, to be understood as the "way," or the "progression" of an Ego in search of its constitutive Self. And it's only in the *living of the experience*, inseparable from its sensed manifestation, that the "metamorphosis" of the "external man" into the "internal man" operates, in Husserl's phenomenological vocabulary.

The gnostic way can lead to an indifference to the world, to mystical acosmism "without a world," "like a stone."[2] It has been argued that existential ontology (Heidegger) and logical phenomenology (Sartre)—by the "strangeness" of the "thrown being in the world" or on the contrary by "engagement"—also miss this *nondual* point of view and *the plurality of worlds* as an "internal genetic pluralization" of the divine, which in contrast the Valentinian theogony proposes.

On the contrary, without knowledge of cosmic Valentinianism,[3] Dostoyevsky the *theologian* borrows from the *dualism of canonical Orthodox Christianity*, whereas the *novelist*, mobilizing understanding, desire, and pleasure, pushes them into their genesis and self-genesis. With the investment into writing—like the acme of his faith—the degenerated world tends to re-integrate itself in and through the regenerated Pleroma of the work.

9.3 Demoniacal Cleavage

In the original outline of *Demons* (1872), Stavrogin has a Christian dimension before becoming a *demoniacal imposter*. Sneering from the height of the "new thoughts" he will embody throughout the novel, he cries: "Oh, he's no dark spirit! He's simply a nasty, scrofulous little demon with a runny nose, a failure." And he calls Satan a "narrow-minded seminarian" with his "suffering from the 1860s" and his "lackey's education." The *diabolical* becomes the central theme of the concluding encounter between this debauched atheist and Tikhon the "so to speak crazy" mad mystic. Though harassed at night by demons that are nothing but "a certain type of hallucination," the exhausting symptoms of his crazy illness, Stavrogin remains Christian while maintaining that he "believes canonically" in the Devil "without believing in God." Rape and murder, a "jouissance that surpasses anything one can imagine," "the instances of transgression when life is in danger," possess him so truly and so violently that he cannot be rid of them, nor does he want to be.

"Demoniacal possession" and practical Satanism: the atheist calls these annihilations of self and others a *freedom*. Unsustainable for the remnants of Christian consciousness still within him: he thinks he is lost. "If you believe in your demon, you are lost," says Dasha, Shatov's sister. Her love could have saved the inflamed nobleman. He refuses it, because "my love will be as shallow as I am myself, and you will be unhappy." And so he deposits his written confession with that "little old man"—"oh, this priest!"—only to be told that "total atheism is more respectable than worldly indifference" and that "a complete atheist stands on the next-to-last upper step to the most complete faith."

His demons decide otherwise: "If I was stealing something, I would feel, while committing the theft, intoxication from the awareness of the depth of my meanness . . . (and it was all based on consciousness!) . . . I am convinced that I could live my whole life as a monk, despite the animal sensuality I am endowed with and which I have always provoked."

Never has an adept of the Crucified One as pathetically carried the Christian cross as the well-named Stavrogin. The cross (*stavros* in Greek) is engraved in his name. "The basic thought of the document is a strange, sincere need of punishment, need of a cross, of all the people's chastisement. And meanwhile this need of a cross is nonetheless in a man who does not believe in the cross," the author explains.[4]

Stavrogin breaks Tikhon's crucifix. The latter detects "something ridiculous" in this twisted confession, "in the style and in the substance." Tikhon, however "imperfect a believer in God," is not "ashamed of the Lord's cross" and asserts that "demons exist" but "the ways they are conceived can be very diverse." "Cursed psychologist" though he is, the confessor nevertheless gratifies his patient with a trenchant interpretation: "There is in front of you an almost unpassable abyss" (*Demons*, 1872).

Gaping cleavage. Abyss of suicide. Doubling and hanging.

The interiorization of the diabolical reaches its apogee in Ivan Fyodorovich Karamazov's nightmare. He also suffers from hallucinations and doubling, which put him face to face with a visitor. No connection to the fact that "devils show their little horns ... from the other world!" This man who had penetrated, "only God alone knows," and in all the senses of the term, into the interior of the second Karamazov son, was "a certain type of Russian gentleman ... *qui frisait la cinquantaine*" (in French in the text).[5] A figure of the old paternal buffoon, destitute and more than old-fashioned, a *has-been*, we would say now, and on top of it all a sponger, with a shameful debonair manner. This spectral, surreptitiously eroticized nightmare in *The Brothers Karamazov* (1881) follows upon the amorous intimacy between the rapist and the shrink in *Demons* (1872), which facilitates the diabolical confession in Tikhon's cell. The fallen angel and Ivan use the familiar form of address immediately, they insult each other, threaten to strike each other to test each other's reality, and finally become one.

"'Not for a single moment do I take you for the real truth,' Ivan cried, somehow even furiously. 'You are a lie, you are my illness, you are a ghost. Only I don't know how to destroy you, and I see I'll have to suffer through it for a while. You are my hallucination. You're the embodiment of myself, but of just one side of me ... of my thoughts and feelings, but only the most vile and stupid of them. From that angle you could even be interesting to me, if I had time to bother with you.'"

"Fool!" this natural sciences student cries.

"Satan *sum et nihil humanum a me alienum puto*," the devil pontificates.

"You are *me*, me and nothing else!" Ivan resists, managing to reason.

But the Devil surpasses him by launching into philosophy in the rationalistic terms demanded by his host and sends him back to what he knows: "Let's say I'm of one philosophy with you, if you like, that would be correct. *Je pense donc je suis*, I'm quite sure of that, but all the rest around me, all those worlds, God, even Satan himself—for me all that is unproven, whether it exists in itself, or is only my emanation, a consistent development of my *I*, which exists pre-temporally and uniquely."

No way you could be more philosophical than the devil! For Satan to triumph, all he needs is for Ivan to believe in his existence "a tiny bit." Doubt once instilled, even at a minimum, will push the poet of the Grand Inquisitor from faith to disbelief and vice-versa, until a "tiny seed of faith" can give him the desire to "truly be assured of his existence," and he "will dine on locusts" and drag himself "to the desert to seek salvation." Understand that the hermit himself is constrained to penitence just to be rid of the devil and only then to deserve God!

Along the way, the "visitor," having become a "guest," demonstrates that the *negativity* he practices with his destructivity is indispensable to the Creation, and that if he had cried "Hosannah!" when the Word who died on the cross was ascending into heaven, "no [further] events [would] occur." *Ergo*, as the devil takes himself for a shadowy agent of the divine, "such a lackey" can only sow confusion in a young soul in ardent expectation of the "new men." So Ivan blocks his ears while the man spells out his demonstration: "a real muddle set in"; "no one believes it"; "there is no need to destroy anything, one need only destroy the idea of God in mankind, that's where the business should start!"

There follows an avalanche of diabolical perspectives. To begin with: "Once mankind has renounced God, one and all (and I believe that this period, analogous to the geological periods, will come), then the entire old world view will fall of itself. Without anthropophagy, and, above all, the entire former morality . . . Man will be exalted with the spirit of divine, titanic pride, and the man-god will appear. Man, his will and his science no longer limited . . . will accept death proudly and calmly."

Then, in a very distant future: "If it does come... anyone who already knows the truth is permitted to settle things for himself, absolutely as he wishes...'everything is permitted to him'... There is no law for God! Where God stands—there is the place of God! Where I stand, there at once will be the foremost place...'everything is permitted,' and that's that!"

Finally, truth will not even be able to count on the Russian people, god-bearing but hooked on "sanction": "It's all very nice; only if one wants to swindle, why, I wonder, should one also need the sanction of truth? But such is the modern little Russian man: without such a sanction, he doesn't even dare to swindle, so much does he love the truth..."

Ivan is so possessed by his satanic double that he feels his legs and arms bound to the guest sitting on the couch across from him. Until Alyosha makes the intruder disappear by rapping on the window to announce from outside that Smerdyakov the bastard has hung himself. Their half-brother, the son of Stinking Lizaveta, materializes like Ivan's second demon at just the right moment, now indubitably embodied. Ivan is actually the one who had the diabolical idea of parricide, of which he accuses himself at the tribunal. But it is Smerdyakov, his inferior "self," who acts on the universal oedipal desire, in this case the desire of the poet inhabited by the Grand Inquisitor, thus proving the very real existence of the Devil lodged within him. It could drive anyone mad, just as Ivan will be soon.

For the carnivalesque theologian that Dostoyevsky was, the diabolical is thus the hidden face of humans who enjoy destructivity to the point of enjoying crime as well as punishment. Freed from God, we have only to believe in this black desire, the terrifying spirituality of nihilism. Stavrogin hasn't reached that point. The guilt with which he carries his cross condemns him to suicide. And Ivan's philosophical deconstructions do not spare him the poison of his unrequited desires.

But the writer's sardonic laugh does not let his diabolical prey go free. After the "death of God" a strong idea remains: the invincible need to believe... in the Devil, as Ivan evinces, martyrized. Yet the cleverest of atheists, the French, laugh "as Voltaire does, [at] the hoofs and tail and horns": "Disbelief in the devil is a French notion, a frivolous idea," which in denying the power of "the stake, the fire," has weakened "the springs of life!" Lebedev, in *The Idiot* (1868) becomes exasperated and prophesizes: the highly prized "speed of communications" is making "the binding principle" disappear, "everything has grown soft." He has already taken the pose of a refractory editorialist unveiling his nihilistic geopolitics:

> The law of self-destruction and the law of self-preservation are equally powerful in humankind! The devil rules over mankind equally until a time that is not revealed to us.
>
> There must have been an idea more powerful than any disaster, famine, torture, plague, leprosy, and all that hell which mankind could not have borne without that one binding idea which directed men's minds and fertilized the springs of life! Show me anything resembling that power in our age of depravity and railways... I meant to say our age of steamships and railways... Show me a force which binds today's humanity together with half the power it possessed in those centuries. And now dare to tell me that the springs of life have not been weakened and tainted under the "star," this net which ensnares the people. And don't try to browbeat me with your prosperity, your riches, the rarity of famine and the speed of communications! The riches are greater but the force is less; there is no more binding principle; everything has grown soft, everything and everyone grown flabby! We've all grown flabby, all, all of us!

This advocate of obscurantism is confused and aggravating. He doesn't know that the "networks" of more and more rapid communication will be capable of incubating if not stoking devious and arrogant hatred. And that mocking the sacred, with its diabolical emanations, does not deny but rather smiles upon the need to believe and invites it to return to its sensed sources.

10

THE PLEASURES OF EVIL AND MISFORTUNE

do you love the damned?
Say, do you know the irremissible?

—Baudelaire

10.1 "This Good and This Evil of the Devil"

The writer lets Zosima speak to re-create the "astonishment, confusion, and joy" of "a certain spiritual perception." At the age of eight, Fyodor-Zosima has his encounter with Job in "a big book, so big": the Bible. To begin with, God speaks with Satan and lets him take His servant:

And God boasted before Satan, pointing to his great and holy servant. And Satan smiled at God's words. "Hand him over to me and you shall see that your servant will begin to murmur and will curse your name." And God handed over his righteous man, whom he loved so, to Satan, and Satan smote his children and his cattle, and scattered his wealth, all suddenly, as if with divine lightning, and Job rent his garments and threw himself to the ground and cried out: "Naked came I out of my mother's womb, and naked shall I return into the earth: the Lord gave and the Lord has taken away." (*The Brothers Karamazov*, 1881)[1]

Dostoyevsky's Christ seems to be closer to Job than to the One tempted in the desert, the one whom the writer leaves to the Grand Inquisitor. Since St. Augustine, in a struggle against Pelagianism, theology interprets the Devil's temptation of Jesus as a "dialectical mediation" between Good and Evil within the Truth of God and the doctrine of predestination. Dostoyevsky's Christ does not reabsorb the Evil One into grace, far from it, nor does he brand him an inferior demiurge. Reading Job imposes on the writer the experience of *turmoil*, the consubstantial inner lining of *joy*: God-and-Satan at the same time as Satan, indispensable *tension* of the generation-degeneration unity. Evil, in a sense, is *positivized*, as if a stakeholder in divine *power*, which is not reducible to an ordinary power but constitutes the very *essence* of *divine tension*, a potentiality as abundant as it is fallible *with* and *in* its plural manifestations-emanations.

In his feverish confession to Alyosha, and before reading him his great "poem," Ivan Karamazov spouts an enigmatic "Who wants to know this damned good and evil at such a price?" It's not a matter of "going beyond" or "dismantling" the dichotomy of ontotheological values from Plato to Hegel that have grounded and constrained thought. But of making "the Euclidian mind" (says Ivan; terrestrial and transitory, Zosima adds) admit that's "why this drivel is needed and created." "Without it, they say, man could not even have lived on earth, for he would not have known good and evil." Now "knowledge" is not worth "the tears of that little child" for "little Jesus." Suffering, revenge, guilt, redemption, forgiveness: is happiness necessarily built upon "the unjustified blood of a tortured child [which the educators of humanity accept], and having accepted it . . . remain forever happy"?[2]

The compassion of the young philosopher-theologian becomes so exalted on hearing the story of the atrocious tortures inflicted on children that it surreptitiously veers toward a viscous complicity with "the good of the Devil."[3]

Homicide, the more intimate *evil of the Devil*, becomes polarized as feminicide with Raskolnikov.[4] He adheres to it absolutely, an irremissible damnation the student needs to survive: inexpressible *jouissance.* His mother and his sister become indifferent to him, because they are incapable of imagining how necessary the crime is for him. His friend Razumikhin doesn't understand anything either, tries to be useful by preaching redemption through charity. Reasoning cannot comprehend the convulsions of murder. Only the humiliation and suffering of a prostitute, Sonya Marmeladova—exiled from this world like the women inhabited by the Demon, women who had joined Jesus—serve as the depository of "that good and that evil of the Devil" which the assassin considers the nucleus of truth. Which has no access to forgiveness: "Oh, how happy he would have been if he could have blamed himself! He could have tolerated everything, even shame and disgrace! But he judged himself severely, and his embittered conscience could find no particularly terrible guilt in his past, aside from his simple *blunder* [Dostoyevsky's emphasis], which could have happened to anyone . . . But he did not feel remorse for his crime."

Could Dostoyevsky's Christocentrism be *cruel?* N. K. Mikhaylovsky had perceived this black sun against which believers that good triumphs over evil struggled; and which Lev Shestov will scrutinize in his reading of Dostoyevsky with Nietzsche.

Suffering is the cornerstone of Dostoyevsky's faith.[5] Lascivious suffering, "no coldness and no disenchantment, nothing of what Byron made popular," but "a thirst for pleasure, excessive and insatiable. Inextinguishable thirst for life," including "pleasure of theft, of banditry, of suicide." It dictates as the ultimate truth of the Dostoyevskian man a rebellious flesh, which profits from not submitting to the Word that bears it and in which it is constituted. Suffering, irreducible to feelings, since it is a primary affect—with its double face of energetic flux and psychic inscription—appears as the ultimate threshold of differentiation and separation between the subject and the other. *Fear* has an object; *rage* explodes; *hate* sets love ablaze; but *suffering* is the first or the last attempt by the subject to affirm its "selfhood," as close as possible to its threatened biological unity and its psychism in the process of blossoming or collapsing. An exorbitant but retarded violence, suffering caresses the putting-to-death of the Self so the Subject may be born: I am no longer crying, I am speaking *my* suffering.

Suffering is the inner lining of my speaking, of my civilization. Only the loss of Self in the night of the body comes before it. Suffering as the inner lining of consciousness? The epileptic seizure imposes this observation: "A fit at 6 o'clock in the morning (the day and almost the hour of Tropman's execution). I did not feel it, awoke after 8 o'clock, with a feeling that I had had a fit. I had a headache and my body was aching all over. N.B. Altogether, the aftereffects of my fits, i.e., nervousness, shortness of memory, an intensified and foggy, quasi contemplative state, persist longer now than in previous years. They used to pass after three days, while now it may take six. Especially at night, by candlelight, an indefinite *hypochondriac melancholy, and as if a red, bloody shade (not color)* upon everything" (emphasis added). Or: "a nervous laughter, and mystic melancholy," he repeats, an implicit reference to the *acedia* of medieval monks. Or: "How to write?" "Suffer, suffer a lot."

This intimacy with suffering probably led the writer to his vision of man's humanity, a humaneness that resides less in the search for a pleasure or a benefice; rather, it definitively overflows as "beyond the pleasure principle" (Freud), as well as in aspiring for a voluptuous suffering. Suffering, a death drive encapsulated in the energy of speaking it, a sadism hampered by the consciousness that watches over the Self now painful and capriciously pensive: "After all, as a result of those damned laws of consciousness, my spite is subject to chemical disintegration. You look—and the object vanishes, the arguments evaporate, a guilty party can't be identified, the offense ceases to be one and becomes a matter of fate, something like a toothache for which no one's to blame" (*Notes from Underground*).

And finally, this plea for suffering worthy of the "metaphysical animal" who suffers from unsatisfied desire, according to Schopenhauer (1819), precursor to "primary masochism" according to Freud (after 1920): "And why are you so firmly, so triumphantly convinced that only the normal and positive—in short, only well-being is advantageous to man? Doesn't reason ever make mistakes about advantage? After all, perhaps man likes something other than well-being?

Perhaps he loves suffering just as much? Perhaps suffering is just as advantageous to him as well-being? Man sometimes loves suffering terribly, to the point of passion, and that's a fact" (*Notes from Underground*, 1864).

Also very Dostoyevskian is the definition of suffering as an affirmed freedom, as a "caprice": "After all, I'm not standing up for suffering here, nor for well-being, either. I'm standing up for ... my own whim and for its being guaranteed to me whenever necessary. For instance, suffering is not permitted in vaudevilles, that I know. It's also inconceivable in the crystal palace; suffering is doubt and negation ... After all, suffering is the sole cause of consciousness. Although I stated earlier that in my opinion consciousness is man's greatest misfortune, still I know that man loves it and would not exchange it for any other sort of satisfaction" (*Notes from Underground*).

10.2 Expressions of Suffering

Suffering as anthropologically essential. Suffering as psychosomatic pain (the author's epilepsy magnified by Kirillov). Suffering as depression. Raskolnikov describes himself as a sad person: "Listen, Razumikhin ... I gave away all my money ... I'm feeling so glum, so very glum. Just like a woman ... I swear!" And his own mother sees him as a melancholic: "You know, Dunya, I was looking at both of you [Raskolnikov and Dunya]. You're the spit and image of him, not merely in your looks as much as in your souls. You're both melancholic, both moody and hot-tempered, both haughty, and both generous" (*Crime and Punishment*, 1866). Suffering, humility and guilt (*Poor Folk*, 1846). Suffering of the doubled Self, fleeing, persecuted-persecuting (*The Double*, 1846; *The Eternal Husband*, 1870; *The Insulted and Injured*, 1861). Expiatory suffering—Nicolay in *Crime and Punishment*, accusing himself of committing a crime when he's innocent: "Do you know ... what the word 'suffering' means for some of these people? It's not exactly for anyone else, but it's simply 'necessary to suffer.' That means to accept suffering; if it's from the powers that be, so much the better," Porfiry explains. These are revelatory indices of the Dostoyevskian Christocentric humanity. They pulverize Christian humanism by introducing into it . . . crime.

Murdering another person protects against suicide, and the crime appears as a defense against suffering. The act of murder extracts the depressive from passive suffering and despondency. In projecting himself into the only desirable alterity and exteriority—the law of the masters ("to become a Napoleon")—Raskolnikov hopes to escape from the category of "ordinary men" charged with the banal reproduction of the species and accede to the category of the "extraordinaries."[6] These are—ultimate turn of the all-powerful— "people who break the law, destroyers or, judging by their abilities, those predisposed to be so." Without the control of this tyrannical and desirable law (Satan *and* God, the good *and* the evil of the Devil), the *object* of the crime, that "vermin," is only an "accident" of the melancholic "principle" whose goal is identical to its source and is nothing but "myself," definitively.

Who is vermin? Is it the victim of the murder or the melancholy student himself, temporarily exalted as a murderer, but one who knows he is profoundly null and abominable? The confusion remains. With clinical precision, Dostoyevsky makes evident the identification of the depressed man with the hated object: "the old woman was merely an illness . . . I wanted to hurry up and overstep . . . I didn't kill a person, I killed a principle!" "There's only one thing that matters, only one: to be able to dare! . . . Not one person had dared or dares, while bypassing all this absurdity, simply to seize it by the tail and heave it to the devil? I . . . I wanted to *dare* and so I killed . . . I went like a clever man, and that's just what destroyed me! . . . Or that if I posed the question, is a person a louse, then of course that person is not a louse *for me*, but is a louse for someone to whom that question never occurs and who acts without asking questions . . . I wanted, Sonya, to kill without casuistry, to kill for myself, for myself alone! . . . I had to find out then, and find out quickly, whether I was a louse like everyone else or a human being? Could I overstep or not?"

And finally: "I killed myself, not the old woman!" "Therefore, therefore, ultimately I'm a louse ... because I myself, perhaps, am even viler and filthier than that murdered louse."

Wickedness, a distorted version of destructivity, a libidinous mask of evil, has accompanied the novelist since childhood. Could it have begun with the severity of the father shamed by his muzhiks and possibly put to death by them? When the diplomatic courier hits the coachman with blows of his fists, the coachman whips all the harder the horses taking young sixteen-year-old Fyodor from Moscow to Saint Petersburg to prepare for engineering school. The scene returns in *Notes from Underground*: "Whip it! Whip it!" the narrator shouts to the coachman taking him to the brothel, where he is looking for his companions to provoke them in a duel. Then, in a dream, Raskolnikov sees himself as a child alongside his father, who remains impassive in front of raging villagers finishing off an old mare.[7] Was Nietzsche, who read Dostoyevsky, haunted by this scene before going mad?

The erotization of suffering plays a part in the "grand mal" (or "*haut mal*" in old French) epileptic aura: an exaltation of humors that inverses the pain into an incommensurable ecstasy. Kirillov describes it triumphantly in the moments that precede the attack ... and suicide:

There are seconds, they come only five or six at a time, and you suddenly feel the presence of eternal harmony, fully achieved. It is nothing earthly; not that it's heavenly, but man cannot endure it in his earthly state. One must change physically or die. The feeling is clear and indisputable ... This ... this is not tenderheartedness ... You don't really love—oh, what is here is higher than love! What's most frightening is that it's so terribly clear, and there's such joy. If it were longer than five seconds—the soul couldn't endure it and would vanish ... To endure ten seconds one would have to change physically. (*Demons*, 1872)

Recent neurological observations maintain that the feeling of harmony and joy is only an imaginary *afterevent following* the attack itself, which attempts to appropriate as positive the "clear" moment, the bedazzlement provoked by discontinuity (violent discharge of energy, disruption of the neuronal and symbolic sequentiality *in* the seizure). Dostoyevsky may have misdirected the observations of the doctors, who then identified "euphoric periods" among epileptics *before* the seizure, whereas these moments of disruption were only painful, according to Dostoyevsky's notebooks.[8]

Did the epileptic attacks begin in prison? Upon his father's death? Or already, muted and unnoticed, during childhood, as suggested in the late narrative, "The Peasant Marey" (1876)?[9]

10.3 The Body of Evil

Notes from a Dead House (1862), the first "book about camps," exposes a "sincere, natural, and Christian" barbarism, as Tolstoy writes to Strakhov.[10] It will be followed by Chekhov's book about Sakhalin Island (1890–1895), by Tolstoy's *Resurrection* (1899), then by the immense literature about deportations by the Nazis and Stalin, as exemplified a hundred years later in Solzhenitsyn's *One Day in the Life of Ivan Denisovich* (1962).

Perverse, boastful, and rancorous, high on their atrocities and intoxicated with laughter, the convicts grumble, whip and get whipped, get drunk and laugh at their crimes, drink like pigs. In their perverse deliriums and remorseless depravations, their bestial tendencies and imbecilic parricides, these cutthroats of little children for the pleasure of cutting throats nonetheless remain zealous interpreters of the Bible. "What marvelous people!" Dostoyevsky writes to his brother.

Had Kryvtsov raped him? And what about the pedophile convict Ivan Karamazov claims to have met "in a penitentiary"? However, it's not the Karamazov son who lived with these people, who say "We're beaten folk . . . we're all beaten up inside, that's why we shout in our sleep," it's actually Fyodor Mikhailovich.

"I am not exaggerating," the memoirist specifies, "I got to know A—v well. He was an example of what the carnal side of man can come to, unrestrained by any inner norm, any lawfulness." He also knew Gazin, "an enormous, gigantic spider the size of a man," and Orlov: "He looked upon everything from some incredible height." But also the "holy old men" and the "naturally good boys": Sirotkin or Sushilov. Prey to "spasmodic anxieties" (Mochulsky) and with "no feeling of friendship," the "convicts are great dreamers," which is "not the case for free people." But the horror comes to be written, interlaced with the tenderness of fleeting contacts with bodies in the baths and "the particular pleasure" given to him by the "splendid Alei."

The writer shares, is subjected to, and embraces the fate of the prisoners; there is neither a denunciation of the "carceral system" nor a theological forgiveness of sinful humanity. Inside and outside: "never would [the convicts] accept me as a comrade," the freed man reminds us, certain all the same to have attained the "kernel" "as closely as possible and without prejudice." Contemplating for the last time the irons that have fallen from him, he is convinced to have noticed "among the people some traits that one had no idea of." Prison will have been for Dostoyevsky a metaphysical laboratory of freedom and transgression. A resurrection from among the dead.

The experience of the *katorga* is an experience of the *bodies of evil*. *Bodies*, in the plural, like the demon whose "name is legion" (Mark 4:9). The prisoner, reprieved, but only to suffer the social death that is the deprivation of freedoms, fully realizes that it is the "house"— the moral and judicial construction—that is *dead*. Whereas, in this deleterious system, jailed, banished, or deported humanity exists only to deploy destructive violence, a contagious, jubilatory vitality. In the porosity of *freedom* and *death*, in frenetic debauchery and thirst for justice, the diary-writing convict and *his* convicts are sur-vivors who defy the banality of *good* as well as *evil*. By inscribing their criminality in the Passion of Christ, which they implore with "voices abrupt, coarse, but as if pleased at something." This contentment— this beatitude?—of "I don't quite know what" is called *freedom*. Promised, missed, mocked. Immanent.

A few late pages discovered in the writer's archives let us hear the convict's emotions. Not having yet found his voice as a reporter, the convict expresses—with the appropriateness, the intonations, and the syncopated cadence of popular speech—the *saintly misfortune* of walled-in humans whose thirst for freedom is the only thing removing them from their programmed condition as caged dogs:

"Bread we eat to live, but life, that's what's not there! But what is true, essential, capital, that's not there, and the convict knows it will never be there; that is, maybe it will be, one day, but when? . . . like a mockery of a promise. . . ."

"Yes, you're just missing one thing: *just to be free*, just to do whatever your heart desires. . . ."

"Policemen caught some loose dogs one night, about thirty, and they put them, all together, all strong and all alive, in a single pile in a covered cart, and took them to the commissariat. Absurd image, disgusting! You can bet that caused havoc! And the two hundred fifty prisoners in the jail, assembled there against their will, from the entire 'kingdom of Russia'—you live as you like to, don't you, but all together and always behind stakes. Isn't that the same covered cart? Of course not, it's even better. There it's just a dog fight, here these are men. *And man is not a dog.* He's a reasoning being, he understands and he feels—at least a little more than a dog . . ."

"Yes, he understands it, he feels it, that he's lost everything, he feels it fully. Look at him, he's singing songs, if it so happens, but it's for the gallery. A cursed life, a life without a dawn! And it's hard to imagine it, this thing, you have to have lived it, to know!"

"But the simple folk, they know about it, and even without the experience. It's not for nothing that they call the prisoners 'the unfortunate ones,' it's not for nothing that they have forgiven them everything, that they feed them and help them. They know it's not the 'great tortures' that count here; it's the prison, here, 'there's nothing else to say but prison!'—and that's what the convicts themselves say."

In this way a central idea of Dostoyevsky's Christology is announced: the idea of a receptacle, an "unfinished and transitory" container whose terrifying intensity is capable of bearing witness, in this world, to the *immortality of the soul*. It will be the people bearer of God, the "theophoric people," whom Dostoyevsky had anticipated in the Omsk prison, without ceasing to live consubstantially with Him through faith in the Russian Christ (the expression doesn't appear until 1868). Shatov, in *Demons* (1872), venerates the God-bearing people and is assassinated by his nihilistic comrades.

The journalist works to clarify, affirm, and impose his spiritual doctrine, while the novelist prefers to probe, breathe, and explode, crying and laughing about it in the polyphony of the writing.

Eager to elucidate this new existential foundation, the ex-convict elaborates his theological theses all through his correspondence and in the articles he rains upon the reviews *Vremya* (Time) and *Epoch*, which he founded with his brother, then on the very conservative *Citizen*. In the last, he begins to publish a column which will become an autonomous periodical called *A Writer's Diary* starting in 1876. He also publishes in *The Russian Messenger*. An early communicator, convinced and prolific, Dostoyevsky publishes his novels in serials whose successes touch the nerve of a new social power: *opinion*. He emerges, formatted by the *press*, and confers on it a status superior to the status of publishers, creditors, and censorship. The enthusiasm of his literary audience can only confirm the writer's faith in the *God-bearing people* whose movements he senses in the public epiphenomenon.

Dostoyevsky's preparatory *Notebooks*, his correspondence, and his early drafts insist on the religious bearing of his writing, even when compressed, as in the rage of the underground man (1864) who desires "something harmful to himself."[11] "But what can be done! The swinish censors, where I mocked everything and sometimes blasphemed *for the sake of effect*—it was permitted, and where I deduced from all of that the need for faith and Christ—it was prohibited" (letter to Mikhail, March 26, 1864). He makes a claim for the *Orthodox source* of this "power of life" that also underlies, paradoxically, the absence of repentance in Raskolnikov in *Crime and Punishment* (1866). He notes that the "idea of the novel" is an "orthodox conception":

"in what does Orthodoxy lie. There is no happiness in comfort, happiness is purchased at the price of suffering... Man is not born for happiness. Man earns happiness, and this always through suffering. There is no injustice here, for the *calling and consciousness of life* are arrived at by experience pro and contra and one must draw this experience upon one's self (by suffering, such is the law of our planet); but this immediate consciousness, which is felt as a living process, is a joy of such great intensity that one can pay for it by years of suffering" (Dostoyevsky, quoted in Mochulsky).

10.4 The Liberated Man: Troubles, Failures, and Luminous Anchorage

The abyss of doubling—personal experience and Orthodox heritage?—nevertheless continues to seek out and deepen the ultimate development of personality that the *Christlike ideal*, the "embodied ideal of man," remains for Dostoyevsky.

The freed convict's experience of love will have been a string of troubles and failures.[12] A soldier at Semipalatinsk, he marries Mme Isayeva in 1856. The jubilatory torments of the ménage à trois will constantly find their way into the writer's pen, culminating in *The Eternal Husband* (1870). The writer then becomes attracted to a libertarian student who loves his work, the impetuous Apollinaria Suslova, eighteen years younger. They share carnal and literary passions, but in provocation, harshness, and resentment, apparently reciprocated. The emancipation of women? Violent arguments: she, the rebel, said to be "too free in her opinions and who doesn't go to church," aligns with the side of the extremists emerging under the reign of Alexander II; he, steeped in desire and the pleasure of being conquered, paradoxical idealist, rather stuck in the "old" world, crazy slave to the *absolute woman*, describes his "eternal lover" in the guise of Natalia Vassilievna in *The Eternal Husband*, like this: "She was of a passionate, cruel and sensual type. She hated depravity, condemned it with unbelievable violence, and—was depraved herself."

The writer finally turns the page of sadness and misfortune. In 1866 his life gains a luminous anchorage when his editor Mikhail Katkov, director of the review *The Russian Messenger*, sends him Anna Grigoryevna Snitkina, a young stenographer, for the dictation of the manuscript of *The Gambler*. She is twenty, he is forty-five. Anna (1846–1918) is intelligent, gentle, and methodical; her father adored *Poor Folk* (1846). The couple marries in 1867. She accepts the misfortunes of the exalted gambler and succeeds in putting the material life of the genius in order, participates in his work, brings him closer to the church (in addition to the faith), and gives him four children: Sonya, Lyubov, Fyodor, and Alexey (Sonya and Alexey will die as babies), as well as a renewed sense of love. Their correspondence and her *Memoirs* about fourteen years of life together tell of this.

The *Meditation Before the Body of Maria Dmitrievna* (April 16, 1864) remains essential, as it is premonitory of the theses Dostoyevsky develops in his Christocentric anthropology and transfigures in his writing.[13] Starting with this postulate, which falls readily into place: the Christian precept "Love thy neighbor as thyself" is impossible because "the law of individuality on earth is the constraint, 'I' is the stumbling block."[14] What law? What individuality? What *I*?

In embracing crime and punishment, gamblers and demons, doubles and undergrounds, the "Selves" that confront and adjust each other in Dostoyevsky's novels give a presentiment of—or even anticipate—the philosophy and the sciences of man and society, born in the disintegration of the theological continent, that mark the end of the nineteenth century. Medico-legal research unveiled the *Psychopathia sexualis* (1886) underlying madness and crime (Richard von Krafft-Ebing); hysterical conversion (Charcot, 1886), the unconscious (Hartmann, 1868), then the fate of sexual drives, repressed according to Freud, the "murder of the father" called the Oedipus complex, the discovery of the death drive, and so on.[15] These are only some of the stages in the knowledge about psychosexuality, all rigorously constituting the unsustainable identity of the Self. Phenomenology on the one hand and general linguistics on the other support and complete these "epistemological divisions." Dostoyevsky slips in the name of the author of *120 Days of Sodom* (1740–1814) in his characters' conversations, and Turgenev calls him "our Sade," but we will have to wait for Leopold von Sacher-Masoch (1836–1895) before Krafft-Ebing feels he must use the term *sadomasochism*. He was to clarify, or outrageously simplify, those voyages to the end of the pleasures and the senses that bereft humans always demand from arts and letters. Which Dostoyevsky's creatures had already abundantly illustrated.

10.5 The Selves in Perpetual Fusion with the All

Dostoyevsky has no interest in this learned harvest of souls that's being prepared all around. Except to make fun of the psychologists he profiles with the judge Porfiry (*Crime and Punishment*, 1866), or even with the Elder Tikhon (*Demons*, 1872). Or he mocks the hyper-specialized European doctors, modest precursors of our scientific advisors who are managing the pandemic with "statistics" and "big data." The novelist makes no bones about sending them to the devil. Who prophesizes:

> I tell you, the old-fashioned doctor who treated all diseases has completely disappeared, now there are only specialists, and they advertise all the time in the newspapers. If your nose hurts, they send you to Paris . . . go to Vienna . . . I resorted to folk remedies . . . and to no avail. In desperation I wrote to Count Mattei in Milan; he sent me a book and some drops, God help him . . . everything went away. I was absolutely determined to thank him publicly in the newspapers . . . but, imagine, that led to another story: not one publisher would take it! "It would be too retrograde, no one will believe it, *le diable n'existe point.*"[16] They advised me to publish it anonymously . . . "In our day," I said, "what's retrograde is believing in God; but I am the devil, it's all right to believe in me." "We understand," they said . . . "But all the same we can't do it, it might harm our tendency. Or perhaps only as a joke?" Well, I thought, as a joke it wouldn't be very witty.

Not without conceding, just a shade ironically, that "psychology prompts novels even from the most serious people" (*The Brothers Karamazov*, 1881).

It's clear: the Selves that inhabit the man of the carnival are part of a Christology that he constructs as a *novel*. They are not content simply to discuss, to analyze, or even to "transvalue" the theological comments of the *thinker* Dostoyevsky. The widowed Self, unable to love (I'm going back to his *Meditation* about his dead wife), "suffers and calls this state a sin." Whereas Raskolnikov, Myshkin, Stavrogin, Nastasya, the Cripple, Dmitri, Ivan, and Alyosha Karamazov *manage and dismantle* the theologian's "principles" by displaying at will their hallucinations, idiocies, pedophilias, humiliations, suicides, parricides, paradoxes and absurdities, vaudevilles and jubilant shame. These masks of the narrator stem from their innards, often invisible and unnamed because they are in osmosis with the foggy landscapes of wet snow, the winding corridors and the staccato, stitched-together narratives. They participate, body and word, in the universal Passion of Christ, temptation included. They are also the Double. Their capacity to penetrate themselves, to let themselves be penetrated and to penetrate others is an exalted pain; their breathless monologues are jubilantly precise as a result of seeking their way. They aggravate me and grab me, impertinent incarnations of the eternal, absurd Word that gives them pleasure and about which, tenderly, seriously, they couldn't care less. They have joined metaphysics in its *site that is the flesh of words*. And they appropriate it for themselves.

So that the Christology they produce and inject into me progressively as I read them reverses itself into carnival—a pitiless, stupefying withdrawal of meaning. And nothing remains, no salvation, except the vibrant heart of this civilization whose palpitations extend to me. To incite me to *situate myself otherwise*, in a *transverse zone*, neither transcendent nor immanent. Eternal *apprentice* that I am, in the *topology* of writing.

The widower's *Meditation* sketches the argument for this novelistic experience, a turnabout that, facing death, turns around to make "where we are already" infinite (Heidegger, *Question 1*, 1968).[17]

Dostoyevsky had been leading the turnabout since he began writing; it will flourish in the great novels. His "double self," with a conviction made of "all the strength of his nature," though worn down by the impossibility of loving another in full consciousness, finds its *plenitude* only by annihilating itself, by giving the self "wholly to each and every one wholeheartedly and selflessly... In this way the law of the *I* merges with the law of humanism, and in the merging both, both the *I* and the all (in appearance two extreme opposites) mutually annihilated for each other, at that same time each apart attains the highest goal of his individual development." I can hear the post-Hegelian tonality of what psychoanalysis after Freud calls the *Subject*, which is precisely not the Self... For Dostoyevsky, this *smelting*, this *alloy in tension* is nothing but the "synthetic nature," "the paradise of Christ."

Terrestrial humanity can only strive "toward the ideal," but not being able to achieve it by "offering his *I*" in sacrifice for another being "(Masha and I)," he/she feels suffering "which is compensated for by the heavenly joy." As for "the attainment of the final goal," which would be "a full synthesis of all being" of our humanity "in development," "unfinished and transitory," it is "in my judgment... completely senseless." "Only one trait" of this "future character of the future being" was announced in the Gospel: farewell to sexual relations, no more men, women, nothing but angels, and as a consequence, "the family is the most sacred thing of man on earth" (at least in 1864!), but "in the name of the final ideal of his goal, man must continuously deny it."

The man who already knows sexual passion with Apollinaria and burns through his money in the casinos doesn't feel ready to become a "glorious body." Is he already thinking about the "fortuitous families" he will reveal in his novels to come (from the Marmeladovs to the Dolgoruky-Versilovs and the Karamazovs), which today are called "recomposed" families, until they disappear?

The bereaved one, however, calls upon doctrines of "immediate divine emanations," upon gnostic "eons," upon the transfigured god of the Gnosis and the Kabbalah, as well as Proudhon's "messianosis,"[18] explicitly named in the *Meditation*, to weave closed the gap constitutive of split, "unfinished" humanity.

If there is "eternal life for every *I*," if the immortality of the soul exists, it would consequently only be of a "symbolic nature" ("a surprising thing" like Christ, writes the widower). But he believes the soul of the Self is "nature" and "symbolic": both a "physical engenderment" (as between terrestrial generations, where the father "transmits to [the son] a part of his own personal individuality") and a moral memory of the great "developers" or "evildoers" of humanity, as "a part of their natures enters in flesh and in spirit into other people." The skeptical meditator warns, however, that "How each *I* is then resurrected into the general Synthesis is difficult to imagine." "And thus on earth mankind strives toward an ideal *opposed* to his nature."

In any case, the sur-viving man condemned to death can only reject "universal inertia" and the "mechanism of matter" induced by "the confusion and uncertainty" of "rational studies of nature." Like Pascal, he wagers, in his fashion, that "we will be *beings in perpetual fusion with everything*"—"otherwise life is without meaning," "it's death." A lost wager, if "one does not contract a carnal union?" Not necessarily; Dostoyevsky's introspection seems to approach the transhumanism of the twenty-first century: "it is no longer necessary to develop [as the man-woman couple does], to pursue the goal through the succession of generations." The meditator has not yet achieved cloning, digital humanity, and artificial intelligence, but he warns that the future being will not bear the name of man, and only "limited natures" are content to "rest" on the "present conceptions" supported by "infinitely too few facts."

Or could it be possible for the terrestrial and transitory Self to prevent (*ia prepiatstvoviet*) investing its carnal desires in language, and only then to tend toward its "plenitude" in the "synthesis with everything," now infinitely namable?

Raskolnikov, who is not a writer but falls ill, feverish and delirious, prophesizes a viral pandemic. Like a new plague, it falls upon the planet like . . . COVID-19: "During his illness he'd dreamt that the whole world was condemned to fall victim to some terrible, previously unknown pestilence, which was moving toward Europe out of the depths of Asia. Everyone would perish except for a chosen few, very few. *Some kind of new trichina had appeared, and the microscopic organisms settled in human bodies.* But these organisms were creatures endowed with intelligence and will. People who were affected immediately became possessed and insane. *But never, never did these people consider themselves as intelligent and as infallible about the truth as when they were infected. Never did they consider their pronouncements, their scientific conclusions, their moral convictions and beliefs so infallible.* Whole populations, whole towns and nations became infected and went insane. Everyone was anxious, no one understood anyone else, each one thought that truth resided in him alone and, regarding all the others, suffered, beat his chest, wept, and wrung his hands. *They didn't know whom to try and how to judge; they couldn't agree on what constituted good and evil.* They didn't know whom to condemn and whom to acquit. People killed each other in senseless rage . . . Everyone was anxious. They forsook the most ordinary trades because everyone proposed his own ideas and suggestions, and they were unable to agree; agriculture was abandoned. In some places people formed into groups, agreed on something together, and swore not to disband—but immediately they began to do something quite different from what they themselves had just proposed. They began to accuse one another . . . Only a few people in the whole world could be saved; these were the pure and chosen, destined to found a new race of people and a new life, to renew and purify the earth, but no one had ever seen these people, no one had ever heard their words or their voices" (*Crime and Punishment*, 1866).

A materialist who develops this reasoning more extensively in "The Sentence" (*A Writer's Diary*, October 1876), who killed himself out of boredom, considers the human condition "a comedy . . . on Nature's part," which has "so brazenly and unceremoniously inflicted this suffering [that I sentence it] to annihilation, along with me." "Since I am unable to destroy Nature"—but we observe today that man has harmed the ecosystem, and the novelist himself was beginning to warn that humanity had given itself the power to destroy its dwelling—"I am destroying only myself, solely out of the weariness of enduring a tyranny in which there is no guilty party."

Dostoyevsky the thinker formulates his theses while never ceasing to question them, in contrast to the "cast-iron sort of person," who wants to "live at all costs," and to the so-called humanists who "plant in the heart of one who has lost his faith the seed of hatred for humanity." He is affirming "without substantiation," he says, but he does it with fervor: "the thought of a genius [who] already envelops everything and everyone" does not die if and only if it flows from a superior idea, the idea of the immortality of the soul. "Without the conviction of his immortality, the links between the person and the earth are broken . . . and the loss of a higher meaning in life . . . surely brings suicide in its wake."

The *writer*, double of the meditating thinker, proposes the idea "without substantiation" and, with crisis upon crisis, at a loss of self and at the limit of life, transfigures death into the pleasure (*naslajdi-enie*) of the text.

THE NATIONAL CHRIST

... to assume completely the form of the genius of other nations in a
reincarnation that is almost total ... is altogether a Russian [capacity],
a national one.

—*A Writer's Diary*, August 1880

11.1 A Mystical Organism

Could it be that the Church, having become "paralytic," was incapable of revealing and teaching the imperious need for shared passions, for ardent communications? An unconscious resurgence of
the gnostic nonduality between worlds, underlying Orthodox faith?
The eschatological tension that animates the "plenitude" and the
"comedy" of the Dostoyevskian Self cannot be contained within the
contours of the unifying, standardized formula for the "personality"
of the person.

The notion of the *individuum* as a "subsisting relation" ontologi-
cally inherent to the "divine tri-personality" (according to Thomas
Aquinas) is elaborated over time first in the trinitary theology, then
in the Christological theology. And it is in the Christian *personalism*
(after Kant, from Péguy to Berdyaev and Etienne Monnier) that the
notion is reaffirmed in opposition to *individualism* and its avatars in
liberal neocapitalism or its annihilation in totalitarian collectivism,

the "banality of evil" included. "Individuality," "thinking subject," "free individual" in the social contract and guaranteed by State legality, "honnête homme" and "rights of man," the philosophy of the Enlightenment makes it the crucial item in social progress, in moral authority, and the law. After having been discerned, in philosophy, by Husserl's transcendental Ego, the *speaking subject* stemming from the Freudian unconscious was to open the person to reconstruction through the *transference*. For us, viralized, pandemicked, the "person" seems self-evident when it claims "freedom of expression," even if it perverts it—all the more so since we don't really know what it consists of.

But the carceral ordeal—the deprivation of freedom and the massification of the work force—made "the child of disbelief and doubt" discover that he needed a *gateway* to establish, maintain, and develop his immortal soul. That will be the *people of God!* An ontological necessity, clarified at the time of his *Meditation* before Masha's remains, that helps the sufferer not succumb to suicide, murder, debauchery, or the "recurring zero." But by passing through each of the emanations that constitute the plenitude of the people of God,[1] and by letting himself be penetrated by them *all*, so as to be *of them* and only thus embody this plenitude.[2]

The people of God have always been around and more so in Russia, where (ever since Photios Christianized the Rus' people of Kyiv in 867) the community of the faithful crowds under the cupolas, kissing the icons and drowning the prayers in their tears. And they kneel better than elsewhere before this Man of Sorrows, at this end of the nineteenth century, while the descendants of the guillotine and the Supreme Being are already preparing the Belle Époque.

But first the pen of this epileptic Fourierist reprieved in the face of the firing squad, having lost his faith, had to pass through the enclosures, the madness, and the crimes of the convicts praying to the Savior son of God to be able to engender this exuberant sacred emanation, this mystical organism, this explosive promise, this poignant aberration that is Christ as a national god. Such as it is celebrated in Dostoyevsky's *messianic popularism* in his cult of the Russian people: "Every great people believes and must believe, if it wants to survive long, that in it and in it alone is contained the means to save the world; that it lives in order to stand at the head of the nations, to bring them all to communion with it and to lead them, in a harmonious choir, toward the ultimate goal for which they are destined" (A Writer's Diary, 1877). "The Russian mission . . . consists of revealing to the world the Russian Christ, who is unknown to the world and whose principle is contained in our native Orthodoxy. In my opinion, that is the entire essence of our future civilizing and resurrecting of at least all of Europe" (letter to Nikolay Strakhov, March 18, 1869).

The journalist constructs his political religion by glorifying the superiority of the Orthodox "Russian idea" that is already anticipated in 1868: "A great renewal through the Russian idea (which is tightly knit together with Orthodoxy, you're right) is being prepared for the whole world, and that will come to pass in a century or so— that is my passionate belief. But in order for this great matter to come to pass, the Great Russian tribe's *political right* and supremacy over the whole Slavic world has to be realized finally and unquestionably" (letter to Apollon Maykov, February 18, 1868).

From the start, he takes a stance as a defender of Christianism in the face of the "bourgeois solution" proper to the West: "our people are infinitely higher, more noble, more honest, more naïve, more capable, and full of a different, very lofty Christian idea, which Europe, with her sickly Catholicism and stupidly contradictory Lutheranism, does not even understand" (letter to Maykov, December 31, 1867); "the moral essence of our judges, and most importantly of our jurors, is infinitely higher than that of the Europeans: the criminal is viewed in a Christian manner"; "And altogether, all Russian moral notions and the goals of Russians are higher than the European world. We have greater spontaneous and noble faith in good as in Christianity, and not as in the bourgeois resolution of the question of comfort" (letter to Maykov, February 18, 1868).

Buttressed by this messianic national consciousness, found or created, the writer wages war against the anti-Christs; his pen will be his sword ("the sword doctrine," he writes in the *Meditation*).[3]

To the aristocratism of the Slavophiles, who idealize the people and "understand nothing about the realities of the time" in "wanting to liberate the rural commune from the Church and the control of the State," he stands opposed like a *pochvenik* (from *pochva*, "soil, terroir"). A Dostoyevsky of his origins, people would say today. The gambler in European casinos, the writer pursued by his creditors, the Russian wandering through Europe pleads *at the same time* for rootedness in the historical and spiritual loam raised to the level of the ontological "truth" he finds deep inside himself. The immersion in popular faith joins and appropriates for itself—projecting itself into it—the chthonian depths of the insulted and injured, capable of reversing culpability into cruelty. As the sects of the *khlysty* do, the "flagellants," as well as the *strastoterptsy*, impassioned about suffering.[4]

The ecstatic passivity and the flood of tears confer a conventionally feminine aspect on the mystical body of the Russian people as Dostoyevsky sees them. A dimension that recalls the Sophia or gnostic Wisdom, instrument of the separation immanent in the divine Self, revealing the weakness intrinsic to the Creator who generates the multitude of His worldly emanations *only through feminine failure*. The docility, the obedience of the people, their "need for a constant discipline, for a permanent effort of self-control" (which Strakhov points out in commenting on his former friend Dostoyevsky) are not only the remnants of Orthodox paternalism. The "spiritual beauty, resigned and sublime," of Pushkin's Tatiana and of the Russian woman in general, which Dostoyevsky praises in his *Speech on Pushkin*, reaches its paroxysm in the sacrificial resignation of "The Meek One" grasping the icon of Mary: well beyond any "servile appearance," ultimate splendor of the divine Sophia.[5]

The intellectual dynamism of the Occidentalists still attracts the former protégé of Belinsky, but the Christian humanists from the 1840s have become too radical, too liberal, even atheistic. With Chernyshevsky and their paper *The Contemporary*, which also radicalizes, the Russian "intelligentsia" (regrettable neologism) imitates the West, which "has lost Christ." More Slavophile than the Slavophiles, more Occidentalist than the Occidentalists, neither the one nor the other,

both at the same time—Dostoyevsky piles on criticisms and approv-
als. The rifts and the surges in his *religious populism* embody the tensions of Petrine, Petersburgian Russia—as well as the convulsions to
come with the Bolshevik Third Rome, which pushed European universalism toward totalitarianism. They look ahead to globalization
today, in contemporary Russia's ambition to embody tendencies that
are shaking up Europe itself, in the form of an opposition against the
East and against the West. The evangelical credo of the populist writer
hardens the ideologies and the morals stemming from the model of the
Creation. Whereas his novelistic "emanations" encourage interrogat-
ing their promises and ferreting out their latent or current threats
more urgently than ever before.

11.2 The Desire for Europe

Never mind! The Russians' national Christ, in the Dostoyevsky
version, has no need to envy "our values," fraternity and universalism included. It is self-evident that the people of Christ, however
national they may be, are imbued with these values and exalt them.
Of all the peoples, the most European, that is to say authentically
fraternal and universal, is them!

"We Russians have two homelands: our own Russia and Europe . . .
The greatest of all the great missions that the Russians realize lies
ahead of them is the common human mission; it is service to humanity as a whole, not merely to Russia, not merely to the Slavs, but to
humanity as a whole . . . Universality is the most important personal
characteristic and purpose of the Russian . . . Many, very many of the
things we took from Europe and transplanted in our own soil . . . were
inoculated into our organism, into our very flesh and blood . . . Every
European poet, thinker, and humanitarian is more clearly and more
intimately understood and received in Russia than he is in any other
country in the world save his own. Shakespeare, Byron, Walter Scott,
Dickens are more akin to the Russians and better understood by
them than they are by the Germans, for example . . . When the French
Convention of 1793 bestowed honorary citizenship *Au poète allemand,*

Schiller, l'ami de l'humanité, it did something admirable, grand and prophetic; yet it did not even suspect that at the other end of Europe, in barbaric Russia, that same Schiller was far more 'national' and far more familiar to the Russian barbarians than he was to France" ("The Death of George Sand," *A Writer's Diary,* June 1876).

Although Europe succumbs to the Antichrist, to Paxton's Crystal Palace (the Universal Exposition in London, 1859–1862), to the reign of money, to pauperization and mediocrity, to anarchists and mad communards, the desire for Europe still gnaws at the convict from Omsk: "they aren't free in the sense we are. Filled with my Russian concern for the world I was the only man in Europe then who was free. It's a strange fact, my boy: in order to serve mankind as a whole and even just France for that matter, a Frenchman must remain thoroughly French. And the same goes for an Englishman or a German. Only a Russian—even as of today, that is, long before the existence of the ideal of universality—can reach his utmost Russian essence solely when he also feels completely European. And this is the most important difference between us and all the others, for we are different from the rest. In France I'm a Frenchman; with a German I'm a German; and faced with an ancient Greek, I would feel like a Hellene. And this way I, a true Russian, am serving Russia best by incarnating her basic idea . . . To a Russian, Europe is just as dear as Russia and every stone there is precious to him. Europe has always been our homeland as much as Russia. In a way, even more so!" (*The Adolescent,* 1875). "Do you know the many tears we shed and the pangs of heart we suffer at the fate of this dear and *native* country, and how frightened we are by the storm clouds that are ever gathering on her horizon?" (*A Writer's Diary,* 1877).

11.3 "A Great People . . . to the Exception of the Others"

In *Demons* (1872), the unfortunate Shatov attributes the idea of the "god-bearing nation" to the "main thought" of Stavrogin, the pedophile nobleman who commits suicide, but Stavrogin could care less and doesn't really recognize his own words, suspecting Slavophile drivel. Shatov carries the idea to its fundamentalist excess in asserting, "as if reciting line by line," that "not one nation has ever set itself up on the principles of science and reason" but that "nations are formed and moved by another ruling and dominating force," quite different (irrational, it is understood), "whose origin is unknown and inexplicable."

You would think you are hearing a *führer*, a *duce*, a generalissimo, or a future supreme calif awakening in the ardent soul of this student born a serf (*carnaval oblige!*) whose gaze "seemed to be ashamed of something." For him, the people are a nondual power, as it should be with Dostoyevsky:[6] both an unquenchable *desire* to arrive at the end and, at the same time, a *negation of all ends* and of all "notions of good and evil," even though each populace possesses its own. In sum, the Spirit of life, even the "rivers of living water," but in the context and meaning of the Apocalypse: both life drive and death drive. This "movement," this "research," this "faith" have a goal: God, which is to say, "the synthetic person of the whole nation, taken from its beginning and to its end."

There is no reducing of God here to the rank of "attribute of nationality," as Stavrogin suspects, with a grimace. On the contrary: "I raise the nation up to God," proclaims the brother of Daria, the ward of Mme Stavrogina who has promised her to her admirer Stepan Trofimovich Verkhovensky. "The nation is the body of God. Any nation is a nation only as long as it has its own particular God and rules out all other gods in the world with no conciliation; as long as it believes that through its God it will be victorious and will drive all other gods from the world . . . There is no going against the fact. The Jews lived only to wait for the true God, and left the true God to the world. The Greeks deified nature, and bequeathed the world their religion, that is, philosophy and art. Rome deified the nation in the state, and bequeathed the state to the nations."

Could French atheism have more "bearing" than Catholicism? Shatov would like to believe it: "France, throughout her whole long history, has simply been the embodiment and development of the idea of the Roman God, and if she has finally flung her Roman God down into the abyss and plunged into atheism, which for the time being they call socialism, that is solely because *atheism is, after all, health-ier than Roman Catholicism*" (emphasis added). A remarkable landing for the carnivalesque theologian.

In conclusion: "If a great nation does not believe that the truth is in it alone (precisely in it alone, and that exclusively) . . . then it at once ceases to be a great nation, and at once turns into ethnographic material and not a great nation . . . Any that loses this faith is no longer a nation" (*Demons*, 1872).

Should Shatov's ideas, revolving around the "god-bearing people," be swept away as their author's was, the liquidation of which was to give the signal for the revolution? Yes, in one sense, and not only. Shatov's "half-science," "insatiable desire," "strength" huddling in "the idea of good and evil" that each nation erects intransigently, this faith in a *God embodied in the nation* preoccupies the publicist as well as the writer. Moral principle or aesthetic principle? A logic turned into a passion, rather. Thus Dostoyevsky opens a page for the phenomenology of the future, inspired by Hegel who identifies the "strength on the back of the concept," or Husserl who unfolds the "pre-predicative sphere" of the transcendental Ego.

Two secondary characters in *The Adolescent*, Kraft (German for "strength") and Vasin take on the "narrow idea of patriotism": "The trouble is that Kraft's conviction is not simply based on logic but rather is a logical conclusion transmuted into an emotional belief. People aren't all the same. In some people a logical conclusion may be transformed into the most violent passion, which often gets hold of the entire personality and becomes very difficult to overcome or even to alter. In order to cure such a man, it is necessary to change that emotional creed, which can only be done by replacing it by another creed, equally absorbing. And that's always difficult to achieve, in many cases impossible." Impossible? Not for the writer, who knows how to breathe his most unfathomable *affects* into "common" (or not) *ideas*. And then, "beyond your confining horizon there are infinite spaces" (*The Adolescent*, 1875).

And yet, the vocation of the *theophoric people* as sole bearer of God, wanting to assimilate the entire world to its idea in a devouring proselytism, remains quite embarrassing. Logically, necessarily, and insatiably, the single-mindedness of this Russian movement should be confronted with the idea of the *chosen people*. An anti-Semitic blindness of the theologian, whose carnivalesque writing alleviates but does not suppress it.[7]

II.4 The Golden Age of the "Russian Type" and the "Jewish Question"

The novelist passes the baton to Andrey Petrovich Versilov, "Russian nobleman" and "philosophical deist," a "peaceful man [seeking only] peace," "the general reconciliation of all existing ideas" (*The Adolescent*, 1875).

Half-ironic, half-bitter, Versilov defines himself as "the only European" who "can reach his utmost Russian essence solely when he also feels completely European," and he proclaims Russian messianism. He is proud to belong to a "Russian type," a "cultural type"—"no more than a thousand representatives of that type." Roaming around Europe, he has already observed the sovereigntist stiffening of Western nationalisms: "they're still too German and too French and they haven't yet finished playing these roles." "Their thoughts and feelings are no longer the same and they no longer treasure their own ancient stones"—and the proof is, they savagely massacred the Tuileries. "Only Russia exists not just for her own sake but for the idea she embodies . . . for Europe" (*The Adolescent*, 1875).

The "nation bearing God" that the feverish muzhik professed is transfigured into a Russian *cultural exception* that relies on "men who remain alone," on the "orphans" of immortality and of God: "We are the bearers of the idea, my dear boy," the genetic father teaches his son Arkady.[8]

In counterpoint to the hustle and bustle of his "accidental family," Versilov holds onto a Christian humanist vision. His aristocratic Russianness does not align with the *dvorianstvo* (from *dvor*, "court"); this Europeanized nobleman has broken with the courtiers taken with feudal power, or more broadly social power. The *idea* he is nostalgic about is the idea of Good, of which the saintly image (*obraz*) is the supreme source; but the only one who can possess it is the "beautiful type" (*blagoobranznii*) issuing from nobility by birth, by ancestry (*blagorodstro*). Versilov well knows that this beautiful type no longer exists, and his "naïve exclamation" makes the adolescent laugh, but the universal Russian, Dostoyevsky-style, doesn't give in: "I'm not talking just of myself, I'm talking about the whole Russian way of thinking," because it embodies and bears "universal suffering for everyone." "Russia has existed in order to produce that thousand men," and he announces, in tears, the "first" or the "last day of European humanity."

Thus "gnawed by the nostalgia for the present," this *citizen of the world*, who anticipates the hardiest promises of globalized beneficence and claims to be able to resorb evil in all its forms, is nevertheless stopped by an irreducible rival: the other people of God, the first. Fascinating and envied, feared, detested. Interminable Apocalypse: "*Un beau matin*, despite all their 'balanced budgets' and 'absence of deficits,' all the governments will get so hopelessly bogged down in their debts that they'll decide to suspend payment and declare themselves bankrupt. Of course, the conservative elements...will be opposed to that declaration because they'll be the shareholders and the creditors of the governments. Then there'll be what we may call a general fermentation: Jews will appear all over the place and Jewish rule will begin...and the struggle will begin...Well, then, after seventy-seven defeats, the beggars will wipe out the shareholders, take their shares away from them, and, of course, become shareholders themselves. Perhaps they'll introduce some innovations, and perhaps they won't. Most likely they'll go bankrupt too. Well, that's as much as I can guess about the future that will change the face of this world of ours. But I suppose I could refer you to the Apocalypse..."

Dostoyevsky's *A Writer's Diary* (March 1877) returns to the "Jewish question" and discusses it in a tone that seeks to appear calm. The publicist's reflections abound in "hatelove" projections on the part of the "people bearers of God" against the "chosen people," alternating between "the for and the against," dwelling on the "*status in statu*," and granting a final, resounding "but long live Brotherhood."

A brother in God with the Israelites, the journalist recognizes their "special, strict, internal makeup" which has constituted "a civilization of forty centuries," "the most rigorous the world has known," as a *status in statu*. Its source is not "the instinct for conservation," indispensable for protection against persecution, as certain superficial approaches have it. But "a certain idea that has a motive power and an attraction . . . on which, perhaps, humanity is still incapable of pronouncing its last word" and whose "predominantly religious character" goes back to "their Providence, under the former, original name of Jehovah." "Besides, it's impossible . . . even to imagine a Jew without God; moreover, I don't believe that there are godless people among educated Jews either: they are all of the same essence, and Lord only knows what the world can expect from these educated Jews!" Be that as it may: "We are talking about the whole and its idea; we are talking about *Yidism* and about the *idea of the Yids*, which is creeping over the whole world in place of 'unsuccessful' Christianity . . ."

"The Russian at least, has no (absolutely no) religious hatred for the Jew." Unless he innocently projects it onto an invading, dominant Israelite: "What if, for some reason, our rural commune, which defends our poor, native peasant . . . should collapse? What if the Jews should descend like a horde upon that liberated peasant who has so little experience, who is so little able to restrain himself from temptation . . . Why, that would be the end of him at once: all his possessions, all his strength would tomorrow pass into the hands of the Jew, and an era would begin that could not be compared with serfdom, or even with the Tatar yoke."

Moved by an ecumenical charity, the polemicist sets aside "the perennial 'resentful affliction' of the Jews toward the tribe of Russians [which may arise from] a prejudice, a 'historical tumor,' *and is not buried among some far deeper mysteries of their law and their makeup*." And he nevertheless hopes that one might "take still more steps forward on the Russian side" for "the complete broadening of the rights of the Jewish race" and for "a complete brotherhood." Which does not prevent the last letters and the *Notebook* of 1880 from denouncing the Jews supporting the nihilists, the bank, and socialism (Lassalle and Karl Marx), because they have "everything to gain from every radical cataclysm and coup d'état" (quoted in Goldstein).

Prophet of "illiberal misfortune," could Dostoyevsky be anticipating the Holocaust? "*The Yids*. And even were they to hold sway over all Russia—with their *kahal* and machinations—and suck the Russian muzhik dry; oh, no, don't breathe a word about it! Otherwise, some *illiberal misfortune* may occur. What won't people say then! That we consider our religion superior to Judaism and oppress them out of religious intolerance. And then what would happen? You can just imagine what would happen!" (quoted in Goldstein).

A pitiable failure of the novelistic genius? And a prophetic, unconscious revelation of the structural gaps and failures inherent in universalist monotheism, which encourage its nihilistic, materialistic, and today technicist derivations to commit crimes.[9]

The theologian of ecumenism Vladimir Solovyov (*Three Speeches on Dostoyevsky*, 1899), who accompanied his friend Dostoyevsky to the Optina monastery, proposes a different vision of the Apocalypse of St. John: he bets on the revolt of the Jews!

The *Antichrist*, having become the universal emperor (with the complicity of the Jews), claims to synthesize the three Christian faiths, of which there remain only three true believers: a Catholic (the pope), a Protestant, and an Orthodox. Scarcely had he declared himself the supreme divinity of the universe "when a new trouble came upon him from a side which nobody had expected: the Jews rose against him." "The boundless and fervent devotion to the savior of Israel, the promised Messiah, gave place to as boundless and as fervent a hatred of the wily deceiver, the impudent impostor [the Antichrist]," Solovyov concludes.

As for the carnivalesque theologian, has he gone astray in the "thirst for sociality" that the novelist attributes to Versilov? His theses betray the theological convulsions of a Christianity at bay, not a "sentimental" one (as Konstantin Leontiev assesses it). But the energy of the vital combat, the *magnum opus* of the novelist, is not in an idyllic reconciliation beyond the destructiveness of apocalypse. It flourishes in the polyphonic dissonance of the writing.[10]

12

CATHOLICISM, ATHEISM, NIHILISM

Socialism must be atheism in its essence.

—Shatov in *Demons*

12.1 Political Religion

The sword thus sharpened attacks two targets as abhorred as they are fascinating: Catholic decadence and the poison of nihilism.

Returning to the homeland in 1871, the author of *Demons* (which is starting to appear as a serial) meets Prince Meshchersky, owner of *The Citizen*, a weekly on the right (aligned with *The Russian Messenger* from Moscow). He becomes its director and meets a collaborator on the review, Konstantin Pobedonostsev, senator, State councilor, and future general procurator of the Holy Synod. Under reciprocal influences and ascendencies, the two men become very "close friends," which continues after Dostoyevsky's departure from *The Citizen*. From their conversations, as Anna Grigoryevna, wife of the author, writes, "he derived keen intellectual enjoyment." "which endured to the day of his death." With censorship gone, the great novelist of the nation has his column, "A Writer's Diary," in each issue of *The Citizen*.

Pobedonostsev brings him into the family of Tsar Alexander II, and the reprieved conspirer is appointed preceptor of the tsarevich.

Konstantin, younger by six years, becomes the symbolic father of Fyodor, who is pleased to play the part of the enthusiastic but dignified adolescent. He remains on his guard, maintaining his "artistic points of view" in the face of the canonical positions of the general procurator, guarantor of Orthodox theology. The *Writer's Diary*, however, shows that a progressive rapprochement occurs between their convictions ("our convictions, dare I say it!" Dostoyevsky emphasizes in a letter to his wife) about faith, the Church, the Vatican, and the "European ideas" of the "nihilist" Peter the Great.

The two friends agree that the fall of Europe is due to the "sin of Rome" which "perverted the image of Christ," and that Catholicism, in transforming itself into socialism, is preparing a "monstrous plot" aiming to "restore Rome!" The article "Three Ideas" in *A Writer's Diary* details the historical and spiritual moments that lead to this observation.

First, caesaropapism, inherited from the Latin empire, tends to impose upon the world a "universal union," a centralized political unity, under the artificial and despotic iron rule of the Vatican. In all seriousness, Dostoyevsky considers French socialism and the Republican motto *Liberté, Égalité, Fraternité* as "the truest and direct continuation of the Catholic idea": "this France, who developed from the ideas of 1789 her own particular French socialism—i.e., the pacification and organization of human society without Christ and outside of Christ, as Catholicism tried but was unable to organize it in Christ, [is] completely contaminated by the spirit and the letter of Catholicism, proclaiming through the mouths of its confirmed atheists: *Liberté, Égalité, Fraternité—ou la mort*, i.e., exactly as the pope himself would have proclaimed had he been compelled to proclaim and formulate a Catholic *liberté, égalité, fraternité* in his style and in his spirit—the actual style and spirit of a pope of the Middle Ages . . . For French socialism is nothing other than the *compulsory* union of humanity, an idea that derived from ancient Rome and that was subsequently preserved completely in Catholicism" (*A Writer's Diary*, January 1877).

This provocative persiflage of pyramidal Republican Jacobinism, blamed on its Latin genealogy, will lead the writer into a passionate rage against the Conventionnels and even the Communards supposedly "infected" with popeism and despotism. The author of *Demons* fails to grasp the Rightful State and the anti-popeism of Voltaire, author of *Fanaticism or Mahomet the Prophet*. He is far from imagining that the "ardent Revolutionary protest," "neither God nor master!" was clearing the way for the always vigilant and unassimilable French *laïcité*.

Dostoyevsky borrows, accentuates, and rationalizes the fascinating repulsion he felt as a European traveler at "Catholicism, Jesuitism, and aristocratism" breathing into Poland "an antipopular, anti-civic, and anti-Christian spirit." And he vigorously denounces this "Catholic propaganda poking its nose into everything, persistent and tireless" (*Winter Notes on Summer Impressions*, 1862). The author had long associated Catholicism with socialism: "Only socialism grew out of Catholic Christianity; brotherhood will grow out of ours"; and this other extravagant rejection of socialism: "Socialism is founded on disrespect for mankind (the herd instinct)" (*Notebook II*, 1863–1864).

In antithesis of the Catholic idea in France, "condemned and waiting in great torment and perplexity," a second one, coming from Protestantism, opposes the German *refusal* to the tyranny of *unity*: the independence of "each person for themselves," that is, a pitiful "atomization" which leads to bourgeois Anglo-Saxon individualism, a secret garden for growing atheism.

Faithful to the "image" of Christ and capable of engendering a "Russian socialism" imbued with fraternity, only the third idea, the Russian Orthodox one, can forge a way out of the apocalyptic fate: "Take a closer look at Orthodoxy: it is by no means only clericalism and ritual; it is a living feeling that our People have transformed into one of those basic living forces without which nations cannot survive" (*A Writer's Diary*, September 1876). "The overwhelming majority of the Russian People are Orthodox and live completely by the idea of Orthodoxy... *In essence* there is nothing at all in our People apart from this 'idea,' and everything stems from it alone" (*A Writer's Diary*, January 1881). The greatest mistake of the liberals and the progressists would be to underestimate this factor, to "not recognize the existence of the church among the Russian People. I am speaking now not about church buildings and not about sermons; I am speaking about our Russian 'socialism'... [about] the ceaseless longing, which has always been inherent in the Russian People, for a great, general, universal union of fellowship in the name of Christ. And if this union does not yet exist, if the church has not yet been fully established—not merely in prayers alone, but in fact—the instinct for this church and the ceaseless longing for it—sometimes even quite unconscious—is still certainly to be found in the hearts of the millions of our People. It is not in communism, not in mechanical forms that we find the socialism of the Russian People: they believe that salvation is ultimately to be found only in *worldwide union in the name of Christ*. That is our Russian Socialism!" (*A Writer's Diary*, January 1881).

So the universalist national religion flourishes as its adversary crystalizes: political universality of Catholicism, of the Vatican, and of the communist International! A conspiracy is already under way, it is the pope's, with "his army of twenty thousand Jesuit combatants, expert at capturing souls," and which could only be reborn in the face of (and with) Karl Marx and Bakunin: "Catholicism knows very well, when it's needed, how to make concessions, consent to everything! But what harm is there in assuring the poor, ignorant people that communism and Christianity are one and the same, and that Christ has always said so? Are there not socialists, intelligent and aware, even, who are already persuaded that the one or the other is the same thing, and who seriously take the Antichrist for Christ?" (*The Citizen*, October 1873).

However, "the evil spirit of revolution," like a satanic double of the Roman idea of universal domination, which can only engender a "general state of insecurity, anxiety, and fatigue" and "increase the number of dissatisfied and furious people" (Pobedonostsev), is already under way.[1] "The new society will *indubitably* triumph, in that it *alone* brings a new positive idea, in that it is the only issue predestined for all of Europe. There is not the least doubt about it. The world will be saved only after having been visited by the evil spirit... And the evil spirit is close by—our children may see it" (*The Citizen*, October 1873).

And the editorialist never stops predicting Orthodoxy's salvation of the "Russian People" and "all humanity": "And perhaps the principal, preordained mission of the Russian People, within the destiny of humanity as a whole, is simply to preserve within it this divine image of Christ in all its purity, and when the time comes, to reveal this image to a world that has lost its way!"

A feint to please the general procurator, get the censors on his side, save the work? Possibly, maybe to begin with. But the double gets taken in, the gambler plunges in, it's a stimulating lash of the whip on the hide of good sense.

Absurdities, theological-political hypnosis? No doubt. With this caustic vision of the *unthought* in current and future political ideologies, the author of *Demons* (1872) discovers and denounces political religion.

The *political* religion of National Socialism, of National Populism, of Fundamentalism, and, in a more dissimulated manner, of Communism as "engineer of the soul" has unraveled, among internauts, into a sort of myth of paradise on earth: immediate happiness and satisfaction, consumerism and social advantages guaranteed. Everyone saved "by bread," which has taken the place of miracles, as Ivan Karamazov's Grand Inquisitor abbreviates it. Ideologies have been constructed and have prospered by seizing hold of the *need to believe* proper to the Man-God, persuaded by the old patriarchal aspiration toward the Absolute, itself supported by the Sovereign pontiff and his terrestrial declinations in Father of the People, *führer, duce,* caesaropapism, brown, red, or black, presidents and even general secretaries of central committees or not ... resulting, yesterday, but still today, in fratricidal, racial, or class struggles, feminicides, infanticides, and so on—more and more armed with ecocidal technologies.

As events progress—the Catholics having taken a position in favor of the Turks in the Russo-Turkish war—Dostoyevsky seems to let himself be impressed: "Roman Catholicism is far from being a vanquished enemy ... its vital powers are phenomenal." And he envisions that only an "all-European war ... will resolve the thousand-year question of

Roman Catholicism, and...a reborn Eastern Christianity will take its place."

The Catholic plot to conquer the world would therefore match that of the atheistic and socialistic Enlightenment—without a Church and without Christ, two faces of the same "anthill." Dostoyevsky's thinking is in line with that of his friend, the young, inspired theologian Vladimir Solovyov, who has been compared to his contemporary, the British cardinal John Henry Newman,[2] when Solovyov denounces "the European socialists [who] demand the forced reduction to the lowest common denominator, so there will remain only satisfied and content workers; they require that the State and society be reduced to the role of simple economical association." Only the high spirituality of Russian socialism can face the challenge and raise the moral level of the Church, and "found a spiritual fraternity, even while preserving social inequality. It requires the spiritualization of the political and social regime, which should embody the truth and the life of Christ."[3]

In discussion with the monk Paissy, Ivan Karamazov inscribes this inspiration in a project that sounds today like a scathing fundamentalist threat: "the Church should contain in itself the whole state and not merely occupy a certain corner of it."

Shatov, before being liquidated, is tasked with taking up this cross again in *Demons* (1872) while attributing it to Stavrogin, who still doesn't find his way there. It's a method among others, novelistic ones, that the writer grants himself to make his own political message pass, though he pulverizes it. Was he giving the reader to understand the ungraspable authenticity of the nihilist martyr? Or did he want to take his distance from his ravaging fanaticism, relativize it, laugh at it? A carnival of Catholicism, of atheism, neither the one nor the other, both at once—up to readers to make their religion out of it, their way.

12.2 The Prophet and the Citizen

I read these lines tracing a faith, its bounds and rebounds, ways, his voice, I hear it, it vibrates, catches fire, goes out...ellipses, and let it explode ... This is not Céline's catastrophic opera, Godless apocalypse and "let nothing exist" ... Dostoyevsky's deluge is an invocation of the invisible that he is not looking for ... he has found it ... he has discovered that sex (which is not pornography) is in the language ... It's the sex of language ... it haunts it ... the drive seeking to say it ... the desire to the death to say it ... it haunts ... it harangues ... it is said and it is contradicted, it charges, it discharges and it threatens ... the doors and the arguments, the links and life ... it huffs, it rolls, and it grabs ... it grabs me ... it aggravates me ... it's too much ... it's that all the same ... injury or magic ... I'm with it.

This *Diary* is a vocal score. The novel orchestrates polyphonies. Dostoyevsky does his Beethoven. The orator with the muffled voice transcends himself as a one-man orchestra in his famous *Speech on Pushkin*, given on June 8, 1880, at the solemn session of the Society of Friends of Russian Literature. It makes the hysterical crowd delirious: "No, Anya, no, you can never conceive of and imagine the effect that it produced! ... I was stopped by thunderous applause on absolutely every page, and sometimes at every sentence ... When I spoke at the end, however, of *the universal unity* of people, the hall was as though in hysteria. When I concluded—I won't tell you about the roar, the outcry of rapture: strangers among the audience wept, sobbed, embraced each other and *swore to one another to be better* ... The meeting's order was violated: everyone rushed toward the platform to see me: highborn ladies, female students, state secretaries, students— they all hugged me and kissed me ... The calls continued for a half an hour; people waved handkerchiefs ...'Prophet, prophet!' people in the crowd shouted. Turgenev, for whom I put in a good word in my speech, rushed to embrace me with tears. Annenkov ran up to shake my hand ...'You're a genius, you're more than a genius!' they both told me" (letter to Anna Dostoyevskya, June 8, 1880).

But his *Diary* is not a personal notepad, it is intended to *profile* the citizen in the public square, in the *news*, the facts and events, to comment and argue his visions and his theses to make them public, publish them, publicize them: *make them sell.* Like Dickens, Dostoyevsky published his novels in serial form. But in contrast to Dickens, who in *establishing* it *constructed* a psychosociology of Victorian England,

Dostoyevsky electrified prerevolutionary Russia in linking the quest for meaning (which he believed in) to the affective underground, which escaped him. His national Christ is also not the *Deus sive Populus* of Joseph de Maistre. He does not possess the scholastic bones of the French providentialist and sovereigntist professing the power *emanating* from God and the *formal* acquiescence of man, nor the satanic bedazzlement of his style.

When the Russian gambler *identifies* the people with the Church, the protective mother, it's the Russian language that invites him to do so. In hearing an echo of the cross (*krest*) in the word *krestianin* ("peasant"), it amalgamates Christ with the earthbound community of the *krestianstvo*, the peasantry. The principles of spirituality thunder and disperse in the dialogic phraseology of the thinker, and the hypnotic ardor of the columnist passes the role of testimony to the passions of the novelist. To make people hear the heretical accents of his original Christianism, its polyphonic plenitude.

Neither the novel *Atheism*, planned for 1868, nor *The Life of a Great Sinner*, intended for 1869, will see the light of day. The torments of the publicist's faith entail the interminable orchestration of his *theses* in Christian anthropology and political religion. These theses sustain his *jouissance* (always this *naslajdienie*) in speaking of them, repeating them, and contradicting them—the only way to leave open the "madness of the Cross," the need to believe, and the sensual quest of the unspeakable that defines "the strength of the Karamazovian baseness." For the novelist (without having read Nietzsche, who did read Dostoyevsky) *saw the death of God* in the Holbein painting and hasn't stopped coddling his own: body and soul, epilepsy and gallows, penal colony, cruel losses of family—father, son, daughter . . . He is probing this moment, this experience—the sole and unique enigma. Enigmatic like the mark he makes: the tear, the in-between, the double, interminable approximation of the void. In epilepsy and cleavage.[4]

Sur-vival can only play at speaking and writing these. Before and beyond worlds and their institutions, religions, rebellions. Beginning with the beginning: engenderment, the father and the son, *hic et nunc*. The nuclear soil of the family, including the underground.

"Accidental" family or not, "everyone wants to kill the father!" It's Ivan Karamazov who says that. We are in 1880, and Freud discovers the Oedipus complex only in 1910 ("On a Particular Type of Object Choice in Man"). To kill the father: the Father, the Creator, God, in the end.

12.3 Did You Say Atheism?

Shatov himself (*Demons*),[5] the fervent apostle of the "theophoric people," convinced that there is no Russian atheist (as there is no Jew without God, according to Dostoyevsky's "Jewish Question"), is not very sure of believing in God. He believes in Russia, in Orthodoxy, in the body of Christ; he believes the "second coming [of Jesus]" will take place in Russia . . .

"But in God? In God?" Stavrogin, his master in atheism, insists.

"I . . . I will believe in God."

With his "extraordinary aptitude for crime," the pedophile nobleman will nevertheless go to the monk Tikhon to read him his confession about the rape of the little Matryosha. Penitence or pride? Tikhon advises against publication. The abuser flies into a rage, seizes a little ivory cross and breaks it. Can one believe in a demon without believing in God at all? Stavrogin is "seeking boundless suffering, seeking it myself." Tikhon replies that "total atheism is more respectable than worldly indifference." The atheist kills himself.[6]

Kirillov is not a rapist; he kills himself because he "[doesn't] understand how . . . an atheist could know there is no God and not kill himself at once" (*Demons*, 1872). His reasoning is based on the (implicit) principle that human consciousness is obligatorily the consciousness of a believer; in taking the place of the God-man, this human becomes necessarily a Man-God. Whatever arrangements he can draw from this glory, this instant of overturning, the mutation *obliges* (the engineer frequently uses this word) this atheistic Man to demonstrate his terrifying freedom as a new god: "'It is my duty to proclaim unbelief,' Kirillov was pacing the room. 'For me no idea is higher than that there is no God. The history of mankind is on my side. Man has done nothing but invent God so as to live without killing himself; in that lies the whole of world history up to now. I alone for the first time in world history did not want to invent God. Let them know once and for all . . . It is in no way possible for man to be without the former God . . . Only this one thing will save all men and in the next generation transform them physically.'" To announce this new humanity, total because totally liberated, Dostoyevsky's ratiocinating engineer needs only an instrument as simple as it is fatal: suicide. The "transhumans" and other such Cyborgs will need the third millennium's technical prowess . . .

The nihilist "has faith that he doesn't have faith": that the Supreme Being doesn't exist. Being is Nothingness, philosophers will say after Kirillov. But he, suicide victim, does not philosophize, his thoughts are depleted in his affects and vice versa.[7] He doesn't reject fear; consumed by his emotions which compress his arguments, he liberates himself from them "monstrously"—by succumbing to annihilation. The exorbitant potency of impotence culminates in the supreme obligation to free oneself from life.

In effect, "everyone is afraid to proclaim self-will . . . [Man] was self-willed only on the margins." No more margins, no more fear; more life, farewell to the "gamin" and other "Russian boys." The shadow of God's death has fallen on his orphans; the "miracle of Him" on the cross will not have taken place, "the word has not been verified." The suicide victim weds the Lost Object, the Lost Father, the Dead Father. Triumphant, melancholy marriage with nothingness, morose victory of faith in the posture of atheism. Stavrogin is not fooled, he sniffs out the believer: "But you don't pray yet?" he teases Kirillov. "I pray to everything." "But since you don't know yet that you believe in God, you don't believe."

Prince Myshkin (The Idiot, 1868) is not "mad about Christ," though he shares the convictions of the journalist: on Catholicism, "an unchristian religion," on atheism, which "just preaches negation," on the pope, with his "earthly throne," his "lies, intrigue, deceit, fanaticism, superstition, and evil-doing," and on the socialism derived from Catholicism. Myshkin is "a totally handsome man,"[8] enamored with a maternal Christ compared to a "mama smiling at her baby." "THE PRINCE IS CHRIST," in capital letters in the preparatory *Notebooks*. But this specimen is an "innocent," a "cursed idiot" (Vanya cries). The one who believes that "beauty [Aglaya's, Nastasya's] will save the world" ends up abandoned, "a being from another eon," according to Mochulsky's apt expression. Whereas Ippolit, who says "best leave religion out of this" but repeats many of the theses of *A Writer's Diary*, decides in his "final explanation" to kill himself. He is convinced that death is "the law of nature" and that any other action is indifferent, including crime. The assassin Rogozhin and his dreamy, abstracted opposite, united by Holbein's *Dead Christ* of which the sinister merchant possesses a copy, are merely "extremes that meet" in the decomposition of faith and of his world. Zosima seems to invert and repair the impotence of belief, neck and neck with atheism. But his cadaver stinks: aberrant, unbearable saintliness.[9]

On the other side, however, those who boast of "new ideas" are recaptured by faith! A certain faith. Stepan Trofimovich Verkhovensky, the failed writer-father of the nihilist Pyotr Verkhovensky, celebrates the amorous dependence that religion and the immortality of the soul procure for him (though he confesses "having lied all his life"): "God will not want to do an injustice and utterly extinguish the fire of love for him once kindled in my heart . . . Love is higher than being, love is the crown of being, and is it possible for being not to bow before it? . . . If there is God, then I am immortal!" (*Demons*, 1872).

Even the deist Versilov, the biological father in *The Adolescent* (1875), calls for Christ to support generations that have become "orphans," in his vibrant homage to Heine: "'Let this be the last day of my life,' every one of them thinks, gazing at the setting sun; 'it doesn't matter, for after I die they'll still be here, and after them there'll be their children . . .' And the thought . . . will take the place of everybody meeting again beyond the grave . . . My faith is quite limited: I'm a deist, a *philosophe* . . . strangely enough, my fantasy almost never stopped there. It mostly ended with Heine's vision of 'Christ on the Baltic Sea' . . . in the end, He appears in the midst of the abandoned men. He comes to them, holds out His hands to them, and says 'How could you forget!' And at once, it's as if the scales fall from their eyes and they break out in a stirring hymn of their new and final resurrection" (*The Adolescent*, 1875).[10]

In the end it comes down to the father, old Fyodor Pavlovich Karamazov, who will be assassinated by one of his sons, to repeat in his turn the eternal torment of the novelist. Karamazov remembers the Marquis de Sade while nursing his cognac and rehearsing the French author's *cochonneries* (in French in the original). To Ivan he says: "'But still, tell me: is there a God or not? But seriously. I want to be serious now.' 'No, there is no God.' 'Alyoshka, is there a God?' 'There is.' 'And is there immortality, Ivan? At least some kind, at least a little, a teeny-tiny one?' 'There is no immortality either.' 'Not of any kind?' 'Not of any kind.' 'Complete zero? Or is there something? Maybe there's some kind of something? At least not nothing!' 'Complete zero.' 'Alyoshka, is there immortality?' 'There is.' 'Both God and immortality?' 'Both God and immortality. Immortality is in God.' 'Hm. More likely Ivan is right.'" (*The Brothers Karamazov*).

That's how the patriarch on borrowed time cuts to the chase, for the time being. It is not the narrator who says it, even less the author, who of course delegates himself in this way, but not entirely. The novel gives Ivan the floor for a long time for his legendary poem *The Grand Inquisitor*, which he reads to his brother Alyosha.[11] The young dissident theologian may well laugh at each page, Ivan doesn't fail to place his text in the gallery of "poetical works" that make the powers of the beyond "descend to earth." "I don't need to mention Dante," *Notre Dame de Paris*, the Apocalypse, Schiller, or "one little monastery poem (from the Greek, of course): *The Mother of God Visits the Torments*."

Ivan's poem has several voices. He *speaks of* the Grand Inquisitor and *makes him speak*. The old man, overexcited, addresses the "prisoner," who is none other than Christ. The poet also adds comments for his little brother (disciple of Zosima the foul-smelling), who will become the future educator of "young boys." Ivan's voice flows into the papal servant's justifications, preparing to burn Jesus on the pyres of the

Inquisition. Is he going to put to death the son of God himself—a parricidal act, the absolute Karamazovian gesture? Not really, they are going to let God escape. *They*: the Inquisitor and the Atheist.

Ivan understands the inquisitorial motivations of the papacy so well that he lends the supposed Torquemada his own libertarian vision of the Temptation of Christ in the desert. In effect, the poet uses the Inquisition to submit Christ to the inquisition of his own questioning. By inflicting on humans the "so terrible burden [of] freedom of choice," is it not He (Jesus) who himself "laid the *foundation for the destruction* of your own kingdom?" For the mystery, the "general and perpetual anguish" of mankind, resides in the painful *concern* to search for oneself, wanting to remain free—but free to prostrate oneself, "obligatorily together," before the "indisputable." A burning paradox from which *doubt* and *rejection* follow.

That said, the Inquisitor's *indictment* accusing Jesus of having overestimated humans in guiding them to a freedom that only leads them to destructive passions in an explosive world where "everything is permitted"—is this only a Catholic construction? The fact is, Jesuits and Dominicans are also inquisitors, ceaselessly *correcting, challenging,* and *betraying* his Work, his Word. Or is this a revolted cry from Ivan's ravaging poetic atheism? Definitive dark plotting maneuver, a pitiful alloy of the Antichrist Inquisitor and Atheism, preparing unspeakable autos-da-fé. Both persuaded definitively that it's You-The Other-Christ who caused the ruin of his own kingdom. The Inquisitor withdraws, but not without kissing his unarrestable prisoner on the lips.

Ivan's "legend" transforms the papist-nihilist conspiracy the journalist Dostoyevsky is obsessed with into an obscure theological-historical fantasy. The poet-student endorses the sayings of the Catholic Caesar, not without imputing them to all the Christian churches that pose as guides for the "Christly herd," in another manner but in the same spirit. A toxic empathy, revealed by his tender compassion for the "sublime sadness" of his strange Torquemada, who boasts he has "refused to serve madness," though he is "at the head of the Roman army" for a future kingdom of the Antichrist. This paradoxical Inquisitor does not condemn to the stake the One who has "come to disturb him" but remains at a loss all the same. "Your suffering Inquisitor is only a fantasy ... Maybe godlessness ... Your Inquisitor doesn't believe in God, that's his whole secret!" Alyosha says incisively.

Broken Ivan, split Ivan—he "swayed as he walked, and ... his right shoulder, seen from behind, appeared lower than his left," his brother had never noticed it before. Nagging duality, inflicted by the "so terrible burden [of] freedom of choice." No institution, whether Church or "common veneration," would be capable of satisfying it. No more than do the painful interrogations of the atheist's questioning conscience. It will become bogged down in conversing with the Devil, before collapsing into madness during the trial of the parricidal son that Ivan accuses himself of being, since he had thought about it, though without acting on it. Another lameness, continual doubling.

13

THE NIHILIST SEEKING GOD

Nihilism appeared in our country because we are *all nihilists*. What frightened us was only the new, original form. . . .

It was comical to see the commotion and the trouble our wise men took to discover: where did these nihilists come from? But you see, they did not come from anywhere; they were all among us, within us, and part of us.

—Dostoyevsky, *Notebooks* (1881)

13.1 Nechaev, Shigalyov, and Lenin

"We"—Russians—torn between Europe and Asia, which attract and repulse each other, each fascinated and baffled by the customs of the other that the long duration of History forged for them. With "our" history, which proceeds by "bursts," gales, catastrophes, and promises, and disperses *duration into instants*. "We," the *Orthodox*, devoted to the *pafos stihii*,[1] cruel underground of passions and of the plaintive adoration of icons, "self-negation" and "self-destruction," "really and truly . . . a village nihilist, a homegrown cynic and thinker" ("Vlas," *A Writer's Diary*, 1873). Necessarily sublime, and preferable to the boring doctrinarians who subscribe to the scholastic pleasures of understanding.

"We"—Fyodor Mikhailovich—sickened by the positivistic socialists who demand "separation from everything," "especially in the Russian manner," "persuaded that on this *tabula rasa* they will immediately build their paradise." "We," the former Fourierist, who lived through the experience of the condemnation to death and the scaffold, were not short on empathy with the nihilists: did he not consider himself a *former Nechaevian?*[2] Better yet: "How do you know that the members of [the Petrashevsky Circle] could not have become Nechaevists,[3] i.e., set off on Nechaev's path, *in the event that things had taken such a turn?* ... Times then were completely different. But let me say one thing about myself alone: a *Nechaev* I probably could never have become, but a *Nechaevist*—well, of that I can't be sure; perhaps I could have become one ... in the days of my youth" (*A Writer's Diary*, 1873).

"We"—"passive" nihilist—whose refusal to believe or lack of aptitude for the sacred in a utilitarianist world is kneaded into *indifference*, based on biological materialism and rational egoism? Or "active" nihilist, like that young man from the "new generation" with "unfinished ideas," vulgar assassin dreaming to be a hero like Napoleon, and who is only a Raskolnikov (from *raskol*, "division, scission," designating the schism between the old Orthodox believers and the official Orthodox Church)?[4] Or even one of "us," the "secret society of incendiary revolutionaries, of mutineers," subject to the charms of Pyotr Verkhovensky, the exalted duplicate of the glacial Shigalyov.[5] Anarchists, *petroleishiki*, those Russian incendiaries who remind him of the insurrection of the Paris Commune burning the Tuileries; who, in *Demons* (1872) murder and set fires to proclaim the great unrest.

Lenin himself admired Nechaev, it seems, before writing his famous Notebook on Hegel's *Dialectic* (1914), before "dialectical materialism" led him to the "dictatorship of the proletariat." The collapse of democracies into totalitarianism—brown or red plagues—but also the sovereigntist excesses, the ultraliberals with their finances, merchandising of bodies, globalized automatization of minds or what remains of them, have their roots in the tragicomic program of the pre-Leninist Shigalyov. Pyotr the activist summarizes:

> He's got each member of society watching the others and
> obliged to inform. Each belongs to all, and all to each. They're
> all slaves and equal in their slavery. Slander and murder in

extreme cases, but above all—equality. First, the level of education, science, and talents is lowered. A high level of science and talents is accessible only to higher abilities—no need for higher abilities! Higher abilities have always seized power and become despots. Higher abilities cannot fail to be despots and have always corrupted rather than been of use; they are to be banished or executed . . . There has never yet been either freedom or equality without despotism, but within a herd there must be equality . . . Only one thing is lacking in the world: obedience. The thirst for education is already an aristocratic thirst . . . We'll extinguish desire: we'll get drinking, gossip, denunciation going; we'll get unheard-of depravity going; we'll stifle every genius in infancy. Everything reduced to a common denominator, complete equality . . . Only the necessary is necessary—henceforth that is the motto of the whole globe. But there is also a need for convulsion; this will be taken care of by us, the rulers. Slaves must have rulers. Complete obedience, complete impersonality, but once every thirty years Shigalyov gets a convulsion going, and they all suddenly start devouring each other, up to a certain point, simply so as not to be bored. Boredom is an aristocratic sensation; in Shigalyovism there will be no desires. Desire and suffering are for us; and for the slaves—Shigalyovism. (*Demons*, 1872)

Pyotr's father Stepan Trofimovich Verkhovensky,[6] for once more laconic, has fun mocking utilitarian happiness, adding to Shigalyovism the "profundity" of the consumer society to come: "Shakespeare or boots, Raphael or petroleum?" (*Demons*, 1872).

Raskolnikov, Stavrogin, Kirillov, Verkhovensky, Ivan Karamazov . . . Dostoyevsky's great heroes are nihilists, atheists, deniers of God, but *up against* him. "You venerate the Holy Spirit without knowing him," Tikhon diagnoses, upon hearing Stavrogin's confession (*Demons*). Kirillov kills himself "without any reason, simply for self-will—only I," but shouting "*Liberté, égalité, fraternité ou la mort!*" As for Pyotr Verkhovensky, it is obvious this "citizen of the world" "believes in God worse than any priest."

13.2 "Line" or "Zone": The Twentieth Century

Orthodox Russia would perhaps not have been the cradle of nihilism if Dostoyevsky's "we are all nihilists" didn't concern us (more seriously, more universally: "all of us"): speaking humanity that "participates" in the nothingness and the nihilism through its "forgetting of the Being limiting [itself] to dealing with things" (Heidegger, *Introduction to Metaphysics*, 1958). Since when? Plato? Aristotle? Since the "history of metaphysics," which "protects nihilism in its heart"? In this way the Heideggerian terminology (*Question I*, 1968) rethinks the reworking of philosophy; it addresses in depth the social and political history of Europe and the planet.

The question of nihilism reemerges in the twentieth century. Ernst Jünger's *The Worker* (1932) uncovers a radically new reality: the "total mobilization put into place since the last world war." The massification of *workers* offers a vast field of experimentation given over to the State and to the temptation to identify technique with ethics. Without justifying the National Socialist or National Bolshevik ideologies, the author maintains that this "world-wide *order* yields to the demands of nihilism and is also a component of his style." In *On Pain* (1934), Jünger recognizes that the "values corresponding [to this 'new' order] have not yet become visible," even judges them to be truly inappropriate, like those promulgated by Nazi Germany. "Pain" is the unique possibility for the individual, testifying to his participation in the process of this technical revolution. In *Über die Linie* (1950) the author goes further yet: a "culmination has occurred," because not only in the ideologies, but "in the human nucleus on which they are founded we have gone beyond zero." The "zero meridian," the zero point of nihilism, has become the "normal state" of humanity, as Nietzsche wrote. Now it's a matter of knowing "if the walk across the desert leads to new wells." Is another experience possible, in this same world, that can "cross the line of nihilism," "the immense force of 'nothingness,'" capable of changing to *plenitude* after annihilation? Our time of coronavirus pandemic, of planetary lockdown, of human, economical, sociopolitical distress, reawakens, in a crucial way, these same questions, decidedly far from being overcome.

Heidegger proposes to abandon the language of metaphysics, in opposition to the philosophy of absolute mobility and of becoming by overcoming (which borrowed from Hegel and Nietzsche): "And if the language of metaphysics, precisely, and metaphysics itself (whether of the living God or the dead God), constituted *as* metaphysics itself the barrier that forbids the passing of the line, in other words the going beyond (*Überwindung*) of nihilism?" Instead of doing an "identification of places" to diagnose the "topography" of nihilism, he announces that he is proceeding to a "topo-logy" that "brings together being and nothingness in its deployment." It is useless to forge an available concept of nothingness-and-being, says the philosopher in substance, in writing B~~ein~~g under erasure, and he asks us to think of an *inclusion of man in nothingness*, as suggested by his formula of man as "a lieutenant of the nothing." Man, in participating in being as well as nothingness and therefore in nihilism, "does not just stay *in* the critical Zone of the line. He is himself, but not himself only in himself, and absolutely not by himself alone, this Zone and consequently the line." I hear this B~~ein~~g under erasure and this man "lieutenant of nothing" as an elucidation of the *split*, the *Spaltung* of the subject according to the latter Freud.[7]

No conceptual "objectifications" of nihilism, then, and no "negativation," *nihil negativum* of the Being, and no "line" either in Heidegger. Let's *speak* nonbeing in figures: *place, situation, Zone*, pro-vocation of thought. "Instead of wanting to overcome nihilism, we should attempt to enter into its essence with contemplation." "That is why Thought and Poetry must return to where they have always already been, in a certain fashion, where in spite of that they have never built." The "will *of* power" appears to him like "the new metaphysics of an accomplished nihilist," in his spiritual fatherland composed of the destructive forces of the nineteenth century. Even though the Nietzschean "will *toward* power" turns—with the death of God—toward the innermost heart of its strength, unveiling itself as the will for life and as life. It is Hölderlin's "wild garden" that Heidegger prefers; those "words of praise arise, like flowers" (in "Bread and Wine").

I read the orchestration of nihilism by Dostoyevsky as the work of an "eternal apprentice" (Heidegger's term) whose writing opens up the freedom to play with "the multiplicity of meanings in the speaking": indefatigable topo-logy from which I retain, definitively, only the oscillation as such, its walk and its song, the "free field of order that makes everything take pleasure." Without a garden, but by an untamed contemplation, Dostoyevsky raises the Speaking of his Thought to the most vehement multiplicity. His walk limps and his song runs out of breath—the better to make the "apprentice" reader that I am understand my cohabitation with nihilism, and only then, "leave nihilism behind us." "Not until it's late do we have the courage of what we *know*. Only recently did I dare to admit to myself that I have always been a profound nihilist," writes Nietzsche in 1887. One year later, it's the collapse.

13.3 Nietzsche and Raskolnikov

Could it have been Lou Salomé who spoke to Nietzsche about Dostoyevsky? "I also knew nothing about Dostoevski until a few weeks ago—uncultivated person that I am, reading no 'periodicals!' In a bookshop my hand just happened to come to rest on *L'Esprit souterrain*, a recent French translation . . . The instinct of affinity (or what shall I call it?) spoke to me instantaneously—my joy was beyond bounds," he writes to his friend Franz Overbeck on February 23, 1887. In a letter to Peter Gast, March 7, 1887, Nietzsche again mentions his discovery, almost in the same terms, and calls *Notes from Underground* a "stroke of psychological genius." His later correspondence insists on his "enthusiastic" reading of the novelist: "any Russian book—above all, Dostoevski (translated into French, for heaven's sake not German!!)—I count among my greatest moments of pleasurable relief." And to Brandes on November 20, 1888, he formulates this solemn and respectful homage: "the most valuable psychological material known to me—I am grateful to him in a remarkable way." While *Twilight of the Idols* (§ 45) intones: "Dostoevski, the only psychologist, incidentally, from whom I had something to learn; he ranks among the most beautiful strokes of fortune in my life."

Nietzsche read *Notes from a Dead House, Notes from Underground, The Insulted and Injured* (1861) as well as the French translation of *Demons* in 1888 from which he feverishly copied pages into his notebook: the seduction of the Antichrist, Stavrogin's letter to Dasha, Stavrogin's denial, Kirillov's epileptic atheism, Shatov's frenzied populism. Perhaps also *The Idiot* (1868), since the "first immoralist" (Nietzsche) calls Christ an idiot in the sense that Prince Myshkin is... Does Dostoyevsky accompany him right up to his last gesture before slipping into madness? I see him in a communion of passion with Raskolnikov—the ultimate spark that unleashes the collapse at the same time as the passionate reflex to protect himself from it.

On January 23, 1889, the philosopher, wandering around Turin, witnesses a Dostoyevskian scene: "[Rodion] runs along the horse's side, rushes ahead, and sees how they are beating her across the eyes, right across her eyes! He starts to cry. His heart rises up in his chest, and his tears begin to flow. One of the men holding a whip lashes the boy across the face; he doesn't feel it; he's wringing his hands, shouting, and then hurls himself at the gray-haired old man with the gray beard, the one who'd been shaking his head before and condemning it all" (*Crime and Punishment*, 1866).

Nietzsche is not reading *Crime and Punishment*, open on his desk, he is not dreaming either. The horse savagely beaten by its coachman is there in front of his eyes, the author of *Beyond Good and Evil* rushes to it and embraces it (like Raskolnikov). Which Dostoyevsky does not do, since he pursues his desire by writing it.[8] Whereas the animal's breath gets the better of the philosopher of the will to power, and he collapses in tears.

A simple coincidence, why not? "Structures in common" to the male passions of two geniuses. Dr. Freud would soon probe the unconscious tendencies of Little Hans (1909), who transferred onto horses his repressed and forbidden sexual desires and pleasures, his phobias. In other words, though not common, the fixation of the libido on the horse is neither incomprehensible nor fatal. And the Nietzschean anxieties did not wait for Raskolnikov's murder of the usurer to change into "transvaluation of [metaphysical] values" capable of *surpassing* nihilism. The two scenes pose face to face the incommensurable complexities of the two men and their two oeuvres confronting nihilism.

That of the *Overman*, which welcomes the *eternal return* through questioning. And that of *dualism* (body-soul, flesh-spirit, good-evil, etc.), reversed into *nonduality* by the polyphony of the writing.[9] The polemicist, seized in an eternal return to metaphysics, lives the fight "that ignited for domination" and understands it, and "he falls along the way."[10] Whereas the writing of the novel, *like a work of poetry*, manages to sublimate madness by "never being concerned with anything other than paying attention to the use of language in thought" (Heidegger).

14

LAUGHTER, SPOKESPERSON FOR THE OBSCENE

Give me a subject, anything... in a second it will be a comedy in five acts, and I swear to you it will be devilishly funny...

—Gogol to Pushkin, October 7, 1835

Millions of the rest of God's creatures... unfinished... created in mockery.

—*The Brothers Karamazov* (1881)

14.1 Spasm of Life

Doubling recomposed as *duality*, the cumulative counterpoints of the ideas, actions, and characters all yield a triumphant spasm that defies unnamable anxiety as much as does His Majesty of Meaning. *It is laughter.* Dostoyevsky's writing doesn't guffaw like Rabelais's juicy fantasies; it doesn't laugh like Dante's divine meditation; it doesn't jubilate like the exuberant comic force of Falstaff; it doesn't ironize like Voltaire's *perfidum ridens.* No dialectical synthesis nor forgetting of fears and ruptures. The imperious, extravagant, impossible Dostoyevskian intimate/extimate dialogue crackles inside the wound (inexpiable suffering) that separates and unites meaning and what can be sensed, the same and the other, the flesh and the word, life and death.

A release of the drive—spasm of life gnawing at the abyss of death—opens up like the inner lining of meaning as it is being constructed, unleashes it from its hinges, and without destroying it, not even necessarily questioning it, sets it in motion. A flowering of interstices and uncertainties, this furtive glimpse of eroticism is neither impossible nor virtual but as real as can be. But unconfinable, tireless, fleeting; ridiculous companion to galloping speech.

Dostoyevsky's discreet, pulsating laugh is not really *reduced*, as Bakhtin thinks (*Dostoevsky's Poetics*); it's an insane respiration that accompanies death and diffracts its advances. This respiration, erogenous zone between the unspeakable and the word to say it, protects from the lack of meaning, from suicide, and from death. When the *laugh* and its inverse, *ridicule*, collapse, the word is lacking and *it kills*. The "Copernican Revolution" of the characters that Bakhtin detects in Dostoyevsky sweeps away their fixed "self-definition," habitually dictated by authors, artificially.[1] Henceforth, the characters escape from the author, self-define as real by the polyphony intrinsic to each of them. Dostoyevsky's Copernican Revolution resides in the *reinvention* of the laugh as a *turn* between the body and language, the flesh and the words. Excited by their multiple facets, the author inscribes his vital energy as the absolute condition of this polyphony, which invites us to live at the ultimate limit and even to surpass it. Misery, horror, comedy, and an odd sort of grace.

14.2 From the "Original Laugh" to a Genealogy of Laughter

Is there any connection with the laugh the goddess Baubo evokes, in the Eleusinian Mysteries, by displaying her vulva topped with a phallic simulacrum? It succeeds in cheering up the anorexic Demeter distraught by the loss of her daughter. Orgasm, masturbation, and female homosexuality are the "original laugh"—a transverse, *a-liminal* conduct between life and death—the dynamics of which are worked out according to various tonalities in the arts and rituals of the European laugh. These *obscene contents* of the Eleusinian Mysteries will be covered up, only the principle of inversion will subsist, *causing laughter at the reversal* of death into life and vice versa: festivals of death-and-resurrection. It also echoes in the laughter of other civilizations, in Asia, Africa, and Latin America.

Patriarchal order replacing the obscure matriarchal period imposes the Adonises and the Dionyses, ceremonies in which dominant masculine sexuality introduces *ravishment* and *fear*: *tremendum* and *fascinans*, potency/impotency. The *masks* of clowns, buffoons, and imps, like a metonymy of the "hidden presence" of the god, sow confusion and chaos: the slippage between two series of independent values provokes a laughter like an intrusion/inclusion of the obscene in the sacred. It is the *inversion-confusion* of differences that is now *logically*, philosophically, morally "obscene," this is what causes laughter and relief, Bergson's *Laughter* (1900) will prove it.

Inversion of moods and norms, the laugh equilibrates the interdictions; in discharging aggressivity, through disguise, it dedramatizes differences and at the same time confirms the right for exceptions. As projections of unconscious feelings onto fantastic figures, comedy and laughter open the identity to its fantasies—I am only "a fiction"—and the social contract to farce. People who applaud see themselves in it and are consoled.

My laughing with Dostoyevsky reawakens this genealogy of laughter when the novelist smothers it (in the sobs of his female characters) or when he makes it tremble (in the tortures and crimes of his doubles).

14.3 Terrible, Ridiculous, Absurd: To Be Reinvented

The *most terrible*: the cascading laughter in Raskolnikov's dream of murdering the old usurious landlady:

> He stood over her. "She's afraid," he thought and quietly freed the axe from its loop and struck the old woman on the crown of her head once and then again . . . He took one look and froze in horror: the old woman was sitting there, laughing—*she was overcome with quiet, inaudible laughter*, trying with all her might to make sure he didn't hear her. Suddenly it seemed that the door to her bedroom was opening slightly and there, too, *someone was laughing and whispering*. Rage overcame him: he began striking the old

woman on the head with all his strength, but with each blow of the axe the *laughter* and whispering from the bedroom sounded *stronger and louder*, and the old woman *shook with mirth*. He tried to flee, but the entire entryway was filled with people . . . His heart skipped a beat, his feet wouldn't budge, and he felt rooted to the spot . . . He wanted to cry out and—woke up. (*Crime and Punishment*, 1866)

These laughs do not make fun of death. Laughter here laughs *from* death, *within* death. Dostoyevsky experienced this laughter, that limit where absolute differences interpenetrate and blend. *Laughing by dint of dying.* The *turn* can only be spoken through shimmerings and twitches. Old Alyona's laugh is a *mask* placed on mute astonishment, the pain-horror, refutation-approbation of nothingness. A species of jouissance. The laughter of the neighbors, a vulgar debauchery that bewilders Rodion, is the echo of his own excitation, projected outward. Rodion is the one who made them all; he is dreaming about them, these demented laughs he sees, hears; they are lodged in him, they inhabit him. Laughs that are blows of the ax, like *apoptosis*, the mortality that sculpts the living, while the epileptic aura transforms them into paradise. Humans then open their gullets to the impossible for a few seconds, the time of a dream.

As for the *ridiculous*, when opposites are confused within me, it is a laugh that does not give its name, which I suppose is evident to others, to their "us-all-ity" to which I do belong, after all. Always inside and outside, the ridiculous is like Kirillov, who kills himself to demonstrate that he is free from God, from nature, from everything:[2] "there's always some new thought here: if one did some villainy or, worse, some shame, that is, disgrace, only very mean and . . . *ludicrous*, so that people would remember it for a thousand years and spit on it for a thousand years, and suddenly comes the thought: 'One blow in the temple, and there will be nothing.' What do I care then about people and how they'll be spitting for a thousand years, right?" (*Demons*, 1872).

The hint of a smile hovers over this "shame," this "villainy" even, which the Man-God inflicts on himself to guarantee his right to freedom. Could the engineer's sacrifice be a wink from the Credo to the "madness of the Cross," to the death Jesus assumes but which makes him obtain immortality, another life after the second death, for himself and for those who follow him? The Son of God must not have felt ridiculous, since he was to sit on the right hand of the Father. Alas, for the nihilist only the risks of freedom remain . . . an *absurd* fate, rather than a *ridiculous* one.

It is a more somber Albert Camus, assiduous reader of Dostoyevsky, who bequeaths to his existentialist friends this narrative of the absurd, as brought to him by Alfred Jarry's *Ubu Roi* (1896), to explore that divorce between "a man and his life." His *Stranger* (1942), who writes that he feels nothing at the death of his mother and "doesn't speak," kills a man in a world without love and deprived of meaning.

Black humor? About the sentimental Kirillov, maybe. But one doesn't laugh on the sandy shores of the existentialist absurd.

Parricide needed a grotesque, absurd character, a Russian Ubu Roi. In contrast to Jarry's burlesque provocateur, assassin of the King of Poland,[3] here "everyone wants to kill the father," Fyodor Pavlovich Karamazov (same first name as Fyodor Dostoyevsky). The most Dostoyevskian of the Dostoyevskians makes one laugh to the point of tears at the *repugnance* he inspires. Papa Fyodor, the predestined target of this murder that the novelist lets us think of as a universal, anthropological component, since it is the foundation of the social contract (*dixit* Freud), is the height of ridicule. Of all the laughs in Dostoyevsky, this is my favorite. A serious, wicked, and sentimental laugh, a tad amusing, deplorable.

Is it because he was abandoned by his first wife, an unwitting feminist? Or because he prides himself on Frenchness, libertinage, and free thinking? More "insolent" than "noble," "wicked and sentimental" (secretly contagious), Karamazov the father truly impresses me when he says Ivan is right in refusing to believe in the immortality of the soul. However, Ivan's "rightness" collapses into dementia. It is Dmitri Karamazov who makes the Karamazovian laugh bounce back, not without having given in to the judicial error that condemns him for parricide (what a joke!). The delusional Mitya had a certain faith: he believed that beauty could reunite the Madonna with Sodom.

So having "developed his special skill at knocking money together, and at knocking it out of other people," Fyodor Pavlovich, this "old buffoon," who "liked to make jokes about his own face," had "an insolent need to make others into buffoons." In a juicy portrait, the sort of physical sketch Dostoyevsky rarely gratifies his characters with, drowning as they usually are in their torrents of speech, he describes this fallacious and salacious wino as having "eternally insolent, suspicious, and leering little eyes." His Adam's apple, "fleshy and oblong like a purse, hung below his sharp chin"; he is "repulsively sensual" with his "long, carnivorous mouth with plump lips" and his Roman nose, giving him "the real physiognomy of an ancient Roman patrician of the decadent period." As sarcastic as he is pretentious, Fyodor suddenly smiles "his long, half-drunken smile, which was not devoid of cunning and drunken slyness," and makes fun of poor Alyosha, his "quiet boy," who "wanted to enter the monastery . . . as a novice." He reveals to him, saucily, that "everybody around knows that only 'monastery wives' live [in the] monastery that has a little village nearby." "The only trouble is this terrible Russianism, there are no French women at all." This before launching into an apparently confused tirade like a dazed alcoholic.

However, speaking ironically about hell, which lacks a ceiling and hooks by which the devil could grab the sinner that he is, this father-to-be-cut-down swallows in one gulp all the finest the West has produced in terms of reformation of faith, disbelief, and illusion. In one swallow, he boos refined, enlightened Lutheranism, then Voltairean deism, and ends up savoring the shadows of the delicate imaginary of Charles Perrault, who was also a father, but of *Cinderella* and *Donkey Skin*:

> "I keep thinking all the time: who is ever going to pray for me? Is there anyone in the world? My dear boy, . . . stupid as I am, I still keep thinking about it . . . that the devils will forget to drag me down to their place with their hooks when I die. And then I think: hooks? Where do they get them? . . . You know, in the monastery the monks probably believe there's a ceiling in hell, for instance. Now me, I'm ready to believe in hell, only there

shouldn't be any ceiling, that would be, as it were, more refined, more *enlightened*, more *Lutheran*, in other words. Does it really make any difference—with a ceiling or without a ceiling? But that's what the damned question is all about! Because if there's no ceiling, there are no hooks. And if there are no hooks, the whole thing falls apart, which, again, is unlikely, because then who will drag me down with hooks, and if they don't drag me down, what then, and where is there any justice in the world? *Il faudrait les inventer*, those hooks, just for me, for me alone, because you have no idea, Alyosha, what a stinker I am . . .!"

"No, there are no hooks there," Alyosha said quietly and seriously, studying his father.

"Yes, yes. Only shadows of hooks. I know, I know. That's how one Frenchman described hell: *J'ai vu l'ombre d'un cocher, qui avec l'ombre d'une brosse frottait l'ombre d'une carosse.*[4] How do you know, my dear, that there are no hooks?" (*The Brothers Karamazov*, 1881)

Philosophism or atheism, who avoids the hooks of evil? They cover the deep, engaging deliquescence of the father. Dostoyevsky lived through this ridicule and reveals it as principal and essential. To be suppressed, then reinvented, endlessly.

14.4 The Salvation of the Man Who Knows He Is Ridiculous

Ridicule can hide so well in *shame* anticipating *humiliation* that it condemns one's speaking to powerlessness. But in Dostoyevsky, the pretense oh so gently reverses into a persistent authenticity. The lures and magic of the incarnate Word.

For example, the maniacal letter-writer Makar Alekseyevich Devushkin in *Poor Folk* (1846):

I live in the kitchen, or rather it would be more correct to put it this way: right next door to the kitchen here there is a room (I should, perhaps, tell you our kitchen is clean, light and excellently appointed), a small room, a modest little corner...i.e. to put it even better, the kitchen has three windows, and I have a partition that runs parallel with the transverse wall, making as it were another room, a supernumerary one; it is spacious and comfortable, there is a window, and everything—all conveniences, in fact. Well, that is my little corner. So, little mother, don't you go away with the idea that I'm hiding something and that there's more to it than what I've described; don't say to yourself: "but it's a kitchen!"—it's perfectly true that I live in the kitchen, behind a partition, but that doesn't matter; I live apart from everyone, so-so, on the quiet. I have provided myself with a bed, a table, a chest of drawers and a couple of chairs, and have hung up an icon. It is true that there are better—possibly even much better—lodgings to be found; but convenience is what matters. And indeed I have done all this for the sake of my own convenience, and you must not think that it has been for any other purpose.

On the contrary, *ridicule does not bring salvation* but is unsustainable; it is consumed, and it disappears when speaking is compressed and killed into silence. Opaque, obtuse tyranny of the husband, who is proud of it, in "The Meek One" (1876):[5] "I'm a master of speaking silently, I've spent my whole life speaking silently and have silently lived through whole tragedies with myself." Incapable of thinking, of speaking from the point of view of the other, of a woman, of his wife, his "unspoken words" intend the tragedy only for *her*: they lead the wife of the "master" to suicide. He, neither tragic nor comic, leads a fantastic existence, in which life and death are blended in silence. No one laughs. Unless it's when the author wrests from the silent husband-narrator this sudden "fantasy": he claims, "she smiled"— finally!—while praying to the icon of the Virgin about ten minutes before her fatal "decision." Regal resignation of the feminine smile, cruel *a posteriori* grimace of masculine impotence.

Ivan Karamazov's bursts of laughter punctuate in untimely fashion the serious indictment of Christianism by the Inquisitor, who himself embodies its essence as well as its corrosive lucidity.[6] Ivan, an improbable burlesque adept of Bergson, tears himself apart with his *double* (even triple) *thoughts* and the *quid pro quos* that enliven his theological polyphony, thus putting into play the dynamic of laughter as decoded by the French philosopher twenty years later.

In addition to the multiplicity of voices into which the despotic and nonetheless suffering "Inquisitor" projects himself, there's the assumed and feared judgment by Alyosha, which, when all is said and done, Ivan also endorses. Then the laugh trembles, scolds, and aggresses him, empties the subject, but also launches it anew: "'Oh, no, I didn't write it,' Ivan laughed . . . [I] memorized it . . . Ivan grinned . . . Ivan laughed . . . he laughed again . . . Ivan was laughing . . . Is he being ironic? Is he laughing?"

The young theologian poetizes only to laugh, his poem vacillates between *fantasy* and *quid pro quos*. What quid pro quos, and who does them, who wants them, these quid pro quos? Ivan? Or the old Inquisitor, he of supreme and abusive paternity, ripe for slaughter? Alyosha, maybe, as judge and alter ego? "'Of course,' he laughed again, 'the man is ninety years old, and might have lost his mind long ago over his idea.'" Who is mocking the subject (Christ, Christianism)? The Inquisitor or Ivan? Jesus, certainly, because while he is not in this *world*, he is let out "into the 'dark squares of the city.'" The Creator, definitely, because he is a God who laughs. He who created humans as "rebels no doubt intended to laugh at them"; he "contributed most of all to this lack of understanding." But Ivan, *a priori*, regains "a firm voice" only by returning to his doublings. Without an axis, or a goal, or a desire to transgress, he accumulates obsessional, fruitless ruminations. Laughter is his respiration, the grimacing jubilation of lameness, of cascading contradictions.

Until the narrator *claims* it: "I am a ridiculous person" ("The Dream of a Ridiculous Man," 1877)—the poor man with his poor people, the writer-convict, the gambler, the wicked underground man, the insulted and injured, the eternal husband, the possessed! Henceforth famous for his *Writer's Diary*, "I" is a "modern Russian progressive," he is no longer tormented in his eternal "poor and small room," but in a chic "armchair . . . a Voltaire one"; he spies on the bedlam that continues as usual on the other side of the partition wall. He "[doesn't] even think, . . . some thoughts wander about," he has felt that "everything in the world should make no difference to me" ("The Dream of a Ridiculous Man").

Similarly, Kirillov, anticipating "beyond good and evil" in his way, draped himself in a kind of nihilistic indifference.[7] He developed a supposed freedom roboticized for egoists who were presumed to have invented justice and who practice it with the guillotine, to preserve its codes. Except that the ridiculous writer-man has overcome all those poses they mocked him for—if indeed he was their dupe, since deep down he was laughing about it. In his *dream* and upon *awaking*—but "what is a dream?"—he is no longer indifferent but simply ridiculous. After having been dead and buried, he was able to "*be* again" . . . on Sirius! Not yet on Mars with Amazon, that's going to come sooner than the narrator imagines, we have proof . . . "Suddenly in one of these [black] spots I noticed a little star," where he found *complete plenitude,* for which he regrets, while also pleased about it, that he was "unable to put it into words." The ridiculous man, without being explicit, lets his readers gather that he is another version of . . . Stavrogin: "the poor little girl whom I had offended"—"I would have shot myself if it hadn't been for that little girl" who "flashed before me."

Dreamed or fantasized, neither hidden nor confessed, not even named, pedophilia is explored in the fiction and takes part in the *plenitude.*[8] A ridiculous function of the writing, with respect to the "cruel sensuality" of earthlings who only believe in the Devil, because they believe "that evil is the normal condition of people." But didn't he himself, the ridiculous man, contribute to corrupting them like that? "Yes, yes, it ended with me corrupting them all . . . like an atom of plague." Whoever they may be, whether they composed "new families" in which "their children were everyone's children" or they considered "consciousness" and "consciousness of life" to be "higher than happiness," the novelist pawns off on us the ridicule of a tamed Stavrogin. His obsessing, sublimated demon, like an unfinished dreamer (*suchestvo neokonchennoe*) constantly under construction, claims he is "going, going, even if it's for a thousand years." "And I found that little girl . . . And I'll go! I'll go!"

How far? To the point of *doing the deed*? The writer apparently boasted of it to Turgenev. Or *writing it*? He had already done so, but Stavrogin's confession, refused by Katkov at the *Russian Messenger* in 1871 (before the awakening of "The Ridiculous Man" in 1877), won't *arrive at destination* until the death of the author. He did manage it, and he made a mockery of his detractors and of censorship: "I love those who laugh at me more than all the rest" ("The Dream of a Ridiculous Man," 1877).

14.5 Laughing Is Over?

Laughter dies in the writing when it broaches the ultimate test: the sacred (with Zosima) and death (with the man condemned to death, according to Myshkin).

In the face of a supposedly saintly monk whose cadaver stinks, the ridiculous and the absurd have nothing to say. No one is laughing, they are staggered. With Zosima, human truth, created "like a sarcasm," pulverizes meaning and the sensible and provokes *fiction*: a *broad* word encompassing the fantastic of the sort Dostoyevsky asserts in his last works.

It is the Christlike idiot Myshkin's task to confront the anguish of death at its paroxysm upon a condemnation to death, to *paint* it at last. The cadaver in Holbein's *Dead Christ*, with no hope of resurrection, had triggered an epileptic seizure in Dostoyevsky. Seeing a copy of the painting at Rogozhin's, the Prince, who represents the author, remembers a "tale of a man dragged to the scaffold." That man: Dostoyevsky! From representative to representative, how can we not make a story? It's the ridiculous Idiot who takes on the challenge that the reprieved man addresses to himself, that the epileptic relives in the "little death" (orgasm), and the author lays down for the reader, in the end. Painting in *words*, transposing, recounting "swiftly and avidly" the promptness of last instants and of *writing*, which lengthen and run out of breath in a fatal acceleration, without tiring or becoming bogged down, by leaping onto the rhythms, the seconds, the beating of the always unfinished and therefore ridiculous thoughts.

For the writer, every utterance that can be written confronts death, and the intent is to make one hear a "distant background, indistinct, subordinate," if only for "the tenth part of an instant." Neither painting nor theater nor décor. Nothing but vibrating concreteness, in noun phrases, short or fumbling, repetitive and striking, banging, stretching into echoes, oscillating and rotating around this point: "You would certainly hear that!"

"It is exactly a minute before death," began the prince perfectly readily, at once carried away by his recollection and apparently oblivious to all else, "just when he has climbed the stair and set foot upon the scaffold. That was when he glanced in my direction; I looked into his face and understood it all... But *how can one convey it?* I would be terribly pleased, terribly pleased if you or anyone else could draw that face! Best of all if it were you! At the time I thought a *picture* would do a lot of good. To do it one really has to *imagine everything* that had taken place earlier, every single thing. He had been living in prison and expecting to wait at least a week before execution... But this time, for some reason, the process was curtailed... Then three or four hours go by on the usual things: the priest, breakfast for which he gets wine, coffee, and beef (well is that a mockery or not? Just think how cruel that is...)... then finally they take him through the town to the scaffold... Ten thousand faces, ten thousand eyes—all that had to be borne, and then worst of all, the thought: 'There's ten thousand of them and not one of them is being executed, but I am!'... Suddenly he begins to weep... this strong and courageous man, a great evil-doer, so they said... The priest, a perceptive man no doubt, stops talking and just keeps offering him the cross to kiss. At the bottom of the ladder he had been very pale, but after he had climbed it and stood on the scaffold, he became white as a sheet all of a sudden, *as white as a sheet of writing paper*... Have you ever felt like that when you've been frightened or in moments of terror, when your reason remains perfectly clear but is no longer in control? ... He kept kissing the cross avidly ... but he would scarcely have felt *anything religious* at that moment ... It's odd but very few people faint in these last seconds! On the contrary, the brain is fearfully alive and active, must be working, working, working, ever so hard, like a *machine*; I can imagine all kinds of thoughts hammering away, all half-formulated, perhaps even *absurd*, irrelevant thoughts like: 'That one staring—he's got a wart on his forehead, the executioner there, he's got a rusty bottom button' ... and all things move and revolve around that point. And to think, this goes on till the last quarter of a second when your head is lying on the block and waiting and ... *knowing*, and all at once it hears the iron sliding above! You would *certainly* hear that! speaking for myself, if I was lying there I would deliberately listen for it and catch the sound! ... And just imagine, people still argue that perhaps the head when it flies off knows for a second that it has done so—what an idea! And what if it were five seconds! ... Draw the scaffold ... *The cross and the head—that's the picture*; the faces of the priest, the executioner, his two assistants and several heads and eyes from below, all that can be drawn in as distant background, indistinct, subordinate. That's the sort of picture it should be." (*The Idiot*, 1868)

In addressing his monologue to the pontificating nitwit valet of the Yepanchins, Myshkin doesn't eliminate the ridiculous. He maintains the carnivalesque *frame* of human exchanges the better to open our eyes to the head about to be cut off. But the laugh returns in the banal or incongruous details, the priest, the cross, the white paper on the secretary's desk, that assail the man awaiting the blade, and it is heard—invisible, unthinkable, but *audible*—especially in the pulsation of the phrasing. "Double thoughts," "all kinds of thoughts hammering away" punctuate a writer "full of life": a discordant, pulsatile music accompanies the criminal to his very last breath, head on the block. And I can hear the novelist writing these lines, this "great criminal" who weeps and speaks to us from beyond his death, for "the rest of eternity to live, the time to arrive there." Had he not written to his brother upon stepping down from the scaffold, on December 22, 1849: "Life is everywhere, life is in us ourselves, and not outside... *On voit le soleil!*"[9]

The Proustian sentence itself was in tune with Dostoyevsky: "its halting quality, its length, its endless yet discreet murmur, as well as its subordinate clauses that put our memory to the test, and its musical alliterations that compensate for our failure to comprehend its logical ramifications... its strange syntactic qualities (which are quite uncharacteristic of French and are thought to be closer to Latin, since the various components of Proust's sentences are separated by unusual distances) that crystallize the aesthetic of 'involuntary memory.'"[10]

The author of *In Search of Lost Time* inserts a parenthesis about "the novel beauty" of the great Russian in the long chat in which he "tried to banish the thought of my mistress [Albertine] and to think only of the musician" whose "little phrase" enchants Swann, the protagonist's double. It's a way of saying that the diverse vocal variations of the Dostoyevsky score are to be heard as identical to the movements of the "lily-white sonata" and the "glowing septet" in the "unsuspected world" of Vinteuil: "those two very dissimilar questions that governed the very different movement of the sonata and the septet, the former interrupting a pure, continuous line with brief calls, the latter welding together into an indivisible structure a medley of scattered fragments—one so calm and shy, almost detached and as if philosophical, the other so urgent, anxious, imploring— were nevertheless the same prayer, bursting forth like different inner sunrises, and merely refracted through the different mediums of other thoughts, of artistic researches carried on through the years in which he had sought to create something new" (Proust, *The Captive*). This dissonance, the mark of the breath and the continually renewed meaning, Proust also hears its "atrocious and spiteful beauty" in Baudelaire's "most energetic lines" about old women, "with no more thought of toning down his language, so as not to scourge the dying." To laugh about pain, the pain of laughing, a pity that takes on the appearance of irony: "divine mystery... The poet tortures us with this sorrow rather than expresses it" (*Against Sainte-Beuve*).

Proust was able to identify them in the Idiot's monologue about the moment of death; the condemned man "would scarcely have felt anything religious at that moment," but "without remembering," "the brain is fearfully alive and active, must be working, working, working, ever so hard, like a machine." You would really have to be an idiot like Myshkin to talk about a machine in a moment like that. Yet another absurd laugh that isn't extinguished but glitters in the vocal tessitura of Dostoyevskian writing, and that the researcher of lost time ends up hearing as an echo to the late quartets of Beethoven.

The polyphonist's laughter is extinguished in the composition, though rarely without exposing itself to ridicule, when the goodness of the just unmasks the heralds infatuated with truth. Like Aglaya provoking Myshkin: "I think it's all very horrid of you, because it's *very ill-bred just to look on and pronounce judgement on a man's soul*, as you judge Ippolit. You have no tenderness in you; *only truth—and that's not justice*" (*The Idiot*, 1868).

When tenderness impregnates the truth, the depths of the soul are no longer obscene, they become sacred, and Aglaya is their sentinel. But this intransigent rebel is capricious, a double of the fiery Nastasya Filippovna, whom she outlives until she succumbs to the influence of Catholicism! Which does not prevent the sarcastic Dostoyevsky from defining his credo in unison with Aglaya's words: "With utter realism *to find the man in man* . . . They call me a *psychologist; this is not true*. I am merely a realist *in the higher sense*, that is, I portray all the *depths of the human soul*."[11]

Do not yield to the facile assertion that this whole Dostoyevskian tribe is seriously perverse. Because you know that, for Freud's posterity, hyperconnected in globalization, "not only does perversion not exist, but we are all perverse."[12] Which is to say, we are *neotenes*, "unfinished ones" (Dostoyevsky the meditator had a liking for the latter expression), dependent on an alterity we are *afraid* of (mamapapa) because it is indispensable to us, and because it installs a "central phobic kernel," a panic without object, that doubles our *appetite for excitation.* Common sense takes fright upon discovering this pan-icky unfinishedness, which the social contract formats insidiously into transgressions, devotions, even per-verse and mother-verse crimes. Combining choler and compassion, Dostoyevsky's laugh, triumphant and guilty, free and full of shame, is never monotonous. "In my position, monotony is ruination," he writes to his brother (letter to Mikhail, October 20, 1846). Laughter, differently than *consciousness* and *knowledge*, is the vibratile key of his polyphony, it puts it into motion, gives it life.

15

"THE NOVEL IS A POEM"

The great unconscious bone-structure underlying the assemblage of deliberate ideas.

—Proust, *Against Sainte-Beuve* (1920)

15.1 *Parodia sacer*

In linking Dostoyevsky to "a certain tradition going back to Socratic dialogue" and to "Menippean satire and the medieval mysteries," Mikhail Bakhtin, in *Problems of Dostoevsky's Poetics*, brilliantly rehabilitated the *carnivalesque perception* of the world and, more profoundly, the *dialogic structure* of language ("I" speaks only with "other"). Decline and renascence, *parodia sacer*, dethroning and profanation, roulette and prison, naturalism and the underworld all express this art of living, of expenditure. The polyphonic novel, ever since its emergence in the fifteenth century, hears them, reflects them back, and abounds in variations.[1] This poetics, providing the principal keys to the Dostoyevskian oeuvre, doesn't only illuminate a literary experience. It unearths the carnivalesque and the dialogic in the social codes of a historical moment (the Renaissance, Europe, Christianity, the technical boom of the nineteenth century) through moral values and their psychosexual specificities. Writing thus understood, a *vertiginous contestation*, which Dostoyevsky invests, affirms, and orchestrates as the fragile constitution of man stabilizes, seizes upon the metaphysical and political labyrinth that precedes and surrounds it, that tortures it and gives it pleasure. A *poetic condensation* emerges from it, to which he submits fragments of theology and philosophy. Orthodoxy and humanism, nihilism and socialism, reason and faith. He consumes them, compact, crumbled, irresistible, unsurpassable. As do the great works of the "discoverers" and the "criminals" Raskolnikov speaks of.

In resisting "socialist realism," on one side, and "religious obscurantism" on the other, Bakhtin occulted *the affective underground of Orthodoxy*, which, in the alchemy of the writing, underlies the philosophical-carnivalesque dualities of ontotheology.

Inheritor of European metaphysics and laughter, the novelist takes his place in the "new world" of Judeo-Christianism, which subsumes them. He grasps its "new and terrible beauty" (as Proust will say): Job and Jesus, gnosis, Churches, deists, atheists, and nihilists. Each reveals its extreme singularity, and all are modulated on musical staffs of whirlwinds, collisions, and adjustments. No simplification, no dispersion of their intimate tremolo as each crosses the others. The author likes complexity, which protects him, André Gide remarked. Because the dialogical resonance of the elements illuminates them reciprocally—a gigantic reverberation in the flood of the novelistic Word. It precipitates the poet, like the reader, into the "pathetic of elements" (*pafos stihii*),[2] beyond language as well as beyond explanation.

15.2 "An Enormous Beast . . . Almost Mystical"

The "ultimate conviction" of Ippolit, whose account of "memories of Siberia" reveals him to be another spokesperson for the writer, proceeds through interminable collages of "prose poems," breathless compressions of childhood phobias and metaphysical anxieties side by side, irrepressible resonances.[3] Repressed sexual excitement, with its retinue of wounds and castrations, and always the inevitable doubling, monstrous cleavage shuddering between a crawling reptile beast and the mother bitch, messengers of devouring Nature. Before the prince charming enters, an angel and idiot of love. The poet, panicked dreamer, flows away in the form of "large quantities of white fluid," strange precursor of Kafka's Gregor Samsa. Another underground, this one psychosomatic, illuminates his "notion of some dark, insolent, senselessly infinite force to which everything is subordinated" (*The Idiot*, 1868). This would be Nature, which Ippolit perceives as a "frightful creature, a sort of monster" that makes you lose your Christian faith:

> I was very much surprised at the prince [Myshkin] guessing the other day that I was having "bad dreams" ... Either he's a doctor or else a man of extraordinary mind who can divine a great many things. (But there cannot be the slightest doubt that in the final analysis he is an "idiot.") ... I fell asleep—I think an hour before he came—and found myself in a room (not my own). It was larger and loftier than mine, better furnished, light and airy ... I saw a *frightful creature, a sort of monster* ... It was brown and had a carapace, *a reptile* about eight inches long, two fingers thick at the head, gradually tapering off towards the tail so that the tip of the tail was no more than a fifth of an inch broad ... The creature was running very swiftly around the room, supported on its claws and *tail*; as it ran, its abdomen and claws wriggled like *little snakes*, with astonishing speed, despite the carapace, and it was most loathsome to watch. I was dreadfully afraid it would sting me ... My mother and a friend of hers came into the room ... At this point, *my mother* opened the door and summoned *our dog Norma*—a huge, shaggy black Newfoundland; she died five years ago. ... The creature halted ... but continued squirming. ... I felt that in Norma's fear there was something very strange, almost something *correspondingly supernatural*, and that she must also be sensing, as I did, that there was something fateful and mysterious about the beast. ... The creature must have jerked itself powerfully free and tried to squirm away, because *Norma* caught it again, this time in the air, and twice more *took it whole into her jaws*, as if

swallowing it. The carapace began cracking under her teeth; the creature's tail and claws thrashed horribly as they dangled from her mouth. All of a sudden, Norma gave a piteous whine: the foul creature had managed to *sting her tongue* after all. She opened her mouth in pain, whining and howling, and I saw the mangled creature was still wriggling across the width of her jaws, emitting large quantities of white fluid from its half-crushed body onto her tongue, like when a cockroach is squashed. . . . That's when I woke up, and the prince came in. (*The Idiot*, 1868)

There is no syncretic spectacle in this polyphonic *flood* because the novel-poem is not a spectacle. Like dreams, Dostoyevsky's images "sting the tongue," they are polyphonic precipitants of the Word. The *spectral visible* turns into the *audible vocal*. And the sex of the voices, haunted by the decomposition-recomposition of shame, of crime, and of pleasure, upsets the ritual spectacle and turns it into a deliverance, thanks to the putting-into-words being shared through a sheaf of dialogues.

There isn't a "new world" (not yet): the worlds of Christocentrism and its Russian Christ have yet to come. And they are tirelessly announced in the eternal return of the writing on the thresholds of *singular intensity* that constitute *tradition* and the *jouissance* (*naslajdienie*) of *speaking* it, thus recomposing it. Neither identity, nor power, nor spiritual scene. The plenitude of this productive power, destruction and infinite elucidation, is the *essential actuosa* of life for Spinoza, a *thought in action* for Dostoyevsky.[4] Another name for writing. It can survive the "death of God" as confirmed by Hans Holbein's *Dead Christ* itself, if one manages to inscribe that death—the indispensable one, the evident one—in the Word. Only thus will the immortality of Christ's message perdure.

So, after having *seen, listen*:

I suddenly recalled the picture I had seen that day at Rogozhin's, above the doorway in one of the gloomiest rooms in his house . . . The picture shows Christ, just taken down from the cross. I believe artists usually depict Christ, whether on the cross or taken down from it, as still retaining a trace of extraordinary beauty in the face ... There was no hint of beauty in Rogozhin's picture; it is an out-and-out depiction of the body of a man who has endured endless torments even before the crucifixion— wounds, torture, beatings from the guards, blows from the popu- lace when he was carrying the cross and fell beneath it, and finally the agony of the cross, lasting six hours (according to my calculations at least) ... But it's odd; as you look at this corpse of a tortured man a most curious question comes to mind: if a corpse like that (and it must certainly have been exactly like that) was seen by all his disciples, ... how could they have believed, looking at such a corpse, that the martyr would rise again? ... Looking at that picture, one has the impression of *nature* as some *enormous*, implacable, dumb *beast*, or more precisely, much more precisely, strange as it may seem—in the guise of a vast modern machine which has pointlessly seized, dismembered, and devoured, in its blind and insensible fashion, a great and priceless being, a being worth all of nature and all her laws worth the entire earth—which indeed was perhaps created solely to prepare for the advent of that being! The picture is, as it were, the medium through which this notion of some dark, insolent, senselessly infinite *force* to which everything is subordinated is unwittingly conveyed. (*The Idiot*, 1868)[5]

The flood of language spares neither nature nor faith, and not death either—neither the resurrection of Judeo-Christianism nor that event unique in the world that it produced: the break with God that left us free from God. The novelist's voices resonate with the passions, narratives, and arguments—intimate because they tell stories—without which the crimes, the misalliances, the grotesque or idiotic sufferings, and Dostoyevsky's ecstatic jubilation could not have blossomed: pleasurable transgressions because they are guilty, torturing.

In delivering them to the Word diffracted from the "multi- toned narration" (Bakhtin), these "communicating vessels" (in the sense of *coincidentia oppositorum*) confer a mysterious eroticism onto "dialogized interior monologue." I perceive them neither as deconstructive philosophical-theological meditations nor as a cynical, grimacing fairground spectacle. The polyphonic opulence of the *contemplative text* carries the rebellious or mystical excesses of faith, of man, of any identity, carnival and Socratic wisdom included—necessarily believing, necessarily criminal—into a nebula of turns of language as they are being composed, not in the least innocent, and necessarily unfinished. The ultimate *sexualization* of the representations, hallucinations, and thoughts is nothing other than the sexualization that is transferred to *invocations*—irresistible flow of approximate words, spontaneous unconscious exactness. The *sex of language* is constructed and transmitted in these breathless operas.

I do mean *sex*. Not at all "sexual freedom"; nor do I mean pornography or "show biz." These are always present when the voice comes up short in the face of crime—murder or pedophilia—to avoid naming them with words that fixate and judge. But rather *sex-outside-of-sex*, appetite of excitement that impregnates man, woman, and child, faith and nihilism, throbbing vitality of the flesh of words, undergrounds and fugues, to be continued, but at what price . . . unique for each reader.

I'm not saying atheistic either, but antitheist in the wake of Spinoza (unknown to Dostoyevsky but a precursor to Nietzsche): the polyphonic convict does not realize he is opening the way, beyond Husserl's transcendental ego, to the transcendental atheism of Freud discovering that "God is unconscious" (as Lacan put it).

15.3 The Unconscious Bone-Structure of Style

Under the carnival masks, under the skin of these poor folks with their Karamazovian sensuality, there is a *music* that makes them live, a music from among those that inspire the European comedy in its universalist design.

When the beautiful stranger, Death, "has taken up residence in [his] brain," Proust wonders "how he can believe in the unity of style, when sensibilities are singular" (*Against Sainte-Beuve*). A profound empathy links him with Dostoyevsky as early as the *Notebook of 1908*, which prepares the way for *In Search of Lost Time*, and through to *Notebook LIX*, the last, written a few months before his death in 1922. Inhabited as he was by the theme of parricide, central to the story of Mlle Vinteuil who causes the death of her father (whose music is related to Dostoyevsky's),[6] he inscribes it on the maternal side, with Charlus's matricidal drives, wanting to see the synagogue with punctured eyes (like Oedipus?) in *Sodom and Gomorrah*, and with the narrator, who compares himself to Orestes.

Dostoyevsky's name is scattered throughout the aesthetic credo elaborated in *Against Sainte-Beuve*. The mixture of admiration and irony the "great Russian" inspires in Proust shows in the connivence between him and Myshkin: the prince breaks the Chinese vase the wife of General Yepanchin prizes; similarly, Bloch, the blundering but subtly endearing Jew of *In Search of Lost Time*, overturns the vase containing the branch that Mme de Villeparisis was in the process of painting at the Verdurins' (*The Guermantes Way*).

Proust's reflections on the limits of the discursive art, associating Baudelaire, Beethoven, and Dostoyevsky, go so far as to project a never-achieved book of criticism on Flaubert, Baudelaire, and Dostoyevsky, imagined in 1921 by Jacques Rivière, who was passionate about Russian orthodoxy: "I can only reply like the prophet Nehemiah (I think) who was on a ladder . . . '*Non possum descendere, magnum opus facio.*'"[7] A swipe here: Dostoyevsky "concentrated, still tense and peevish, a great deal of what was to blossom later on in Tolstoy"; "proleptic gloom of the primitives which the disciples will brighten and dispel" (*The Captive*). Admiring details there: "In Dostoievsky I find the deepest wells of insight but only into certain isolated regions of the human soul." Proust doesn't enthuse. Because he's in Dostoyevsky's debt?

And yet, finally, all the threads are tied to make of Dostoyevsky the hero—the pivot—of the implausible lovers' explanation between the narrator and Albertine, in the posthumous text of *The Captive*. "The unique thing that Dostoievsky has given to the world" is not only "a frieze interrupted and resumed in which the theme of vengeance and expiation is unfolded." The narrator and his Albertine—a "being in flight" and initiated into Dostoyevsky for the circumstance—slip into it in search of "mysterious," "unintellectual" movements. What "defies analysis" about parricide, dreadful torture, is relayed by a "new beauty": "the Dostoievsky woman (as distinctive as a Rembrandt woman)," "good nature . . . only play-acting, terrible insolence." Since "it's possible that creative writers are tempted by certain forms of life of which they have no personal experience," the narrator has Albertine ask: "But did he ever murder anyone, Dostoievsky?" And still today, other Albertines may ask: did he himself commit the crime of pedophilia? "And perhaps it wasn't necessary for him to be criminal himself," the "little Marcel" slips in, knowing the underground of writing.

It is not so much the religious atmosphere of cruel moral beauty that floods the last lines of Proust's writing as the "unanalyzable" breath of the creative art: "mysterious, grandiose, august."

Once again, compared to Elstir, the impressionist painter from *Within a Budding Grove*, Dostoyevsky's characters and their actions "seem to us as deceptive as those effects in Elstir's pictures where the sea appears to be in the sky." Even more stupefying, the irruption of the favorite author of the narrator's grandmother, "a great artist of the same family as a painter whom I was to meet at Balbec and who had such a profound influence on my way of seeing things: Elstir." This is Mme de Sévigné. She, "like Dostoievsky, instead of presenting things in their logical sequence, that is to say beginning with the cause, shows us first of all the effect, the illusion that strikes us," which destabilizes and grabs us. Albertine, disbelieving, asks for an example of this discordance, which her interlocutor promises and which never comes, *The Captive* being unfinished.

So I return to the first appearance of the famous letter-writer in *In Search of Lost Time*: "But already that afternoon in the railway carriage, on re-reading that letter in which the moonlight appears—'I could not resist the temptation: I put on all my bonnets and cloaks, though there is no need of them, I walk along this mall, where the air is as sweet as that of my chamber; I find a thousand phantasms, *monks white and black, nuns grey and white, linen cast here and there on the ground, men enshrouded upright against the tree-trunks'*—I was enraptured by what, a little later, I should have described (for does not she draw land-scapes in the same way as he draws characters?) as the Dostoievsky side of Mme de Sévigné's Letters" (*Within a Budding Grove*).

Proust is quoting from memory, and he rewrites the fabulous marquise, adding witticisms of his own to the sparkling style of the great letter-writer, guided by the singular, even illusory, *perception* instead of by the *cause*. Dostoyevsky, fascinated, on the other hand, but still doubled, insists on his "terrible, unmasterable, incredible distaste for letter-writing... I *cannot* write letters: I cannot write about myself and be just."[8] Raging with jealousy against the marquise: "You can never write anything in a letter. That's why I can't stand Mme de Sévigné. She wrote letters entirely too well" (letter to Apollon Maykov, January 18, 1856).

No "received ideas," no utilitarian narrative delivered "in a measured way." What remains, as the last horizon: the late quartets of Beethoven, considered in tandem with Baudelaire. They form an uninterrupted musical fabric, slippages without directional intention, and from time to time they let us hear the infinite. Whatever the medium (language, sound, or image), style is an "unconscious bone-structure underlying the assemblage of deliberate ideas" (Proust, *Against Sainte-Beuve*). "Double view," "vision," and transgression of limits, this "total theater" is in unison with the "rhythmic motifs of the being," as Mallarmé pointed out. The joining of scattered fragments, of elements of narrative, of take-offs and reprieves supports the "mystic hope" of "the formula, eternally true and for ever fertile." Proust leans on Dostoyevsky, projecting himself into him, to praise "the hallucinatory power of his imagination" (*Against Sainte-Beuve*): "This evolution of a thought, I did not intend to analyze it abstractly but to recreate it, make it live" (Proust and Rivière, *Correspondance*, 2–3).

The political-historical bearing is part of it, war and revolution inscribed in it, glimpsed, sketched, guessed: "And even if war were scientific, it would still be right to paint it as Elstir painted the sea, by reversing the real and the apparent, starting from illusions and beliefs which one then slowly brings into line with the truth, which is the manner in which Dostoievsky tells the story of a life. Quite certainly, however, war is not strategic, it might better be described as a pathological condition, because it admits of accidents which even a skilled physician could not have foreseen, such as the Russian Revolution" (Proust, *Time Regained*).

Like Elstir, like Vinteuil, Dostoyevsky painted these accidents, but with the flesh of words, which lets one hear the infinite in the human comedy. His joy is delirious; he makes his score vibrate and laugh, incorporating it into the passions, into the history of religions, into the deflagration of ideologies. His poetics is none other than this polyphony and polyrhythm, music whose dissonances, irreducibly individual, rejoin "that great poet" Proust speaks of "who has been fundamentally one, since the world began" (*Against Sainte-Beuve*). We call him Dostoyevsky, Sévigné, Baudelaire, Proust, Beethoven, Shakespeare . . . His metaphysical undulations defy the spiritual, linguistic, and sexual misery of a world laboring to manage its viral, digital age.

NOTES

Many of Dostoyevsky's novels have been translated under different names: for example, *Demons* has also been translated as *The Possessed*. I retain only the titles of the versions from which I have retrieved cited passages. These translated texts are listed in the bibliography. —TRANS.

1. The Condemned Man, the Sacred Malady, and the Sun

1. One more minute, Mr. Executioner, one more minute!
2. Cf. chapter 5.2, "Proud 'Little Demons' and 'Firm Like Saints.'"
3. You can see the sun!
4. Kristeva is referring to the book collection from the French publisher Buchet/Chastel with the series title "The Authors of My Life." Her contribution to the series, *Dostoyevsky*, was translated into English by Jody Gladding and published by Columbia University Press in 2022. —TRANS.

5. Cf. chapter 13.3, "Nietzsche and Raskolnikov."

6. Cf. chapter 14.5, "Laughing Is Over?"; chapter 15.3, "The Unconscious Bone-Structure of Style."

2. Dostoyevsky, "Author of My Life"

1. Passages quoted in this section are from Mikhail Bakhtin, *Problems of Dostoevsky's Poetics*, trans. Caryl Emerson (Minneapolis: University of Minnesota Press, 1984).

2. Cf. chapter 1.1, "December 22, 1849."

3. Cf. chapter 13, "The Nihilist Seeking God."

4. A portmanteau coinage by Kristeva, semanalysis is a theory of the signification of speech and writing that takes the speaking subject into account. —TRANS.

3. In the Steps of the Liberated Convict

1. Cf. chapter 1.2, "The Ultra-Deep Song of Beings."

2. Cf. chapter 10.4, "The Liberated Man: Troubles, Failures, and Luminous Anchorage."

3. Cf. chapter 10.4, "The Liberated Man."

4. Cf. chapter 3.1, "Passions Played/Played-Out."

4. Beyond Neurosis

1. Coined by Jacques Lacan around 1975, *parlêtre* combines *parler*, "to speak," with *être*, "to be" or "being."

2. Cf. chapter 2.4, "Freud: Reader of Dostoyevsky."

3. " 'Perhaps, reader, you would have me invoke hatred at the opening of this work!' . . . He later perceived he was born wicked." Lautréamont, *Maldoror and the Complete Works of the Comte de Lautréamont*, trans. Alexis Lykiard (Cambridge, MA: Exact Change, 1994), 28–29;

"Two enormous towers.... Multiplying them by two, the product was four ... but I could scarcely perceive the need for this arithmetical process" (137).

4. The writer makes this claim in his correspondence with the General Procurator of the Holy Synod, Konstantin Pobedonostsev. Cf. chapter 12.1, "Political Religion."

5. Cf. chapter 8.5, "What Freedom? Digressions on the 'Religious Pathetic' (*pafos stihíí*)," *Per Fílium* section.

6. Julia Kristeva, *Powers of Horror: An Essay on Abjection*, trans. Leon Roudiez (New York: Columbia University Press, 1982).

5. The God-Man, the Man-God

1. Cf. chapter 12.3, "Did You Say Atheism?"

2. This eroticization of suffering, parallel to a rejection of capital punishment, evokes analogous positions in the Marquis de Sade. Dostoyevsky's contemporaries established similarities between the two writers, not without a certain ill will. Thus Turgenev notes that Dostoyevsky, like Sade, describes "the pleasures of sensual people" and becomes indignant about the fact that "the most important priests in the Russian Orthodox Church sang requiem masses for our de Sade and even read sermons on this universal man's love of all humanity! We really do live in strange times!" (letter from Ivan Turgenev to M. Y. Saltykov-Shchedrin, October 6, 1882).

3. Cf. chapter 14.5, "Laughing Is Over?"

4. Cf. chapter 10.5, "The Selves in Perpetual Fusion with the All."

5. Cf. chapter 10, "The Pleasures of Evil and Misfortune," and chapter 13, "The Nihilist Seeking God."

6. Cf. chapter 5.3, "Children, Loves, and Cruelties"; chapter 6.3, "The Violence of the Trauma: Things and Words"; chapter 7.6, "The Madonna, Sodom, and the 'Ode to Joy'"; chapter 10.1, "This Good and This Evil of the Devil"; chapter 10.3, "The Body of Evil"; and chapter 14.4, "The Salvation of the Man Who Knows He Is Ridiculous."

7. Kristeva, *The Severed Head: Capital Visions*, trans. Jody Gladding (New York: Columbia University Press, 2012).

8. Cf. chapter 8.5, "What Freedom? Digressions on the 'Religious Pathetic' (*pafos stihii*)," "The Icon Is Not an Image" section.

9. Cf. chapter 12.3, "Did You Say Atheism?"

10. Cf. chapter 11.4, "The Golden Age of the 'Russian Type' and the 'Jewish Question.'"

11. Cf. chapter 7.2, "The Grand Inquisitor"; and chapter 12.1, "Political Religion."

12. Cf. chapter 5.1, "Memories of Childhood: Marey and Vlas."

13. The scene of sexual abuse, narrated in the chapter "At Tikhon's," impossible to publish under the censorship reigning at that time in prudish Russia, was not retained by the *Russian Courier* (December 1871), which was publishing *Demons* in episodes. The complete version appeared for the first time in French in the translation by André Markowicz (Actes Sud, Babel, 1995).

14. Cf. chapter 5.1, "The Mortal Male, Thinking and Ridiculous"; chapter 5.3, "An Extraordinary Aptitude for Crime: Pedophilia"; chapter 12.3, "Did You Say Atheism?"; and chapter 13.1, "Nechaev, Shigalyov, and Lenin."

6. The Purloined Letter

1. Cf. chapter 9.2, "The Valentinian Gnosis," and chapter 9.3, "Demoniacal Cleavage."

2. Cf. chapter 5.3, "Children, Loves, and Cruelties."

3. Cf. chapter 5.3, "An Extraordinary Aptitude for Crime: Pedophilia."

4. Cf. chapter 5.2, "Nastasya Filippovna: 'Heaven Alone Knows What Is Living Within Me Instead.'"

5. Cf. chapter 5.3, "An Extraordinary Aptitude for Crime: Pedophilia."

6. Quoted in Joseph Frank, *Dostoevsky: The Miraculous Years, 1865–1871* (Princeton, NJ: Princeton University Press, 1995), 22.

7. Cf. chapter 3.2, "Crystal Palaces."
8. Cf. chapter 6.1, "Jouissance."

7. Everything Is Permitted

1. Cf. chapter 11.4, "The Golden Age of the 'Russian Type' and the 'Jewish Question.'"
2. Cf. chapter 8.5, "What Freedom? Digressions on the 'Religious Pathetic' (*pafos stíhii*)," "The Icon Is Not an Image" section.
3. Cf. the Idea, chapter 5.1, "Language, an Eroticism Without an Organ," and chapter 15.2, "'An Enormous Beast...Almost Mystical.'"
4. Cf. chapter 6.3, "The Violence of the Trauma: Things and Words."
5. Cf. chapter 5.3, "The 'Ones Thirsty for Flesh.'"
6. Cf. chapter 2.4, "Freud: Reader of Dostoyevsky."
7. Cf. chapter 12.3, "Did You Say Atheism?"
8. Cf. chapter 5.2, "Proud 'Little Demons' and 'Firm Like Saints.'"
9. Cf. chapter 5.1, "The Mortal Male, Thinking and Ridiculous"; chapter 5.3, "An Extraordinary Aptitude for Crime"; chapter 10.2, "Expressions of Suffering"; chapter 12.3, "Did You Say Atheism?"; chapter 13.1, "Nechaev, Shigalyov, and Lenin."
10. Cf. chapter 5.1, "Same, Sameness, 'Self-Love.'"
11. Cf. chapter 5.1, "Memories of Childhood: Marey and Vlas."
12. Cf. chapter 5.2, "The Cripple: Delirium or Pain?"
13. Cf. chapter 13, "The Nihilist Seeking God."
14. Cf. chapter 5.2, "Grushenka: A 'Bitchy' Shame."

8. The Russian Virus

1. Pierre Pascal, *Dostoïevski* (Paris: Desclée de Brouwer, 1969), 60.
2. Cf. chapter 2.1, "Outside the Limits"; chapter 2.2, "Polyphony According to Bakhtin"; chapter 2.3, "Seriousness of the Carnival."
3. Cf. chapter 13.2, "'Line' or 'Zone': The Twentieth Century."

4. Cf. chapter 15.3, "The Unconscious Bone-Structure of Style."

5. Cf. chapter 8.5, "What Freedom? Digressions on the 'Religious Pathetic' (*pafos stihii*)."

6. Cf. chapter 5.1, "Language, an Eroticism Without an Organ."

7. See Julia Kristeva, *The Sense and Non-sense of Revolt*, trans. Jeanine Herman (New York: Columbia University Press, 2001) and *Intimate Revolt*, trans. Jeanine Herman (New York: Columbia University Press, 2003).

8. Julia Kristeva, "Europe Divided: Politics, Ethics, Religion," in *Crisis of the European Subject*, trans. Susan Fairfield (New York: Other Press, 2000), 111–62.

9. From the Greek *hesychia*, silence and peace in the union with God.

10. Martin Heidegger, *The Essence of Human Freedom: An Introduction to Modern Philosophy* (1930), trans. Ted Sadler (New York: Continuum, 2002).

11. Julia Kristeva, *New Maladies of the Soul*, trans. Ross Guberman (New York: Columbia University Press, 1997).

12. Cf. chapter 13, "The Nihilist Seeking God."

13. Cf. chapter 14.2, "From the 'Original Laugh' to a Genealogy of Laughter."

14. Olivier Clément, *The Church of Orthodoxy* (New York: Chelsea House, 2001).

15. Google, Apple, Facebook, Amazon. —TRANS.

16. Vladimir Lossky, *The Mystical Theology of the Eastern Church* (Yonkers, NY: St. Vladimir's Seminary Press, 1976).

17. Cf. chapter 13.2, " 'Line' or 'Zone': The Twentieth Century."

18. Cf. chapter 9.2, "The Valentinian Gnosis."

19. Marie-José Mondzain, *Image, Icon, Economy: The Byzantine Origins of the Contemporary Imaginary*, trans. Rico Franses (Palo Alto, CA: Stanford University Press, 2004).

20. Cf. chapter 5.1, "Language, an Eroticism Without an Organ."

21. Cf. chapter 8.5, "What Freedom?"

22. Cf. chapter 7.6, "The Madonna, Sodom, and the 'Ode to Joy' "; chapter 9, "Christocentrism"; chapter 11, "The National Christ."

23. To disappear, to annihilate oneself. Cf. chapter 2.1, "Outside the Limits."

9. Christocentrism

1. "Between justice and my mother, I choose my mother." That is how the popular imagination has retained the Nobel Prize–winning writer's comments addressed to Swedish students: "At this moment bombs are being planted in the trams in Algiers. My mother could be on one of those trams. If that is justice, I prefer my mother."

2. Henri-Charles Puech; Hans Jonas; Nathalie Depraz.

3. Cosmic Valentinianism will be accessible after the discovery in 1945 of the fourth-century manuscripts of Nag Hammadi in upper Egypt, which yield documents directly issuing from the gnostic sects.

4. Quoted in Konstantin Mochulsky, *Dostoevsky: His Life and Work*, trans. Michael A. Minihan (Princeton, NJ: Princeton University Press, 1967), 460.

5. That is, "approximately fifty years old."

10. The Pleasures of Evil and Misfortune

1. Cf. chapter 1, "The Condemned Man, Sacred Evil, and the Sun"; chapter 3.4, "The Whims of Chance: Money and the Synagogue"; chapter 7.4, "Zosima: 'Life Is Paradise, and We Are All in Paradise.'"

2. Cf. chapter 5.3, "Children, Loves, and Cruelties."

3. Cf. chapter 9.3, "Demoniacal Cleavage."

4. Cf. chapter 4.2, "Matricide, Crime, and Forgiveness."

5. See Kristeva, "Dostoyevsky, the Writing of Suffering and Forgiveness," in *Black Sun: Depression and Melancholia*, trans. Leon Roudiez (New York: Columbia University Press, 1989), 173–218.

6. Cf. chapter 4.2, "Matricide, Crime, and Forgiveness"; chapter 4.3, "The Unnamable and the Atoms of Silence."

7. Cf. chapter 13.3, "Nietzsche and Raskolnikov."

8. On Dostoyevsky's epilepsy, see Jacques Catteau, *Dostoyevsky and the Process of Literary Creation*, trans. Audrey Littlewood (Cambridge: Cambridge University Press, 1989), 90–134.

9. Cf. chapter 5.1, "Memories of Childhood: Marey and Vlas."

10. Cf. chapter 3.1, "Passions Played/Played-Out"; chapter 3.4, "The Whims of Chance: Money and the Synagogue"; chapter 5.1, "Memories of Childhood: Marey and Vlas"; chapter 6.3, "The Violence of the Trauma: Things and Words."

11. Cf. chapter 4.1, "'At the Bottom of the Stinking, Abject Underground.'"

12. Cf. chapter 3.1, "Passions Played/Played-Out"; chapter 3.3, "The 'Hampered Ego.'"

13. Cf. chapter 5.1, "The Mortal Male, Thinking and Ridiculous"; chapter 10.5, "The Selves in Perpetual Fusion with the All."

14. Cf. chapter 3.3, "The 'Hampered Ego.'"

15. Cf. chapter 2.4, "Freud: Reader of Dostoyevsky."

16. "The devil doesn't exist."

17. Cf. chapter 3.3, "The 'Hampered Ego'"; chapter 5.1, "The Mortal Male, Thinking and Ridiculous"; chapter 13.2, "'Line' or 'Zone': The Twentieth Century."

18. A word forged by Proudhon from "messiah" and "apotheosis." It refers to the social creation of the Messiah. —TRANS.

11. The National Christ

1. Cf. chapter 9.2, "The Valentinian Gnosis."

2. Cf. chapter 10.4, "The Liberated Man: Troubles, Failures and Luminous Anchorage," and chapter 10.5, "The Selves in Perpetual Fusion with the All."

3. Cf. chapter 3.3, "The 'Hampered Ego.'"

4. Cf. chapter 8.5, "What Freedom? Digressions on the 'Religious Pathetic' (*pafos stihii*)," "*Per Filium*" section.

5. Cf. chapter 3.5, "The Carnival of the Couple: An Underground Laugh," and chapter 5.2, "Disfigured Destinies of the Second Sex," "'The Meek One,' or 'There Is No Sexual Relation'" sections.

6. Cf. chapter 9.2, "The Valentinian Gnosis."

7. See David I. Goldstein, *Dostoyevsky and the Jews* (Austin: University of Texas Press, 1981).

8. Cf. chapter 7.1, "From the Dead Father to the Murder of the Father."

9. Cf. chapter 3.4, "The Whims of Chance: Money and the Synagogue," and chapter 5.2, "Disfigured Destinies of the Second Sex," "Proud 'Little Demons' and 'Firm Like Saints'" section.

10. Cf. chapter 14, "Laughter, Spokesperson for the Obscene," and chapter 15, "The Novel Is a Poem."

12. Catholicism, Atheism, Nihilism

1. Cf. chapter 2.3, "Seriousness of the Carnival," and Tzvetan Stoyanov, *Le génie et son maître* (Paris: L'Esprit des Péninsules, 2000), 101.

2. Cf. J. Kristeva, "Moi-même et mon Créateur, selon J. H. Newman," 2013. Solovyov is the author of a "Speech on the Incarnation" and a "Speech on the Memory of Dostoyevsky," 1883.

3. Cf. chapter 11.3, "'A Great People . . . to the Exception of the Others.'"

4. Cf. chapter 2.4, "Freud: Reader of Dostoyevsky," and chapter 2.5, "The Flesh of the Infinite Void and of Words."

5. Cf. chapter 5.1, "The Mortal Male, Thinking and Ridiculous"; chapter 5.2, "The Cripple: Delirium or Pain?"; chapter 7.1, "From the Dead Father to the Murder of the Father"; chapter 11.3, "'A Great People . . . to the Exception of the Others.'"

6. Cf. chapter 5.3, "An Extraordinary Aptitude for Crime: Pedophilia," and chapter 7.5, "The Serpent, a Mother Alone, and Shakespeare."

7. Cf. chapter 13, "The Nihilist Seeking God."

8. Cf. chapter 5.1, "His Characters, His Doubles," and chapter 11.4, "The Golden Age of the 'Russian Type' and the 'Jewish Question.'"

9. Cf. chapter 7.4, "Zosima: 'Life Is Paradise, and We Are All in Paradise.'"

10. Cf. chapter 7.1, "From the Dead Father to the Murder of the Father."

11. Cf. chapter 7.2, "The Grand Inquisitor," and chapter 14.4, "The Salvation of the Man Who Knows He Is Ridiculous."

13. The Nihilist Seeking God

1. Solzhenitsyn's term; cf. chapter 8.5, "What Freedom? Digressions on the 'Religious Pathetic' (*pafos stihii*)."
2. Sergey Nechaev (1847–1882), Russian nihilist partisan of terrorism.
3. Mikhail Petrashevsky (1821–1866), militant Russian utopian, founder of the circle of intellectuals that Dostoyevsky had participated in.
4. Cf. chapter 4.2, "Matricide, Crime, and Forgiveness," and 4.3, "The Unnamable and the Atoms of Silence."
5. Cf. chapter 7.3, "Shigalyov: 'Desire—We Will Kill It.'"
6. Cf. chapter 7.1, "From the Dead Father to the Murder of the Father."
7. Cf. chapter 2.4, "Freud: Reader of Dostoyevsky," and 2.5, "The Flesh of the Infinite Void and of Words."
8. Cf. chapter 4.2, "Matricide, Crime, and Forgiveness," and chapter 7.1, "From the Dead Father to the Murder of the Father."
9. Cf. chapter 9.2, "The Valentinian Gnosis."
10. Cf. chapter 15.3, "The Unconscious Bone-Structure of Style."

14. Laughter, Spokesperson for the Obscene

1. Mikhail Bakhtin, *Problems of Dostoevsky's Poetics*, trans. Caryl Emerson (Minneapolis: University of Minnesota Press, 1984), 49.
2. Cf. chapter 5.1, "The Mortal Male, Thinking and Ridiculous"; chapter 5.3, "An Extraordinary Aptitude for Crime: Pedophilia"; and chapter 12.3, "Did You Say Atheism?"
3. Cf. chapter 7.1, "From the Dead Father to the Murder of the Father"; chapter 7.6, "The Madonna, Sodom, and the 'Ode to Joy'"; and chapter 12.3, "Did You Say Atheism?"
4. "I saw the shade of a coachman scrubbing the shade of a carriage with the shade of a brush." A popular quotation from a

seventeenth-century French parody of the *Aeneid* (book 6, the descent to the underworld) by Charles Perrault and others.

5. Cf. chapter 5.2, "'The Meek One,' or 'There Is No Sexual Relation.'"

6. Cf. chapter 7.2, "The Grand Inquisitor."

7. Cf. chapter 10.2, "Expressions of Suffering"; chapter 12.3, "Did You Say Atheism?"

8. Cf. chapter 5.3, "Children, Loves, and Cruelties"—"An Extraordinary Aptitude for Crime: Pedophilia"; chapter 6.2, "The Ravished Young Girl"; and 6.3, "The Violence of the Trauma: Things and Words."

9. "You can see the sun!" Cf. chapter 1, "The Condemned Man, the Sacred Malady, and the Sun."

10. Julia Kristeva, *Time and Sense: Proust and the Experience of Literature,* trans. Ross Guberman (New York: Columbia University Press, 1996), 279.

11. *Biography, Letters and Notes from the Notebook of F. M. Dostoevsky* (St. Petersburg, 1883), 373, quoted in Bakhtin, *Problems,* 60.

12. Julia Kristeva, "On Mother-Version," *Talks on Psychoanalysis,* International Psychoanalytical Association, 1982, http://www.kristeva.fr/ipa-talks-on-psychoanalysis.html.

15. "The Novel Is a Poem"

1. See Julia Kristeva, "Adolescent Novel," in *New Maladies of the Soul,* trans. Ross Guberman (New York: Columbia University Press, 1997).

2. Cf. chapter 8.5, "What Freedom? Digressions on the 'Religious Pathetic' (*pafos stihii*)."

3. Cf. chapter 5.1, "The Mortal Male, Thinking and Ridiculous," and chapter 12.3, "Did You Say Atheism?"

4. Cf. chapter 5.1, "Language, an Eroticism Without an Organ."

5. Cf. chapter 5.1, "Holbein's *Dead Christ*" and "Language, an Eroticism Without an Organ"; chapter 6.4, "Writing and For-giveness."

6. Cf. chapter 14.5, "Laughing Is Over?"

7. Marcel Proust and Jacques Rivière, *Correspondance 1914–1922* (Paris: Sillage, 2013).

8. Quoted in André Gide, *Dostoevsky*, ed. Arnold Bennett (New York: New Directions, 1961), 20–21.

BIBLIOGRAPHY

Works by Fyodor Mikhailovich Dostoyevsky

The Adolescent. Trans. Andrew R. MacAndrew. New York: Doubleday, 1971.

The Brothers Karamazov. Trans. Richard Pevear and Larissa Volokhonsky. New York: Farrar, Straus & Giroux, 1990.

Complete Letters. 5 vols. Ed. and trans. David Lowe and Ronald Meyer. Ann Arbor, MI: Ardis, 1988–1991.

Crime and Punishment. Trans. Michael Katz. New York: Norton, 2019.

Demons. Trans. Richard Pevear and Larissa Volokhonsky. New York: Knopf, 1994.

The Double and *The Gambler.* Trans. Richard Pevear and Larissa Volokhonsky. New York: Knopf Everyman's Library, 2005.

The Eternal Husband and Other Stories. Trans. Richard Pevear and Larissa Volokhonsky. New York: Bantam, 1997.

The Idiot. Trans. Alan Myers. Oxford: Oxford University Press, 1992.

The Insulted and Injured. Trans. Boris Jakim. Grand Rapids, MI: Eerdmans, 2011.

Netochka Nezvanova. Trans. Ann Dunnigan. Englewood Cliffs, NJ: Prentice-Hall, 1970.

The Notebooks for The Possessed. Trans. Victor Terras, ed. Edward Wasiolek. Chicago: University of Chicago Press, 1968.

Notes from a Dead House. Trans. Richard Pevear and Larissa Volokhonsky. New York: Knopf, 2015.

Notes from Underground. Trans. and ed. Michael Katz. New York: Norton, 1989.

"Petersburg Dreams in Verse and Prose." Trans. David Foreman. *New Zealand Slavonic Journal* (2003): 281–99.

The Unpublished Dostoevsky: Diaries and Notebooks. 3 vols. Ed. Carl R. Proffer. Ann Arbor, MI: Ardis, 1973.

White Nights and Other Stories. The Novels of Fyodor Dostoevsky, vol. X. Trans. Constance Garnett. https://www.gutenberg.org/ebooks/36034.

Winter Notes on Summer Impressions. Trans. David Patterson. Evanston, IL: Northwestern University Press, 1988.

A Writer's Diary. 2 vols. Trans. Kenneth Lantz, intro. Gary Saul Morson. Evanston, IL: Northwestern University Press, 1993–1994.

Other Sources

Bakhtin, Mikhail. *Problems of Dostoevsky's Poetics.* Trans. Caryl Emerson. Minneapolis: University of Minnesota Press, 1984.

Bataille, Georges. *Inner Experience.* Trans. Stuart Kendall. Albany: State University of New York Press, 2014.

Beauvoir, Simone de. "Pyrrhus and Cineas." In *Philosophical Writings,* ed. Sylvie Le Bon, trans. Mary Beth Timmerman, 77–150. Urbana: University of Illinois Press, 2005.

Carrère, Emmanuel. *Limonov.* Trans. John Lambert. New York: Farrar, Straus & Giroux, 2014.

Catteau, Jacques. *Dostoyevsky and the Process of Literary Creation.* Trans. Audrey Littlewood. Cambridge: Cambridge University Press, 1989.

Chekhov, Anton. "On the Road." In *The Chorus Girl and Other Stories*. Trans. Constance Garnett. https://www.gutenberg.org/ebooks/13418.

Clément, Olivier. *The Church of Orthodoxy*. New York: Chelsea House, 2001.

Depraz, Natalie. "Le statut phénoménologique du monde dans la Gnose: Du dualisme à la non-dualité." *Foi et Raison* 52, no. 3 (October 1996): 625–47.

Dostoevsky, Anna. *Dostoevsky: Reminiscences*. Trans. Beatrice Stillman. New York: Liveright, 1975.

Frank, Joseph. *Dostoevsky: The Miraculous Years, 1865–1871*. Princeton, NJ: Princeton University Press, 1995.

Freud, Sigmund. "Dostoevsky and Parricide." Trans. James Strachey. In the *Standard Edition of the Works of Sigmund Freud*, vol. 21, 173–94. London: Hogarth, 1928.

——. "Formulations on the Two Principles of Mental Functioning." Trans. James Strachey. In the *Standard Edition of the Works of Sigmund Freud*, vol. 12, 213–26. London: Hogarth, 1911.

——. "Neurosis and Psychosis." In the *Standard Edition of the Works of Sigmund Freud*, vol. 19, 149–53. London: Hogarth, 1934.

Gide, André. *Dostoevsky*. Ed. Arnold Bennett. New York: New Directions, 1961.

Goldstein, David I. *Dostoyevsky and the Jews*. Austin: University of Texas Press, 1981.

Hegel, G. W. F. *The Phenomenology of Spirit*. 1807. Trans. Terry Pinkard and Michael Baur. New York: Cambridge University Press, 2018.

Heidegger, Martin. *The Essence of Human Freedom: An Introduction to Modern Philosophy*. 1930. Trans. Ted Sadler. New York: Continuum, 2002.

——. *Introduction to Metaphysics*. Trans. Gregory Fried and Richard Polt. New Haven, CT: Yale University Press, 2000.

Jonas, Hans. *The Gnostic Religion: The Message of the Alien God and the Beginnings of Christianity*. Boston: Beacon, 1963.

Kristeva, Julia. "The Adolescent Novel." In *New Maladies of the Soul*, 135–53. Trans. Ross Guberman. New York: Columbia University Press, 1997.

——. "Bulgaria, My Suffering." In *Crisis of the European Subject*, 163–83. Trans. Susan Fairfield. New York: Other Press, 2000.

——. *Dostoyevsky, or the Flood of Language*. Trans. Jody Gladding. Foreword Rowan Williams. New York: Columbia University Press, 2022.

——. "Dostoyevsky, the Writing of Suffering, and Forgiveness." In *Black Sun: Depression and Melancholia*, 173–218. Trans. Leon Roudiez. New York: Columbia University Press, 1989.

——. "Europe Divided: Politics, Ethics, Religion." In *Crisis of the European Subject*, 111–62. Trans. Susan Fairfield. New York: Other Press, 2000.

——. *Intimate Revolt*. Trans. Jeanine Herman. New York: Columbia University Press, 2003.

——. "Moi-même et mon Créateur, selon J. H. Newman." In *Pulsions du temps*, 421–34. Paris: Fayard, 2013.

——. *New Maladies of the Soul*. Trans. Ross Guberman. New York: Columbia University Press, 1997.

——. "On Mother-Version." In *Talks on Psychoanalysis*, ed. International Psychoanalytical Association. 1982. http://www.kristeva.fr/ipa-talks -on-psychoanalysis.html.

——. *Powers of Horror: An Essay on Abjection*. Trans. Leon Roudiez. New York: Columbia University Press, 1982.

——. *The Sense and Non-sense of Revolt*. Trans. Jeanine Herman. New York: Columbia University Press, 2001.

——. *The Severed Head: Capital Visions*. Trans. Jody Gladding. New York: Columbia University Press, 2012.

——. *Time and Sense: Proust and the Experience of Literature*. Trans. Ross Guberman. New York: Columbia University Press, 1996.

Lautréamont. *Maldoror and the Complete Works of the Comte de Lautréamont*. Trans. Alexis Lykiard. Cambridge, MA: Exact Change, 1994.

Lossky, Vladimir. *The Mystical Theology of the Eastern Church*. Yonkers, NY: St. Vladimir's Seminary Press, 1976.

Mochulsky, Konstantin. *Dostoevsky. His Life and Work*. Trans. Michael A. Minihan. Princeton, NJ: Princeton University Press, 1967.

Mondzain, Marie-José. *Image, Icon, Economy: The Byzantine Origins of the Contemporary Imaginary*. Trans. Rico Franses. Palo Alto, CA: Stanford University Press, 2004.

Nabokov, Vladimir. *Lectures on Russian Literature*. New York: Harcourt Brace Jovanovich, 1981.

Nietzsche, Friedrich. *Nietzsche: A Self-Portrait from His Letters*. Ed. and trans. Peter Fuss and Henry Shapiro. Cambridge, MA: Harvard University Press, 1971.

——. *The Portable Nietzsche*. Trans. Walter Kaufmann. New York: Viking, 1968.

——. *Selected Letters*. Ed. and trans. Christopher Middleton. Chicago: University of Chicago Press, 1969.

Pascal, Pierre. *Dostoïevski*. Paris: Desclée de Brouwer, 1969.

Power, Arthur. *Conversations with James Joyce*. London: Millington, 1974. Chapter 4 excerpted at https://www.reddit.com/r/dostoevsky/comments /nqxgqa/james_joyce_on_dostoevsky/.

Proust, Marcel. *Against Sainte-Beuve and Other Essays*. Trans. John Sturrock. London: Penguin, 1988.

——. *In Search of Lost Time*. Trans. C. K. Scott-Moncrieff, Terence Kilmartin, and D. J. Enright. New York: Modern Library, 1992.

Proust, Marcel, and Jacques Rivière. *Correspondance 1914–1922*. Paris: Sillage, 2013.

Puech, Henri-Charles. *En quête de la Gnose*. Paris: Gallimard, 1978.

Solovyov, Vladimir. "A Short Story of the Anti-Christ." Trans. Alexander Bakshy. In *War, Progress, and the End of History: Three Conversations, Including a Short Story of the Anti-Christ*, 114–38. Hudson, NY: Lindisfarne, 1990.

Stoyanov, Tzvetan. *Le génie et son maître*. Paris: L'Esprit des Péninsules, 2000.

Suslova, Apollinaria. *Polina Suslova's Diary*, in F. M. Dostoyevsky, *The Gambler*, 199–302. Trans. Victor Terras. Chicago: University of Chicago Press, 1972.

Turgenev, Ivan. *Turgenev's Letters*. Trans. A. V. Knowles. London: Athlone, 1983.

INDEX

Céline, Louis-Ferdinand, 21, 30
censorship, 42, 114, 298n13
Chaplin, Charlie, 8
Charcot, Jean-Martin, 227
Chekhov, Anton, 170–71, 186, 222
childhood, children and, in Dostoyevsky works: barbarism and cruelty against, 106; in *The Brothers Karamazov*, 105–6; in *Crime and Punishment*, 105; in *Demons*, 107; in *The Insulted and Injured*, 105; in *Notes from a Dead House*, 81–83; pedophilia and, 107–11; purity of, 104–5; rape of young girls, 107; "ravished young girl," 116–20; in *A Writer's Diary*, 81–83. *See also* adolescence
Christian humanism, 205; in *The Brothers Karamazov*, 147; post-Christian humanism, 106
Christianism: in *The Brothers Karamazov*, 144–45; in canonical Orthodox Christianity, 209; Creation in, 208; Dostoyevsky, F., as defender of, 236; dualism as part of, 208–9; Ego and, 209; freedom and, 73; Gnosis of Valentinus and, 208–9; laughter and, 275–76; Nietzsche on, 72; origins of, 204; post-Christian humanism, 106; psychology of, 72; transvaluation of, 43; vocabulary of, 204
Christianity: morality and, 141–42; personalism and, 234
Christian socialism, 135
Christocentrism, xiv; in *The Brothers Karamazov*, 211–13; confession in, 206; in *Crime and Punishment*, 207; cruelty of, 217; demoniacal possession, 209–14; in *Demons*, 209–11; destructive violence of, 204; "humanitarism" and, 205, 207; in *The Idiot*, 214; jouissance and, 204; nature themes and, 287; necessity of God in, 207; in *Notes*

from a Dead House, 204; obscurantism and, 214; in *Poor Folk*, 203; vocabulary of, 204; in *A Writer's Diary*, 203, 205
Christology: bodies of evil and, 224–25; the Self in, 229
Cicero, 85
Citizen, The, 15, 42, 246–47, 249–50. *See also* *Writer's Diary, A*
Civilization and Its Discontents (Freud), 31, 128
Claudel, Paul, 21
Coetzee, J. M., 21
Cold War, Soviet Union during, 172, 178
Colette, 30
comedy, as literary genre, 27
Communism, as political religion, 250
confession: in Christocentrism, 206; in *Crime and Punishment*, 56, 150; in *The Idiot*, 20; *Stavrogin's Confession*, 112
consciousness: in *Crime and Punishment*, 58–59; in *Demons*, 80
Constantine (emperor), 179
Contemporary, The, 15, 42, 237
"Copernican revolution," 183, 269
Cosmic Valentinianism, 301n3
creativity, of Dostoyevsky, F., xiii, 32
crime, as literary theme: consciousness and, 58–59; in *Crime and Punishment*, 55–61; in Dostoyevsky works, 18–21; etymological origins of, 57; forgiveness in, 18
Crime and Punishment (Dostoyevsky, F.), 20; aesthetics in, 64–65; antihero in, 61; "atoms of silence" in, 61–65; children in, 105; Christocentrism in, 207; confession in, 56, 150; consciousness of behavior in, 58–59; crime as theme in, 55–61; critiques of, 65; deus ex machina in, 64; Ego in, 63; extraordinaries in, 58; forgiveness themes in, 55–61, 63; Greek literary influences in,

crime themes in, 18–21; criticism of, 21; as "cursed Russian," xii; dialogism of, 30, 160–61; Dickens compared to, 252–53; on education of women, 39; ego for, 43–44; as epileptic, 13–14; in Europe, 40–42; feminism and, 11; Freud on, xii–xiii, 30–34; gambling for, 41; historical literary context for, xi–xiv; imprisonment of, xii, 3, 16; letters of, 12–13, 202–4, 236, 252, 283, 292, 297n2; marriages of, xiii, 16, 43, 77, 200; Maykov and, xi; messianic popularism of, 235–36; moralism of, xiii, 32; narrative style for, 289–93; neologisms for, 23, 201; neuroticism of, xiii, 32; oedipal themes for, 31–32; Orthodox Christianity criticized by, 3; in periodical media, 15; political religion of, 246–51; on polyphonic novel, xii, 27, 30; as prophet, 251–54; psychosexuality of, 199; religious convictions of, 199; Russian legacy of, 169, 235–36; as "Russian ogre," xi; in Siberian jail, 16; as sinner, xiii, 32; Snitkina as wife of, xiii, 41, 47–49, 123, 200, 227, 246; translations of, 16, 19, 22–23; tropisms of, 20–21; works as mix of literary genres, 27–28. *See also specific topics; specific works*

"Dostoyevsky and Parricide" (Freud), 31

"Dostoyevsky, Freud, Roulette" (Sollers), 21

Double, The (Dostoyevsky, F.), 9, 24, 32; dialogic structure of, 26; laughter in, 50

doubling, in novels, xiii

"Dream of a Ridiculous Man, The" (Dostoyevsky, F.), 72, 118–19

dualism: Christianity and, 208–9; of theology, xiv

Dudintsev, Vladimir, 173

Durand, Claude, 195

Eckhart, Meister, 178

economy, as concept, 86

Ego: annihilation of, 43; Christianity and, 209; in *Crime and Punishment*, 63; for Dostoyevsky, F., 43–44; homoeroticism and, 70; Husserl on, 235, 289; Ideal of the Ego, 70; limits of, 76; sacrifice of, 77–78; transcendental, 235, 289

Egyptian Nights (Pushkin), 114

Ehrenburg, Ilya, 173

Epoch, The, 15, 42, 225

eroticism: in language, 85–89; without organs, 86–89; roots of, 84; suffering and, 221, 297n2

Eternal Husband, The (Dostoyevsky, F.), 16–17, 32, 226; gambling in, 44; jouissance in, 115; laughing symbolism in, 49–50; laughter in, 49–50; love triangles in, 40; neuroticism in, 52; suffering in, 219

Ethics III (Spinoza), 79

Ethics IV (Spinoza), 79–80

Eugénie Grandet (Balzac), 7

Eurasianism, 194

Europe: Catholicism in, 236; Dostoyevsky, F., tour of, 40–42; humanism in, 180; Lutheranism in, 236; Russia's relationship with, 238–39; in *A Writer's Diary*, 238–39

evil: Arendt on, 183; bodies of, 222–26; in *The Brothers Karamazov*, 160–61, 215–19; in *Hamlet*, 160; homicide as, 216–17; in *Notes from Underground*, 53–54; radical, 183; unlinking good from, 53–54; wickedness and, 221

"Execution of Stepan Razin, The" (Yevtushenko), 173–74

existentialism, humanism and, 106
extraordinaries, in *Crime and Punishment*, 58

Fadeev, Alexander, 171
faith, sin and, 50
Fanaticism or Mahomet the Prophet (Voltaire), 248
fathers, in Dostoyevsky works. *See* paternal figures
Father/Son paradigm, in Russian Orthodox Christianity, 187–90
feminicide: in *Crime and Punishment*, 216–17; escalation of, xiii
feminine jouissance, 118, 162–63
feminism, Sand and, 11
fetishism, fetishization and, in *The Gambler*, 39
"Figura" (Auerbach), 85, 193
figures, figurism and, 86–87; etymological origins of, 85
Finnegans Wake (Joyce), 33–34
Flaubert, Gustave, 13, 290
Flight from Byzantium (Brodsky), 169
Flowers of Evil (Baudelaire), 205
Fontaine, Jean de la, 22, 24
foreclusion, 32
forgiveness, as theme: in *The Adolescent*, 125; in *The Brothers Karamazov*, 124–27; in *Crime and Punishment*, 55–61, 63; in *Demons*, 124; in *The Idiot*, 124; jouissance and, 124–25; trans-identitarians and, 124
formalism, Russian Formalism, 29
"Formulations on the Two Principles of Mental Functioning" (Freud), 32–33
France: atheism in, 240–41; Catholicism in, 241; Christianity in, 176; Convention of 1793, 238; Declaration of the Rights of Man and of the Citizen, 175, 181; French Revolution, 175, 181; Gothic

Catholicism in, 176; Jacobinism in, 248; laicity in, 175–76, 248; Paris Commune, 42; Russia influenced by, 175–78; secularization of, 175; socialism in, 41–42, 247; social sciences in, 176
freedom: Christianism and, 73; in *Dead Christ*, 73; Heidegger on, 182; Kant on, 181–82; in Russia, 181–84; suffering as, 219
free will, Kant on, 195
French Convention of 1793, 238
French Revolution, Declaration of the Rights of Man and of the Citizen and, 175, 181
French structuralism, in polyphonic novel, 25
Freud, Sigmund: *Beyond the Pleasure Principle*, 31–32; *Civilization and Its Discontents*, 31, 128; on Dostoyevsky, F., xii–xiii, 30–34; "Dostoevsky and Parricide," 31; "Formulations on the Two Principles of Mental Functioning," 32–33; Jung and, 167; Oedipus complex and, 129, 139–40, 142, 156, 183, 254; *Oedipus the King* and, 156; on parricide, 156; pleasure principle for, 218; on repression, 266; on sex haunted by language, 30–31; on suffering, 218; *Summary of Psychoanalysis*, 156; on unconscious, 60
"Frieden" (Heine), 135
fundamentalism, nihilism and, xii
fundamentalist transhumanism, 44
Fyodorov, Nikolai, 76, 190–91

Gambler, The (Dostoyevsky, F.), 17, 32, 95, 227; anti-Semitism in, 47; fetishism in, 39; gambling themes in, 44; jouissance in, 40; maternal dominion in, 44, 46–47; money as

Russian Orthodox Christianity (*cont.*)